4-8-15

THE NEW CREATION STORY

Spirit, Eros, & Climate Chaos

TRILOGY BY ANDREW F. BEATH

BOOK THREE

THE ECOLOGICAL EPOCH

DEDICATION AND ACKNOWLEDGMENTS

I recently wrote the dedication for this trilogy's volume one and volume two, so I had the opportunity to thank those involved in all three books, including my son, Leonardo, my daughter, AnaSophia, and my former life-travel companion and current editor, Cynthia Mathis Beath. A few minutes ago, during a short meditation, I thought, "Who has not been thanked sufficiently?" An answer came in short order: "The whales, elephants, and other large-brained mammals, in appreciation for their beauty and their companionship as fellow planetary travelers."

In addition, there is a contingent of fellow social justice/environmental activists that has given me strength and courage through their own dedication to their ecological work. Some are close friends; some are acquaintances that have inspired me. I include a partial list here as a thank you and ask forgiveness from those I have inadvertently omitted: John Mack, John Picone, Atossa Soltani, John Seed, Randy Hayes, Jim Gollin, Joanna Macy, Lorin Lindner, Brian Swimme, Andy Lipkis, Joel Solomon, Dave Henson, Brock Dolman, Josh Mailman, Vijali Hamilton, Danny Sheehan, Mike Roselle, Celia Alario, Harriet Crosby, Rebecca Dmytryk, Rosa Jordan, Peter Levitt, Ralph Metzner, Gigi Coyle, Lynn Twiste, Eric Seifert, and Tom Hayden.

Leigh J. McCloskey provided the images used for the book's cover and the interior. He is a visionary artist and philosopher. Leigh has deeply explored the archetypal and hidden aspects of the psyche through his visual art works and writing. The works that are included here come from Leigh's *Codex Tor* illuminated books and *Grimoire* (Book of Spells). Georgianne Cowen took the Chapter Eight photo of her daughter, Serina, with Leigh McCloskey's studio as the setting. Steve Chapple took the author's photo that appears on the back cover.

TABLE OF CONTENTS

BOOK THREE

THE ECOLOGICAL EPOCH

PREFACE

A person with a strong ego usually has confidence in his abilities, knows his strengths, and, as a result, functions successfully in the world. Someone who wants to find more meaning in his life, to grow beyond this everyday competency, at some point begins to look for spiritual meaning. I was a good student and successful athlete in high school and college; I went on to obtain a graduate degree from an Ivy League university; I married a beautiful girl from a "good" Southern family; and within a few years of starting my first corporate job, I was given important responsibility and a high salary.

All of this created a healthy, competent ego but did not provide a meaningful life. It seemed as though I were a character in a dramatic play, portraying an image—a façade to fit the expectations of my corporate culture and my new "in-laws." It took me about five years to grow through this cultural morass, leave my job, and begin to travel the world in search of *je ne sais quoi*.

No matter how competent the ego, it is a "front man," hiding a more authentic being that resides behind the mask. My own personal growth demanded I crack open that façade so I could see the world from a pluralistic perspective—one that holds multiple viewpoints at the same time. There is no "right" or "wrong." There are multiple sides to each story.

From birth through childhood and adulthood, one's emotional conflicts cause wounds, pain, and suffering. Too much emotional stress causes mental illness. Entire wars are started because a "leader" has a damaged psyche. I refused to go to fight in Vietnam; it just didn't feel like it made sense. I left the corporate world for the same reason; it didn't feel good. Deconstructing the ego takes time and effort, especially if you don't consciously know that's what you're doing.

I traveled the world for ten years, learned to write poetry, studied with spiritual masters, and, eventually, started a not-for-profit organization to try to "serve life" in some positive ways. From this pluralistic perspective, I was usually able to discern when other people had self-serving, ulterior motives in personal relationships, business activities, and large-scale cultural dynamics. I began to recognize the traps they set, the wars they start, and the patriotism or "corporatism" they promote need not influence my life decisions.

As a result, my own psychological, emotional, and behavioral patterns have become more visible to me. I came to realize that my ego identity is a product of enculturation and circumstance. To understand another culture, indeed to see any other worldview, it is important to break through one's confining ego-shell, which usually produces greater personal awareness.

I call this big-picture perspective "Ecological Epoch consciousness." Its defining characteristics include an ongoing awareness of how important interrelationship is for one's healthy functioning; being fully present; an appreciation for life; living in integrated, sacred reciprocity with one's surroundings; realizing the profound depth that intimacy provides; and being grateful for the gift of life. Unity and diversity are a connected, fluid spectrum—as are seemingly disparate "ideas." Metaphorically speaking, "light" and "dark" compose one unified reality that is only partially knowable to the human mind. This complexity adds a mystical element, as well as depth and richness, to life. Sacred creativity is manifested everywhere around and within me. I am a part, yet I am also the whole.

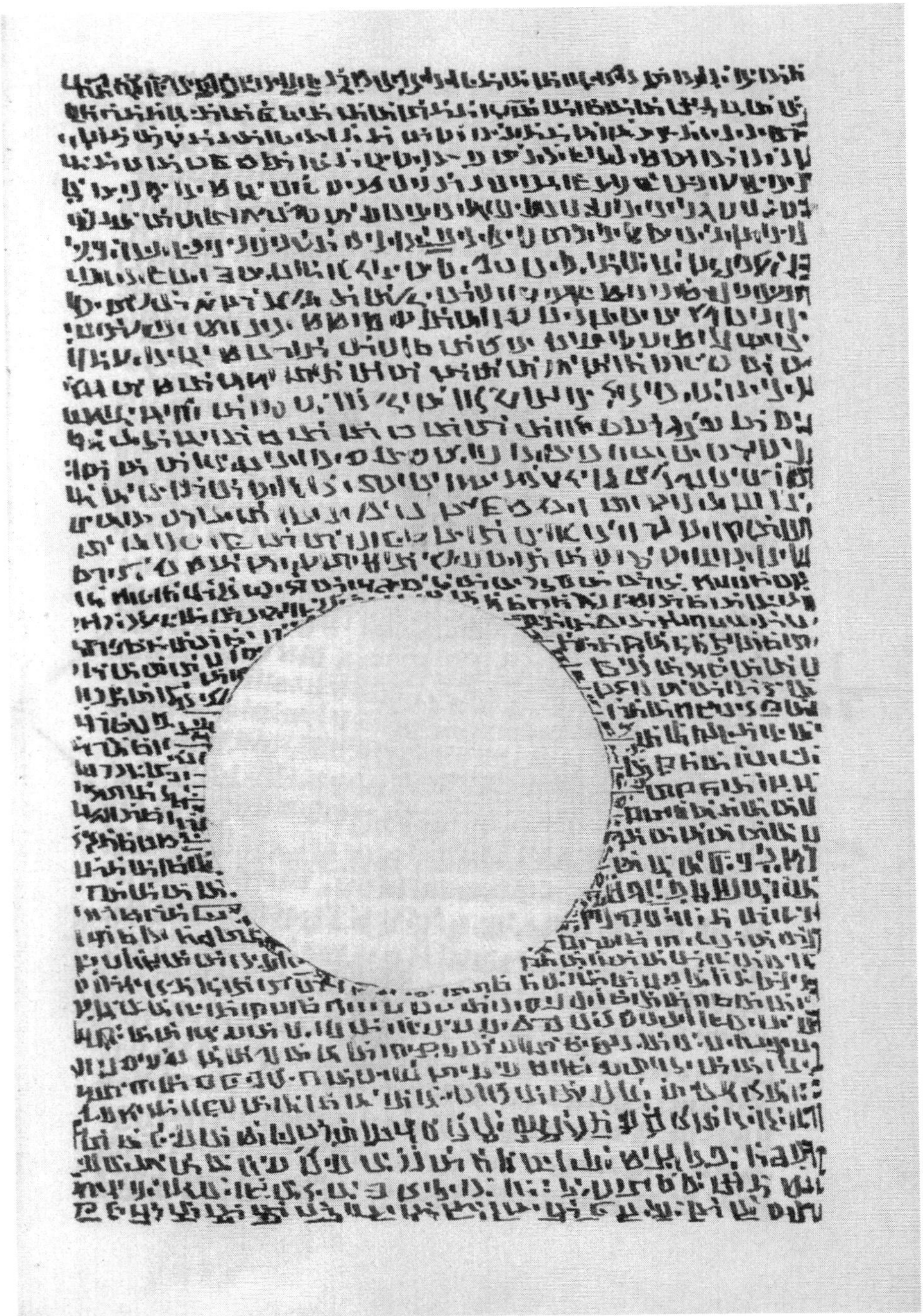

INTRODUCTION

The New Creation Story helps define who we are as individuals and as a species. It also addresses an important question: Where have we come from? This new story is about expanding awareness that enables us to transcend personal, ego-driven decisions and thereby deepen our relationship with all creation. In this story, the term "Natural Harmony" refers to our planet's interactive, living systems that have been developing during the past 3.8 billion years and hold the interrelationship among all life on Earth in sacred trust.

Both as individuals and as a species, we can create a future story that is different from our past story—one that is not confined by the past. As we grow and expand our own nature, we free ourselves from the constraints that limit our future success. In addition, we remove divisions; we more readily integrate with other people and with Earth's other creatures. This is how intimacies grow. Today's expanding climate chaos is more a crisis of consciousness than of malicious intent, and consciousness is expanding to meet the crisis. The times are changing.

We are now birthing the next step in the evolution of human consciousness. For those who are aware of our dire predicament, the ecological destruction we are causing is painful—just as human birth is difficult, traumatic, and dangerous for the mother and infant. The Ecological Epoch has arrived. Its values eventually will be integrated into our social behavior, our politics, and our business activities—but at what cost?

Our near-term, society-wide response to global warming will determine whether we wake up soon enough to transition into this new epoch with grace or with trauma. Will the mother and infant survive the birthing process?

In our Creation Story, we demonstrate the necessity for sustainable economies so that our children might inherit a thriving planet, not a withering wasteland. In recent generations, humanity's remarkably productive scientific accomplishments have constrained our intuition and our big-vision focus. With our new inventions, products, and endless consumption, we are not just consuming "goods"; we are also consuming the world around us. In prior centuries, tuberculosis, a public health epidemic, was called "consumption." It was a virulent, "wasting away" disease. Our consumer society is in the midst of a public health epidemic, one that is causing the Earth to waste away.

For the past seventy years, we have been consuming our surroundings, as a parasite consumes its host, so we can increase population, create more "stuff," and accumulate more possessions. The larger Earth community is now suffering our excesses and is withering, yet we are mostly blind to what we are doing. To participate in the Ecological Epoch is to live in Natural Harmony. Just as a caterpillar, enclosed in a chrysalis, eventually emerges as a butterfly, the human species is preparing to transform; however, today's mindset—how we see the world—must suffer through death and rebirth so that a new human species is able to emerge and spread its colorful wings.

The old is dying and giving birth to new human consciousness, one whose priority is to support others—not just our family and friends, not just humans, but all living things—and to make decisions based on what is best for the planet's life-giving systems: the air, the water, and the mountains. Although we don't yet recognize it, we humans are supported by the entire Earth community and cannot exist in a healthy way without this mutual interrelationship. Ecological consciousness will change our behavior and restore health to the planet so that our children can live gracefully.

Stories that are frequently repeated in our culture influence our beliefs and priorities to such an extent that the story itself becomes the subsurface operating system that ultimately drives an individual's actions and a community's social behavior. These influences are frequently subconscious, and, for lack of more focused stories to accurately interpret past and present events, society is often swept along in a river of unintended compliance, resulting in behavior that is based on prior epoch's mythologies whose influences are counterproductive to contemporary circumstances. This is precisely our present day situation.

We each create the universe we see, primarily from our own worldview: that is, our ways of seeing things and our attitudes toward life. Sometimes this re-creation is consistent with that of our neighbor, sometimes less so. Societies in distant lands often have much different stories about where the world came from, the meaning of life, and how people should behave. The most profound stories are ones that touch common ground and, therefore, benefit far-flung societies, individuals, the earth, and all living things. These commonalities can't be found without delving into the deepest core that human intuition, intellect, and emotion can access. This manuscript is *Book Three* of a trilogy. This volume is called *The New Creation Story, Book Three, the Ecological Epoch*. The two prior volumes are: *The New Creation Story, Book Two*, with the subtitle *Consciousness*; *Book One*'s subtitle is *In the Beginning*.

The narrative presented to you in these pages, provides ways to interpret reality—the universe of objects, thoughts, and feelings we each experience for ourselves. To the extent that it suggests alternative perspectives that lead to more health, happiness and well-being for a person, and, therefore, assists our planet's regeneration, then to that extent it has fulfilled its purpose. The ongoing, myth-like narrative, the Creation Story, is indented as a substory to distinguish it from the traditional descriptive format, which is presented as normal paragraphs and fonts; as such, there are two parallel presentations. Each "story" segment is numbered, starting with the book's number within the trilogy, *Book Three* in this case. The second number denotes the story sequence within the book. For example, (3:1) denotes this Creation Story's first *Book Three* installment. Since (3:36) is the final segment, there are 36 individual installments.

Coming to know our human story in the fullest possible way is part of a transformation process. As described in *Book Two*, consciousness epochs continue to unfold; the Ecological Epoch is the most recent. As cultures come and go, cycles occur that flip between male-dominated epochs, in which men control almost all the group decisions, and gender-balanced epochs, in which women have equal social influence with men. Likewise, feminine and masculine values cycle in and out of prominence with each new consciousness epoch. Interestingly, a male-dominated political cycle is not necessarily controlled by masculine values; for example, as we saw in *Book Two*, men led the Philosophical Epoch that began around 600 BCE; however, its values were feminine, as our continuing Creation Story describes:

(3:1) About thirteen thousand years ago, near the end of the Ice Age's most recent cold cycle, people with **Earth-Honoring Mythology** built large ceremonial sites for spiritual practice and ritual. The carved images that remain show both male and female human figures, often merged with animal totems. There is no anthropological evidence indicating that men controlled these cultures—there may have been shared, gender-balanced social influences. Soon after this Ice Age cycle ended, humans learned to grow crops, and agriculture provided the sustenance needed for villages to multiply. This was the New Stone Age. Cultivated earth yielded grains that sustained a growing human population. Fertility goddesses became the spiritual focus; they represented good harvests, more children, and ubiquitous creativity.

Thus began the **Goddess Mythological Epoch**; however, as domestication progressed, something was lost. Both emotional and physical barriers were erected. The people began fencing themselves in, surrounded by their newly tamed agricultural lands, separated from the wild lands and forests. Generations passed. The unfamiliar, wild woodlands became feared. Within a few thousand years, villages begat towns and later became cities, supported by croplands and cattle. Men and women shared authority. Women excelled in medicine, agriculture, and spiritual guidance. They were highly respected for these many contributions. In this respect, the culture was "gender-balanced." Feminine, relational values took precedence over masculine, dominating values.

About five thousand years ago, a cultural transformation began to sweep away these established cultures. The **Patriarchal Mythological Epoch** had arrived. Using newly invented weapons and worshipping aggressive male deities, this exclusively male authority came to prominence. The alphabet was developed, and linear, rational thought helped install hierarchical, authoritarian leaders. Encouraged by warrior gods, men controlled the culture, and empire building began in earnest. Masculine principles repressed feminine values in social organizations.

After about four thousand years of domination and empire building, a new consciousness evolved, setting the stage for the **Philosophical Epoch** to emerge. Feminine values once again came to the forefront in a new culture that began around 600 BCE, a few hundred years after the Axial Age appeared; however, this consciousness epoch retained men as its leaders. Male philosophers with political influence introduced compassion and concern for others as important ethical standards.

Increasing rationality and scientific discovery created the next consciousness stage, the **Scientific Epoch**, which gave birth to the Scientific Revolution and produced the many inventions that eventually created our consumer-oriented society. Another cycle came into play in the Scientific Epoch: men not only dominated society, they also prioritized masculine values. The feminine influence was once again subjugated and repressed. In both the Philosophical and the Scientific epochs, the "sacred, natural world" was diminished in the human mind. Time passed. Science's "shadow side" developed the "bomb," polluted the atmosphere, acidified the oceans, and depleted many of Earth's animal species—rationality had run amok.

During our entire scientific endeavor, we have never fully engaged our intellectual skills to deeply understand our relationship to the earth's "aliveness" and health; however, we've now come to a crossroads, and ongoing worldwide ecological devastation is forcing us to engage with the Earth. In recent years we have begun to bring our scientific endeavor into alignment with Natural Harmony and thereby started to transform our culture; unfortunately the current industrial momentum and its associated consumerism continue to exact a huge toll. Earth-life is now withering, but the consciousness pendulum has swung in the other direction, revealing new ways to "see" life on Earth.

We have recently emerged from the Scientific Epoch and entered into the **Ecological Epoch,** in which feminine values have regained primary influence. New solutions are being revealed and implemented, thereby originating what will once again become a gender-balanced society. Creating a new relationship between humans and the living Earth is the current generation's challenge so that the Earth will be allowed to heal, human population will stabilize at a sustainable level, and resources will be distributed equitably. If in the near term we are able to incorporate a gender-balanced social structure that incorporates feminine values, perhaps we can avoid social chaos; however, if we fail, our children may face the greatest tragedy to ever befall the human species.

CHAPTER 1

THE STATE OF THE WORLD

We live amid incredible beauty; sadly, our natural world is withering around us—when we eventually are able to "see" the beauty, we will finally recognize the damage we have done.

This Creation Story is a story about "becoming". The Ecological Epoch has arrived, although it may not seem that way. Corporations rapaciously grow, and financial institutions continue to gain a disproportionate share of the economy's wealth and profits. The average person falls further behind. However, it is important to remember Rachel Carson's book *Silent Spring* was published as recently as 1962, describing the damage DDT and other chemical toxins were causing the environment. This was a wake-up bell, extolling the absolute necessity for an ecological truce. It heralded the new millennium. By the year 2000, experts in every discipline were emphasizing the dangers we are creating from our insatiable production and consumption economies.

We have entered this new epoch in a harrowing circumstance. The world's politicians are either oblivious to the impending environmental

1

and social chaos, or they are paralyzed by it. There is evidence all around us. Related newspaper articles appear daily: On August 22, 2012, the *Los Angeles Times* reported the following: "The world urgently needs to adopt drought management policies as farmers from Africa to India struggle with lack of rainfall and the United States endures its worst drought in decades, top officials with the United Nations weather agency said. Climate change is projected to increase the frequency, intensity, and duration of droughts, with impacts in many sectors, in particular food, water, health, and energy, said the World Meteorological Organization's Secretary General, Michel Jarraud."

A United Nations Conference on Sustainable Development was held in 1992 in Rio de Janeiro, Brazil. A follow-up conference called Rio+20 was held June 20–22, 2012. The 1992 conference ended with hope and confidence that the world's social and environmental problems would be solved in the following decades. Five hundred issues were identified as needing improvement to create a sustainable world. At Rio+20, it was determined that only four of the five hundred had improved significantly, leaving the remaining 496 issues without progress. The 2012 conference ended in disappointment, with almost no new initiatives or solutions.

Our New Creation Story is embedded in this particular context. There are critical reasons for our story's revelation at this time. The most compelling is that man-made climate change has, beginning with the Industrial Revolution, been ongoing for many decades. In actuality, climate change is becoming climate chaos. Carbon has risen to more than 400 parts per million (ppm) in the atmosphere, well above the 350 ppm that might be a "safe" level. The world's climate scientists now agree that a two-degree (Celsius) or 3.6-degree (Fahrenheit) increase in global temperature is the absolute maximum level that will enable the earth's systems to operate without major disruption. Even at a two-degree increase, the odds are only 80 percent that calamity can be averted.

If we exceed this two-degree level, climate chaos is likely to become social chaos, creating agricultural failure and massive famine, igniting resource wars for food and water, and producing many millions of environmental refugees. Governments and social systems will fail, replaced by anarchy in some locations and fundamentalist dictators in others. This is currently happening in some less-developed countries. The curve for this trend is climbing upward. Now that experts have informed us about the climate change's severity, what are we doing to rein it in?

The earth's atmospheric temperature has already increased 0.8°C from industrial activity. Arctic ice is disappearing at an alarming rate. The oceans have become more acidic, causing coral reefs to die and mollusk shells to atrophy. Mountain glaciers are disappearing, causing rivers to lose the downstream volume needed to grow enough crops to successfully feed the massive populations that rely on this water. Given these results and many more ecological disruptions, most environmentalists think that even a two-degree Celsius increase will be a recipe for disaster.

Yet carbon emissions are not declining; they are increasing. We are not moving down toward the required 350-ppm level; we are accelerating above the 400-ppm level. In 2011, the International Energy Agency reported that CO_2 emissions were about 31 gigatons (each gigaton equals one billion tons), more than 3 percent higher than the prior year. The 3-percent-per-year increase has been typical, and as of 2014 there are no signs that this increase is abating.

Scientists from the Lawrence Berkeley National Laboratory concur with climate experts in multiple national and international agencies: after more than forty sophisticated computer simulations, there is agreement that the atmosphere can absorb only about 565 more gigatons of CO_2 before the two-degree increase is exceeded. According to climate activist Bill McKibben, at the 3-percent-growth rate, we will add 565 gigatons in the next sixteen years. Even assuming a small decrease in carbon emissions, we will exceed the 565 number before midcentury. My eight-year-old daughter will be forty-five years old by then. She will be required to deal with multiple dire consequences created by my generation's carbon-use decisions.

Should we be scared about where we're leading our children, hand in hand? You bet we should! And here's why. We learn from a *Carbon Tracker Initiative* article published in the *Business Spectator* that current oil, coal, and gas reserves amount to 2,795 gigatons.[1] Yes, this is about five times the amount that can be used safely while still protecting the planet's flora and fauna. Human beings are in danger. The current atmospheric carbon buildup rate is heading toward not a two-degree increase but rather a six-degree (Celsius) temperature increase (equal to 11°F) by midcentury, *which will turn our Garden of Eden into a hellish, unrecognizable ecological disaster— accompanied by economic collapse and social chaos.*

These 2,795 gigatons represent the currently recoverable fossil fuel reserves—that is, energy resources that have been located already and are now available to be extracted and burned. These are the published reserves that investors have used to value a company's stock. Fossil-fuel reservoirs are the main assets of numerous corporations and oil-rich governments. The world's decision makers and the financial markets are definitely planning on using these reserves. There is no current mechanism to prevent their use—not even to slow down this worldwide burning, not to mention that billions of dollars are being spent yearly to find more reserves.

The International Energy Agency (IEA), based in Paris, France, represents twenty-eight nations. In November 2012, the IEA predicted in a report that the United States would find and produce so much new oil and gas that it would surpass Saudi Arabia to become the world's top oil source by 2020. The organization refers to an "energy renaissance" from new technologies, including hydraulic fracturing (fracking) and horizontal drilling. Oil production was less than 10 million barrels per day in the

---

1 James Leaton, Carbon Tracker Initiative, March 23, 2012, Business Spectator, Climate Spectator: Popping the carbon bubble

United States when it peaked in 1970. It fell to 5 million barrels per day in 2008 and then began to increase; the 2015 level will exceed 10 million barrels and increase further by 2020 to 11.1 million barrels. The report states that worldwide oil production, based on consumer demand, will be 99.7 million barrels per day in 2035, a 15 percent increase from today.

We also see our culture's craziness reflected in the report's additional information: This increasing energy production and oil use will use up more than 15 percent of the world's water resources and cause higher CO_2 concentrations in the atmosphere, resulting in a *6.5-degree (Celsius) temperature increase*. This is well beyond the "safe" level—yet the world's fossil-fuel locomotive is barely challenged. Fossil fuels received a 30 percent increase in government subsidies last year, which represents cultural psychosis. In this context, we desperately need new stories that redefine who we are—not by how we've behaved in the recent past, but by how we will build a sustainable, concerned, and compassionate future. When a person awakens into Ecological Epoch consciousness, the way she perceives the world is transformed; her relationship to the living Earth becomes fresh, exciting, and protective.

Climate Change: A World without Ice

During the George W. Bush administration in the United States, there was public confusion about whether or not global warming was "manmade" or a naturally occurring cyclical change. If natural, there was no impetus to modify our "business as usual" approach to energy and manufacturing policies—big business would benefit by not having to expend profits to reduce their CO_2 emissions and other pollutants. Most of the confusion arose from questionable scientific reports paid for by the polluting industries. They were attempting to prove that the rising CO_2 was a natural phenomenon. Thankfully, that period of obfuscation is behind us; the public now acknowledges that we humans are causing climate change by converting fossil fuels from nature's underground reservoirs and depositing their chemicals into the atmosphere. This causes a "greenhouse" effect—denser CO_2 concentrations, methane, and other gases are trapping heat from sunlight that used to radiate back into space.

An environmental organization started by Bill McKibben called "350. org" brings attention to the fact that CO_2 concentrations in the atmosphere must be held to 350 ppm to maintain a stable climate. At the beginning of the twentieth century, industrialization was in its infancy, and CO_2 was well below 350ppm; in fact, as shown by arctic ice cores, levels have been more or less stable below this level for more than four hundred thousand years. In the past fifty years, CO_2 concentrations have grown abruptly. In 2014, carbon dioxide concentrations are above 400 ppm and rising quickly.

Some environmentalists are adamant that we have to reduce the presence of polluting gases to "save the planet." This is not the case—the planet will be fine. It is our children and grandchildren who will suffer, along with a large percentage of all living species that we will be ushering into extinction. The planet has had much higher CO_2 levels during its four-and-a-half billion-year history. A geologic investigation of a period fifty-six million years ago in Wyoming's Big Horn Basin is presented in a fascinating work, as described in a 2011 *National Geographic* article titled "World without Ice."[2] This may seem like a long time ago; however, in geologic time, fifty-six million years is slightly more than 1 percent of the planet's current age.

Nine million years after the dinosaurs disappeared, there was a sudden and dramatic spike in the atmosphere's CO_2 levels—a period called the Paleocene–Eocene Thermal Maximum, or PETM for short. Although causes for the sudden increase are not known, the interesting parallel with today's circumstance is that the CO_2 concentrations at PETM were similar to what scientists estimate they will be *if* we burn all of the known and currently available fossil-fuel reserves—oil, coal, and natural gas—depositing

---

2. Robert Kunzig, "World without Ice," *National Geographic*, October, 2011.

their pollution into the atmosphere. Of course, this is the very path we are on; even though alternative fuels are being developed, there is little political will to eliminate fossil-fuel use—unfortunately, the conversation is about slowing its use so the reserves last longer, while alternatives are gradually developed.

A hybrid car might travel fifty miles to a gallon instead of twenty-five, thereby taking twice as many years to convert the same amount of fossil fuel into the atmosphere; however, it makes no difference to the atmosphere whether these chemicals are added to the air in fifty years or a hundred years; the effects will be the same—massive disruption. During PETM, the earth's temperature rose 9° Fahrenheit; there was no ocean ice, and water temperatures in the Arctic Ocean reached 74° Fahrenheit, similar to the mid-Atlantic summertime temperatures now. CO_2 spiked from 1,000 ppm to 1,500 ppm. The Earth has self-regulating mechanisms: Over time, rain "scrubs" CO_2 from the air. In addition, "weathering" eventually sequesters CO_2 from the air and combines it into rocks; however, during PETM, this process took more than 150,000 years before concentrations returned to earlier levels.

The world changed during PETM: Most coral and shell animals disappeared because excessive CO_2 permeated the oceans all the way to the ocean floor, acidifying the water and dissolving the shells. As temperatures rose, wildfires devastated most older forests, eliminating the habitat for existing species and opening niches for new life forms; "greenhouse" conditions heated up the land; rainfall declined by 40 percent in the Big Horn Basin, drying out the soil; insect populations expanded; existing species either adapted or disappeared and were replaced by new ones; and plants with smaller leaves prevailed because they were able to retain moisture. One horse-like species adapted in the Big Horn by evolving over time to the size of a large cat, possibly because food supplies were less available and not as nutritious.

Interestingly, PETM was not a mass extinction period because the warming took place slowly over a ten-thousand year-period. Most flora and fauna, like the Big Horn Basin horse, were able to adapt. They had time to migrate or physically change and, thereby, survive. This is not the case with today's warming episode. It is occurring more than ten times faster than the pace of change during PETM. There is not enough time for most species to adapt, and a vast number will go extinct.

During PETM, some extinction occurred, but many new life forms emerged. It could be said that life on Earth eventually benefited. Many of today's modern mammals took on their current form during this hot period, including the primates that are our direct ancestors; in fact, *Homo sapiens* may not have come to exist except for this Paleocene–Eocene Thermal Maximum. So PETM was a good thing for our primate ancestors; however, another such episode of planet-wide ecological change likely would result in a major contraction of our species, which could occur rapidly.

Our food sources, especially those in coastal areas that will be inundated with rising sea levels, are too delicate to withstand rapid climate change; most of the earth's productive lands are occupied. Our population is massive and rising; there is no place for "climate refugees" to go. Do we want our children and grandchildren to have to live through a "pruning" of our species and a life of trauma? In this coming, sudden, high-carbon geologic episode, most existing species will not survive.

We currently have choices: We can mobilize our creativity, revamp our economies, provide alternative fuels, recycle industrial materials, and eliminate most pollutants, thereby minimizing atmospheric CO_2 increases and their concurrent disruptions. *Or* we can proceed with business as usual. According to "World without Ice," we have burned about 300 billion tons of CO_2 into the atmosphere during the industrial period. That is only 10 percent of the earth's estimated fossil deposits, so we have some distance to go before PETM's nine-degree temperature increases; however, we have already set in place the groundwork for an unavoidable two- to three-degree (Fahrenheit) increase. The effects are just beginning to show, and we are currently on a trajectory to an increase of somewhere between four and seven degrees over the next fifty years.

Our New Creation Story provides several choices for the future we are in the process of creating, including an apocalyptic one that could come to pass if we do not immediately begin to reduce the increase in CO_2 that our human activities are causing:

(3:2) Humans can survive this potential upheaval, but the planet could not sustain the eight to ten billion humans that it is capable of feeding with a stable climate. As temperatures increase, some pathogens will run rampant. With the current small increase, we have seen the Pine Beetle destroy vast swaths of forest. New viruses and bacteria will attack cattle and chickens. Wheat and rice will not be immune. In some respects, evolution welcomes change; life forms that have dominated are eliminated or trimmed back to more reasonable levels, opening ecological space for forms that are better adapted to the new conditions.

Our food is grown on just 3 percent of the planet's surface (about 12 percent of the land mass). Climate change will eliminate many of these fertile areas; some will become desert; monsoon deluges will erode others. Steady rains suitable for agriculture will begin to fall on new areas, some fertile but many infertile. Glaciers will disappear, the rivers they fed will run dry, and downstream farms will lay fallow. These changes can occur relatively quickly, even by human time scales.

The sea is rising; problems this creates are likely to take hold in just a few decades. Low-lying rice fields in Asia will be rendered useless from salt intrusion. People by the hundreds of millions will be displaced. Disruption to modern agriculture is beginning to occur now. In the heavily populated Asian countries, environmental refugees will cause massive impacts upon the social systems and governmental order. Currently in the developed Western world, locations that used to receive good agricultural rainfall are drying up; topsoil is blowing away. Deserts are encroaching onto farmlands. Our agricultural economy hangs in a delicate balance while trying to feed a world population that is approaching eight billion.

Our banking and financial systems are so burdened with debt that they are on shaky ground. Entire regional economies are teetering. It will not take much ecological disruption to collapse various components of the world's economy. When a hundred million people cannot survive in their homeland, and these many millions pull up stakes to relocate, they will have no place to go—there are no regions that will welcome and feed them. Their vast numbers will create social and political instability. Economies will begin to collapse; jobs will contract drastically; social services will be cut; there will be hunger, unrest, and social chaos.

Although tolerated now, the disparity between rich and poor will not be tolerated when the poor cannot feed their children. Starvation still exists even in today's relatively wealthy economic conditions; as less food is available, deaths from starvation will increase; the human population will begin to decline from social unrest and from insufficient food. Social order will be restructured. We all will be dramatically affected. No country will be spared.

This apocalyptic vision is the direction we are collectively heading, but it is not inevitable; our story has several possible outcomes. There is no right or wrong. We are participating in an unfolding consciousness process that will be whatever it becomes; however, we do have economic, social, and governmental choices that will affect our story's ending and determine the planet's near-term health—and our species' future.

Violence against People/Violence against Nature

I often hear people say things like, "We'll always have war because that's just human nature; it's the way we are." In a similar vein, a person's angry behavior is often dismissed as "passion," as though it were justified; retribution is idealized, but forgiveness is not—just survey today's popular films to weigh the balance. My clear position is that violence against other people or against nature is a matter of attitude and worldview. It is possible to change, and this transformation can be made quickly if necessary.

In the mid-1940s, Japan was a belligerent aggressor on the world stage; the Japanese attacked their neighbors ruthlessly and committed multiple atrocities. They behaved badly. Eventually they were soundly defeated; the final blow was Hiroshima and Nagasaki's barbaric bombing after Japan had been rendered defenseless, their air force destroyed. The war experience, the destruction wrought from nuclear retribution and its annihilation, changed their aggressive culture from violent to peaceful. Over the next few decades, the Japanese became model world citizens with no aggression toward others and almost no violence within their own borders. They are an educated and creative society; their creativity was redirected from weapons to consumer goods, from warplanes to the world's most innovative automobiles.

Japan was humbled and, through this humility, became a changed culture; the country currently ranks near the top of the world's countries on a "peacefulness" index. On the other hand, America's perception that it "won" the war with Japan, and its failure to acknowledge the barbaric nuclear attacks helped transform that nation into a global policeman and the planet's most aggressive "world power," qualities that came back to haunt the country in Vietnam, Iraq, and Afghanistan.

What if we were to "scale up" this example and imagine a nuclear war? It almost happened in 1962. According to interview tapes released in September 2011, Jackie Kennedy, the president's wife, with inside information about the possibility of a nuclear attack, told her husband that if the war happened, she wanted to die in Washington with him, not be "sent away." We were that close. Currently, in 2014, more than five thousand nuclear warheads are stockpiled in the United States alone; Russia has many more, and various smaller countries, such as Pakistan, have nuclear armaments. Even a "small" nuclear exchange between developing counties like India and Pakistan would have a tremendous ripple effect on global economies and on the world psyche.

Were the United States to be involved in a nuclear exchange, we would be a humbled people, ready to redefine government's authority to wage war. Climate change is like a slow-motion nuclear buildup; remember those nuclear bomb tests that the US military exploded in the atmosphere? The current CO_2 buildup is similar but even more insidious because global warming is less visible to most people than the nuclear mushroom cloud.

We have stopped nuclear testing and given lip service to eliminating the weapons arsenal, but more countries have developed or otherwise attained these nightmarish devices as part of their "defense" strategy. What happened to Japan was not enough to dissuade North Korea and other "rogue" countries with unstable leaders from attempting to become nuclear states. A nuclear-bomb episode, were one to occur, would force any country to reassess its priorities. Will it take a climate-change weather holocaust to transform today's world culture, or can we be proactive and make adult choices that prevent this result?

Change happens; Japan changed. The main theme for this Creation Story is that human consciousness has always been changing and is currently in the midst of a "sea change"—we are being forced to take the next step in the evolution of human consciousness. This is occurring now! Are we physiologically, emotionally, and mentally capable of squeezing through this needle's eye and avoiding the otherwise dire consequences? An article titled "In the Minds of Men" in *Science and Spirit* magazine provides insight to demonstrate that we are not biologically programmed for violence; rather; it is a cultural choice affected by how we are governed, as well as by our child-drearing techniques, educational system, criminal-justice policies, economic structures, religions, freedoms, distribution of wealth, and other variables.[3] North Korea has an aggressive culture; Bhutan has a peaceful culture.

Contrary to mass-media and government apologists for attacking the Middle East, there is evidence that we humans are *not* predisposed to belligerence and warfare; that is, this is not how we "have always been." Rather, it is cultural, and culture can change. *Homo sapiens* are a two-hundred-thousand-year-old species. This represents almost ten thousand generations of changing DNA and accumulated wisdom that have made us what we are

---

3 Jenny Desai, In the Minds of Men, March 2005, Science and Spirit magazine

today. We know little about our emotional and psychological development prior to about ten thousand years ago because there is no written history or literature that dates back this far; however, we do have artwork, ceremonial sites, and anthropological artifacts to inform us about our deep past.

What were we like for the prior 190,000 years? If we can't answer this question, then we can't claim to know what predispositions we have as a species. This Creation Story emphasizes what we are becoming. Consciousness moves in cycles over time; nurturing qualities are sometimes most influential, while at other times, dominating qualities prevail. Cycles can take several thousand years to play out; one or two cycles do not define our species, yet the most recent historical periods are the limit of what the general population knows.

We are almost seven million years removed from the other primates. We cannot be defined by studying their behavior. Yes, chimps can be belligerent and sometimes form rudimentary "war parties" to attack other bands; however, bonobos are just as closely related to us and act entirely differently. They are peace loving and sensual. Orca whales are sometimes needlessly aggressive toward other species, but this is an exception—other whales are not. Elephants and other large-brained mammals are not combative. "Animal Planet" films show lions attacking their prey; this is how these animals obtain food. We let the slaughterhouse kill for us. Predators seeking food do not conduct war; many defend territory for reproduction "rights"; however, our brains, neural structures, and consciousness are many millions of years departed from these primate relatives. During this time frame, *Homo sapiens* have developed a biological filter to help us make constructive choices.

Humans' prefrontal lobes act as a censoring gate between angry emotions and overly aggressive behavior. This provides one element of our "free will." We have been given gifts unlike other animals: self-reflective consciousness, ingenious creativity, and free choice. Developing the prefrontal lobe's filtering function was essential to this biological evolution's success. Naturally, aberrations occur. According to the article "In the Minds of Men," in several different studies, the brains of murderers and other violent people were scanned using positron emission tomography. Results showed there were aberrations associated with various brain structures that normally regulate aggression, including "the orbital frontal cortex, associated with the ability to resist our physiological urges; the anterior cingulate cortex, involved in learning and pain perception; and the amygdala, linked to emotional modulation."

These physiological exceptions, often with a genetic or mental-illness basis, are not the norm; however, when social media focus on an abnormal person's behavior, without providing proper context, people generally come to believe that these dysfunctional actions are more ingrained in our society than they actually are. Given the appropriate resources, dysfunctional people can often be cured, sparing us from many episodes of social chaos, including children killing children in the classroom. A kinder society, one that the Ecological Epoch will create, can provide a different cultural milieu, one that will spawn fewer abnormal episodes.

It is also likely an aberrant, power-hungry person is more likely to covet authority than is a more normal peace-loving person. As a society, it is important to be vigilant so that we are not drawn into international conflicts, as has occurred in the past, by the fears and aggressive predilection of individuals with structurally deficient brains.

It's coming to America first,
the cradle of the best and of the worst.
It's here they got the range
and the machinery for change
and it's here they got the spiritual thirst.
It's here the family's broken
and it's here the lonely say
that the heart has got to open

in a fundamental way:
Democracy is coming to the USA.
—Leonard Cohen, from the song "Democracy"

The State of the Political World

It's important to remember that the world's seven-billion-plus people are spread across a large spectrum when considering access to wealth, nutrition, health care, education, and perhaps most important, information, including the Internet and all of its social-networking influences. The top one billion people also control almost all of the world's resources and means of production.

Barack Obama was reelected for a second presidential term on November 6, 2012. Prior to the election, he held three debates with his Republican challenger, Mitt Romney. Over the total four-and-a-half-hours of debating, neither candidate made any substantial reference to our planet's declining environmental health. The ice is melting, the seas are rising, entire animal species are disappearing, floods and droughts are rearing up more frequently, clean water is harder to come by, world population is exceeding sustainable limits, and there is increasing social unrest, but all we heard from both candidates was how to increase job creation to amp up the economy and how to quell increasing terrorism and its concurrent social unrest.

Obama was supposed to be a visionary president, yet during his reelection he was afraid to address the most severe challenge of our human era. Corporations provide huge political contributions. There is such a strong corporate resistance to climate-change legislation that Obama was unwilling to broach the issue until after he was reelected. During his second term, he gave lip service to climate-change issues; however, a weak environmental protection program will not suffice.

With atmospheric CO_2 concentrations at more than 400 ppm and climbing, we cannot afford to convert *any more* carbon from the ground into the atmosphere. Yet Obama's plans included increases in oil production, in addition to developing alternative energy sources. He is a caring, intelligent man. It is likely he will be personally saddened and heartbroken with remorse a decade from now when he realizes that he was the world's most powerful man, yet he did little to solve the world's greatest problem—one that will cause his children and grandchildren to suffer the consequences.

As I write, the political world is becoming more and more unstable due to scarce resources, including oil and water wars. Russia has invaded its neighbor. There have been extended wars in Iraq, Afghanistan, Libya, and Syria and violent government changes in Egypt, and other Arabic countries, as well as continuing Israeli–Arab tensions: oil wars, fundamentalist religious wars, and wealthy-versus-poor wars. This violence is mostly about worldwide wealth distribution. Each group is trying to protect or improve its own lifestyle and presumed *right* to pollute the air, change the climate, and sacrifice other species to accumulate more *stuff*.

On April 30, 2011, the world learned that a United Nations missile strike had attacked Muammar Gaddafi at his son's home. The Libyan leader was not hurt; his son and his son's three children, all were younger than twelve years old, were killed. Many Libyans rejoiced in the streets, celebrating the pain imposed on Gaddafi by this loss of his family members. Many Westerners, the attackers, felt like something positive had been achieved because Gaddafi was generally considered a rogue and enemy; at the same time, many had a distasteful gut feeling that we Westerners had "gotten away" with a terribly wrong action that killed young children. There was almost no international discussion or recrimination for this attack. But the gut reaction tells us something was wrong with a military action that purposefully targeted a household full of children. Soon thereafter, Muammar Gaddafi was deposed, located by a mob, and killed on the spot. Four years later the Libyan political unrest continues to build. In one country after another, religious fundamentalists are gaining ground.

In another incident, elite US Navy SEALs stormed Osama bin Laden's compound in Pakistan and apparently executed everyone inside. Five or six people were killed, including bin Laden's son and his female companion. Bin Laden was shot multiple times at close range. This time, it was the Westerners who celebrated in the streets, yelling, "USA! USA!"—again that sickening feeling welled up in many caring individuals.

On May 5, 2011, *The New York Times* reported the following: "Some Americans celebrated the killing of Osama bin Laden loudly, with chanting and frat-party revelry in the streets. Others were appalled—not by the killing, but by the celebrations." My friend, Michael Walbolt, a US Army veteran, wrote to me: "Being gone, I just got this news. The mood around me here on Cat Island didn't fit mine. Bin Laden was a profoundly cruel person, but I also believe that gleefully cheering his death and demanding his head on a stake says more about our collective dehumanization than his."

Was there any attempt to capture bin Laden and put him on trial? There's something amiss, something very wrong on both sides of the conflicts, including the insane resource wars that governmental and international corporations are promoting and pursuing. When we begin to fully use our collective creativity and our compassionate concern for all people, we will provide the needed resources for everyone—without wars. We know how to produce alternative energy. We also know that women's education and improved income opportunities in the poor regions will lower the world's population, allowing us to sustain everyone and begin to heal the planet.

Drone missiles, fired remotely from US bases, have become a primary weapon to attack those considered to be US enemies. There are no trials, no combat, and too little consideration for "collateral damage" that kills children and civilians. In Pakistan, the drone program led to a major deterioration of a formerly friendly relationship between the two countries. Notwithstanding the fact that the military target might be valid, the killing of innocent bystanders is murder by the state—a war crime. It is more evidence that we have lost our collective way. Five decades before Osama bin Laden, Martin Luther King, Jr. said, "I mourn the loss of thousands of precious lives, but I will not rejoice in the death of one, not even an enemy. Returning hate for hate multiplies hate, adding deeper darkness to a night already devoid of stars. Darkness cannot drive out darkness: only light can do that. Hate cannot drive out hate: only love can do that."

It's extremely difficult to change the mind of a fundamentalist who is on either side of a charged issue. The human population is growing. The media-driven desire for more cars, refrigerators, and televisions is multiplying; pollution is increasing. As long as we retain our current cultural mindset, all of these conditions mean that political conflicts over scarce resources will also increase. There is no easy political solution. Nothing less than changing how we see the world, our worldview, will solve the current dilemmas. This new story adds perspective that will help to integrate Ecological Epoch consciousness (EE consciousness) into our political and social landscape, thereby providing a lens through which we are able to see the myopic political propaganda and corporate greed that are currently creating irreversible ecological damage and leading us into to social chaos.

For a person to be as alive as it is possible to be, to fully express his or her humanity and experience his or her body, mind, and spirit in their most profound essence, it is important to participate in the Ecological Epoch, including an immersion in its ideas and emotions. The Ecological Epoch expresses a new, evolved worldview, both intellectual and intuitive, and provides guidelines for social behavior that respect and protect all life.

Integrating EE Consciousness

EE consciousness integrates all prior human consciousness stages—that is, all knowledge and consciousness that is now, and has ever been, available to humankind. Individuals perceive their surroundings through a personal, culturally bound worldview; as such, each person's world is at least partially an illusion created from his or her own biases. Entire societies and cultures follow suit. We each have our own unique physiological, emotional, and intellectual information-gathering skills. To the extent that a person successfully understands the connections that are inherent in Natural Harmony, his or her EE consciousness expands.

Changing our cultural biases and creating sustainable economies is daunting; in fact, it is overwhelming when considered as a task or responsibility. There is no evidence that the political and corporate policies currently in place are changing in ways that can possibly solve our looming challenges. In reality, things seem to be getting worse; this includes our governing policies, business ethics, and, more importantly, our collective attitude toward the looming dangers. Many are in denial, unwilling to face up to the issues because the consequences will occur down the road, not today. Others are purposefully choosing bottom-line profits with full knowledge that irreparable damage will occur from their business decisions.

Sometimes we change before we're forced to change; usually we do not. In today's political climate, jobs trump the earth's ecological health. Stockholders and voters want immediate results. It matters little which party is in power. Although structural problems within our worldwide economies will not change until our cultural perceptions and attitudes change, many people have changed and see the waterfall looming ahead. Therefore, political solutions are not impossible. Although there are barriers for politicians to make major changes on their own initiative, with enough public pressure, elected officials will follow the people's lead.

There are many good reasons for each of us to do our part in finding and implementing solutions—most compelling is that life becomes more meaningful. But what about hope? Even though we know how to solve our challenges, there is no rational reason to think we can implement the necessary changes in time; however, there are irrational reasons. The human species has amazing ingenuity. Change happens when least expected. The Berlin Wall tumbled down practically overnight. Individuals can beat addiction and transform themselves. So, too, can whole societies.

Entrenched special interests, especially those represented by people who own the mega-wealthy chemical, oil, and gas industries, not only *buy* political candidates with election contributions, they also *fund* scientific research. As would be expected from self-interest, the businesses fund scientists whose research results are expected to support their clients' business objectives. For example, Charles Koch is one of the wealthiest billionaire oilmen in the United States. His tax-exempt foundation paid for a $6 million research project by Richard A. Muller, who is a professor of physics at UC Berkeley and cofounder of the Berkeley EarthSurface Temperature Project. At the time, Muller was the highest-profile and most attention-grabbing "climate-change denier" in the country.

Although the United Nations Intergovernmental Panel on Climate Change and 98 percent of all climate scientists agree that global warming is now occurring and is caused by human activity, Muller made headlines by disagreeing. He claimed the changes were due to natural cycles and said they were not man-made. His lofty academic position and attention-getting style helped confuse the public and dilute governmental pressure for change. So he got the Koch money. He did his studies, and a remarkable thing happened: he changed.

Muller wrote in *The New York Times*: "Three years ago, I identified problems in previous climate studies that, in my mind, threw doubt on the very existence of global warming. Last year...I concluded that global warming was real and that the prior estimates of the rate of warming were correct. I'm now going a step further: Humans are almost entirely the cause.... The average temperature of the earth's land has risen by 2.5 degrees Fahrenheit over the past 250 years, including an increase of 1.5 degrees over the most recent fifty years. Moreover, it appears likely that essentially all of this increase results from the human emission of greenhouse gases."

He was *converted*. Muller uses that word himself to describe his turnaround. This incident has more significance than just its scientific research results. It represents awakening awareness—an important scientist's movement away from the Scientific Epoch and into the Ecological Epoch. Muller's heart and spirit were somehow affected, not just his intellect—thus he used the term "converted" to refer to himself. Because he is an important climate scientist who represented the far end of the global warming debate, *and he changed*, it shows that anything is possible. Hope exists. A grand transformation can occur.

Surely other politicians and corporate executives will have similar sudden conversions. This is where our hope for the future resides—in the unexpected, in the irrational, in the intuitive. Mostly, our hope comes from faith in the human capacity to find a way through, to be brilliant when circumstances require brilliance, because we are standing on a precipice that will destroy us unless we act brilliantly—now.

Enlightened Masculine and Divine Feminine

Last spring, my eighty-year-old friends renewed their marriage vows in a ceremony attended by one hundred people. It was held under a massive five-hundred-year-old oak tree at a beautiful environmental retreat center called the Ojai Foundation. The ceremony was a ritual to honor equality in the male-female, feminine-masculine coming together. This couple is truly merged in love and partnership. They are two wise elders, a psychiatrist and an innovative educator whose blended lives, according to their own description, have created a "third" entity that represents their commonalities. Likewise, *the Ecological Epoch is characterized by the marriage of the enlightened masculine with the divine feminine*. This coming together was inevitable. Our story describes the ways in which we now see that our world has more depth than we have previously known, and it reveals the new epoch we have entered.

In the *New Creation Story, Book One*, I introduced readers to a "wisdom guide" named Sophia who has presented herself to me during various meditations over the years. I sometimes encounter her in my dreams and daydreams, also. When I'm pondering a question, I often ask for her advice. Sometimes I hear her advice without asking. Sophia continues to provide guidance within our current story:

(3:3) As I sat near the tree trunk looking skyward through the high, ancient branches, Sophia came into my awareness—at that moment my consciousness was drawn down into the oak's deeply embedded root system and concurrently upward to the brilliant sun, whose rays were filtered by the oak leaves. Aw, yes! Sophia and the tall oak for me, in that moment, became a bridge from Earth to sky, from dark to light. The oak's chlorophyll, coupling with the sun's photons to draw carbon into its giant body, builds its earthly form. In the recent past, this same tree sustained indigenous people, providing acorns to eat and protection from rain, wind, and sun. The ceremony, occurring a few meters away, extolled beauty within one's heart and mind. It was a love crucible to promote healthy relationship and this coupling's captivating, deepening intimacy.

Earth-honoring mythologies of past epochs described goddesses and gods with both otherworldly and human qualities. Some deities championed the Earth and its plants and animals; for example, the goddess Inanna knew how to descend into the underworld and return, bringing new life with her. Times passed; cultures changed. Patriarchal mythologies honored transcendent sky gods and goddesses. When connections to the Darkness and the goddess were lost, repressed, and denied, the masculine principle became distorted. These newer, male-dominated cultures were often absent-hearted in their exuberance; however, they eventually gave us science, literature, complex music, and spaceships to Mars—a necessary progression as we evolved toward the Ecological Epoch.

The disconnected masculine embraces domination. This sometimes results in wholesale destruction—evidence that respect for the feminine has been lost. Woman, in particular, have suffered from this disconnect. The patriarchal cycle is now in its death throes; we have begun the next cycle. It will be integrated. We have a choice of methods: either through divine inspiration or through pain and trauma. Whichever occurs, we humans will soon see the world differently. Change is upon us.

Our generation's most important question begs answers: "What new relationship with Mother Earth is needed to defuse the dangerous challenges we face? When will we see that changing the planet's atmosphere will be disastrous for today's life on Earth?" Fortunately, we do have answers: energy systems can be replaced on a wholesale basis; man-made toxins can be removed from our everyday lives so they no longer foul our bodies, water, land, and air; and wealth can be more fairly distributed, thus reducing family sizes and overall population. These changes will come about from *seeing* the nature of reality more deeply. How long will it take to transform our culture and our economies? This answer will determine how much suffering my children and grandchildren will have to endure. We are now charting a new course for Spaceship Earth.

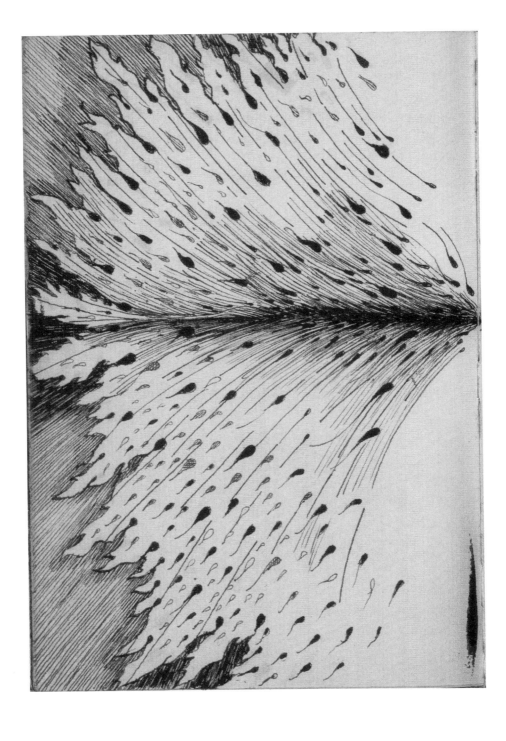

CHAPTER 2

POPULATION GROWTH AND CONSCIOUSNESS

Today's world population is moving toward eight billion, continuing to grow rapidly. The best projections are that it will increase to nine billion by the year 2050. The current rate of increase for the wealthiest countries is less than half a percent per year and falling, so a stable balance has almost been achieved; the rate for the poorest countries is 2.3 percent per year, about six times as much. Almost all of the increase by 2050 will occur in the developing world. Does this mean that the poor are responsible for causing overpopulation and its consequent environmental damage? Let's look further, comparing the *poorest one billion* to the wealthiest: Wealthy populations have six times the number of phones, five times the number of Internet users; fifty times the number of computers, and seventy-five times the number of automobiles, and they produce thirteen times the amount of CO_2 emissions per person. This means, in terms of industrial pollution, one newborn in the United States is equivalent to thirteen new children in a poor country.

Two percent of the world's seven billion-plus people own 50 percent of the world's wealth. About five billion people have incomes of less than $4,000 per year. The remaining two billion have incomes exceeding $4,000. This higher-income group, about 30 percent of the world's people, has greater life expectancy, much lower childhood mortality, better access to good sanitation (toilets and clean water), and lower death rates from infectious diseases. Fertility rates are directly correlated to infant mortality, education, and income opportunities. More education for women equates to a much lower fertility rate.

People in developing countries do not require automobiles, phones, and computers for fertility rates to decline. What's needed is literacy, education, access to birth control, and basic income opportunities for women. These requirements are not too expensive when compared to, for instance, worldwide military budgets.

Ecological damage and climate chaos are less a function of human population than of human consumption. The average person in the United States uses six times as much of the Earth's resources when compared to worldwide individual consumption. Most of the world's seven billion-plus people live simple lives because they have no choice; however, a large number, about two billion, are on the cusp of obtaining the necessary wealth to purchase and consume more. Fueling this dangerous expansion in China, for example, are numerous coal-burning electrical plants, the most polluting energy source. Coal-energy plants are being constructed to satisfy that country's consumer-goods aspirations. China is also a leader in solar energy technology, less for ecological reasons than for practical ones. Their economy is growing so quickly that they need all the energy sources they can develop.

In Alberta, Canada, tar-sands oil production is almost as dirty and destructive as China's coal. It is massive in every respect; the world's largest trucks are filled from Earthmovers as big as a three-story house. Tar-sands oil production uses the energy equivalent of one barrel of oil to create three new barrels, creating massive CO_2 emissions in the process. It destroys the intact, virgin boreal forests that cover the sands. Massive clean-water resources are turned to industrial waste and stored in huge, unlined "tailing" dams, causing toxic liquid to leach downward into the water table. The tar sands are remotely located so extensive pipelines are needed to get the oil to markets. Accidents and spills cause more environmental damage, native communities suffer, and pristine rivers become polluted. The corporations involved have plans to triple tar-sands oil production in the near term.

According to Robert Kennedy, Jr., senior attorney for a large environmental protection group: "Those tar sands contain a carbon reservoir equivalent to all the carbon burned in human history.... (The new pipeline) will light the fuse on that carbon bomb and trigger still more climate upheaval." The Alberta tar-sands project is the most impactful single-location, man-made environmental destruction the world has ever seen. Even worse, the engineers operating this project have developed technology that is spreading to other countries. The United States is pursuing similar tar-sand oil production on a smaller scale in Utah. Other states and countries are following suit. Recently, the US has also authorized expanded oil production in the pristine Alaska wilderness.

Creation stories are born from their own era's consciousness stage. The Bible's Genesis story encourages people to be profligate and populate the land. It also gives the people permission to rule over the "beasts" of the land.

(3:4) This Genesis story was created at a time when the earth's population was less than two hundred million individuals. Most of the world was wild, containing forests and mountainous areas where "beasts" ruled. Time passed. The human species spectacularly proliferated, multiplying more than thirty-five times. Soon there were more than seven billion people—the one beget the many and became the thirty-five. Wildness shrunk away until it now exists primarily in special "protected" areas that are barely wild at all. In a desire to entertain each other, to live grandly, and to move around the globe, a small number of the more than seven billion people continue to "use up" the world, and now entire ecological systems have become unbalanced and verge on collapse. The beasts have been bound in zoos and animal parks, fulfilling the creation story's mandate.

The three-thousand-year-old Genesis creation story had a major impact on the people and the planet. In the most recent one hundred years another myth gained prominence; it promotes production and consumption and is layered on top of the *profligate* story, adding insult to the Earth's ongoing injury: *As industry booms, personal income expands apace, bringing more cars, more factories, and more climate chaos. This is the story of a psychotic human animal that, in its craziness, ate its own children. Economic growth at the expense of the planet's ability to sustain life is the most shortsighted objective imaginable. It is an uninformed story espoused by highly educated, intelligent people who are ignoring the impending decline; as such, they have become ignorant. The mother of depression hovers in the shadows.*

The Ecological Epoch provides a different story, one that is needed because Earth's living systems are deteriorating. Human consciousness has recently attained another stage:

(3:5) Our story proposes a future based on a new worldview: one that values the Earth and all its human and animal inhabitants so much that the wealthy are willing to forgo what they do not need in order to help the less fortunate to live in abundant simplicity. A few decades before our current time, we began to hear stories of dire scenarios to come because human population was soon to reach twelve billion. But something shifted in the wealthier European countries: Women became more educated, and larger numbers entered into careers; birth control became widely available and accepted; women's incomes rose, and the number of children per household began to decline. Without government directives, many countries leveled their population growth, and some, including Italy and Russia, began to lose population. In Asia, China discouraged large families through government policy. But the economically disadvantaged majority in Asia, Africa, and South America continued to produce a great many children in hopes that their offspring would provide some old-age security for them. Poor conditions for women create population growth. Women don't want to be exclusively tied to the home with too many children and no other life opportunities. As occurred in Europe, population will stabilize without government intervention if women are provided birth-control methods, basic education, and satisfactory income-earning opportunities. World population is a global issue that affects all nations. The wealthy will improve their children's futures by helping the poor attain stability, thereby reducing planet-wide overpopulation. For a time, there will continue to be wealthy people and countries; however, their concern for the planet and for others in the new epoch will mean that eventually everyone will have enough for shelter, food, and healthy living conditions. Population will, thereafter, decline spontaneously. When global population stabilizes, the planet and all its people will benefit.

Human population is a problem, but it's not *the* problem—that honor goes to overconsumption, which we will address in detail. But first, let's look at our astonishing population history. In the first millennium, beginning at the time of Jesus of Nazareth, in the year 1 CE (of the Common Era), the world population was about two hundred million. It took until 1800 CE to reach one billion for the first time. To state this numerical concept in another way, humans separated from the other primates almost seven million years ago; therefore, it took this entire time span to accumulate one billion individuals for the first time. The year was 1800.

It took 130 years to add an additional billion people, for a total of two billion by the year 1930. The Scientific Revolution set the stage for massive industrial expansion, which led to wealth creation and better healthcare for the wealthy; the average life span increased in Sweden, for example, from thirty-two years in 1800 CE to eighty-two years today. After staying relatively steady for about eight thousand generations since *Homo sapiens* first appeared, lifespans in the wealthy nations have gone into orbit in the past eight generations.

As wealth accumulated, a growing middle class had the means to feed and house more children, and infant mortality rates declined. The next billion people appeared in thirty years—by 1960, we totaled three billion; another fourteen years to 1974 added a billion more, now four billion total;

the next billion took thirteen years, so in 1987 we were five billion; by millennium's end in 1999, we had become six billion; and as I write in 2014, we have recently surpassed seven billion people.

To put this population growth into human consciousness terms, consider this: It was 1677 when Antoni van Leeuwenhoek created improved lenses for microscopes and determined that human sperm contained millions of living, swimming cells that he called "animalcules." It was about 150 years later, around 1820, when scientists "discovered" human egg cells and thereby finally realized how an embryo came into being. The population was just above one billion. Two hundred years later, we will be about eight billion. How recently removed are we from the innocent ignorance of our species!

Demographic Transition

What population changes are likely to occur in the near future? Experts recently predicted there will be about nine billion people by midcentury. A billion people were added in twelve years between 1999 and 2011. Along with this prediction, there was optimism that the nine billion level would be the maximum and that a decline would then take hold; however, in the spring of 2011, projections by the United Nations population division, a group that has an excellent track record, estimated additional growth to 10.3 billion by the year 2100. They prophesize growth will end in 2100, and some retraction in numbers will occur thereafter. That time frame is just three generations away.

A demographic transition is occurring throughout the world. Health care is improving, and child mortality is falling. Better sanitation and food availability will extend any given population's life span; people live longer, thus expanding population even as birthrates decline. A generation or two ago, a typical woman in a poor country might have borne six children because she expected to lose three or four of them. Having lots of children was also old-age insurance for the parents. In most countries, conditions have improved; when women have choices, including access to contraception and education, they have fewer children.

There is a lag time of a generation or two from the point where conditions improve, resulting in longer life spans, and the point where birthrates decline. A large part of the planet's population increase will occur in Africa, with gains of 2.6 billion people by 2100. Countries like Nigeria and other midcontinent African states have the highest birth rates, and the population is now living longer—a formula for drastic overpopulation. Nigeria is projected to double its population by 2050, adding 160 million people (almost half the current US population) in a land with minimal resources to provide for all those new appetites.

Some countries, including Brazil and the United States, have falling birthrates; however, the population continues to grow because, with longevity increasing, births are still more numerous than the replacement rate at which new births balance with the number of people who die. Of course, net immigration also increases a country's population. The United States is expected to add 113 million people by 2050, a one-third increase. Russia, Italy, and Japan have an aging population due to improved socioeconomic conditions. Each country has birthrates that have declined enough so that they balance with deaths, resulting in no population growth.

A few decades ago, China had a major population growth problem. Starting in 1979, the government implemented directives that penalized families with more than one child; one generation later, population growth was under control. The birth/death rate is now below replacement level, and the population is beginning to stabilize. Although growth will continue through 2050, a significant decline is projected thereafter.

India has tried for decades to get its growth under control, without success. It is expected to add more than one half a billion people by 2050, an incredible number for a country struggling with poverty. The state of Kerala in southern India is a notable exception. This region is not wealthy;

however, the government has focused on women's education, high literacy rates, and concern-for-all welfare policies, and the population has stabilized.

The international community knows what is needed. As early as 1994, the United Nations International Conference on Population and Development recognized two priorities. One was stabilizing world population, and the other was creating sustainable economic development and growth. Twenty years down the road, we have accomplished little on either front. Our experts know what is needed, but the powers that be thwart the necessary changes and blunt the resolve of the few visionary politicians in office.

As the United Nations statement points out, population growth is not the only issue to be solved in our quest for a sustainable world that can support future generations without further degradation. Appropriate economic systems and pollution reduction are just as critical. Many critics from wealthier countries decry population growth in the developing nations as an impending "population bomb"; however, the ecological footprint of the world's poorest two billion people is negligible when compared to that of wealthy nations.

The United States makes up about 4 percent of the world's population and uses 25 percent of its energy, thereby far exceeding the world's average. When compared to the planet's lowest one-third income earners, the typical US person uses twenty to one hundred times more resources. And the United States is continuing to expand its population with aspirations to consume even more per person! There is little talk about leveling off, or sustainability, or living with less, or simplifying one's lifestyle. It's bad politics for candidates or elected officials to do so—even anathema to the American *way of life*. Our story faces a paradox:

(3:6) Wealthy peoples' consumption creates climate chaos, melting ice, and rising oceans. The poor are more affected than the rich because the poor have almost no assets; therefore, no margin of error. A small sea-level rise will wipe out a large percentage of rice production in low-lying countries such as Bangladesh, India, and Vietnam. The poor become more destabilized from harsher conditions. Floods, droughts, and hurricanes reduce their food and health security. They continue to have larger families to compensate for losses. The solution is to improve poor peoples' living standard, but the earth's resources are now being utilized in excess—that is, faster than they can be replenished.

An intractable conundrum exists: Population growth in the developing world and in the wealthier nations is a critical issue that directly impacts the earth's health. Even small growth in high-consuming societies has a huge effect. And large population growth in low-income areas also carries an ecological toll—people cut the trees for firewood to cook a simple meal; wild animals are displaced as larger human populations look for homes to sustain their families in the remotest Amazonian jungles; species extinctions continue to mount.

There is now a "consumption bomb" ticking away along with the earlier recognized population bomb. These are the two sides of the same coin, which is buying economic collapse and worldwide depression. How could it be otherwise? The year 1945 was a watershed in which world economies and the atomic bomb began to overwhelm the earth's supportive resources; by 1983, we were consuming 100 percent of what was "restorable"; today we would need 1.4 Earths to provide and then restore what we are consuming. We are using up the Earth at a rapid pace. It's easy to see that this cannot proceed for long.

In newly developing countries like China and Brazil, the movement out of poverty is achieved by burning more polluting coal or damming large, wild rivers, as is occurring now with Brazil's massive Belo Monte dam. This and a series of other dams planned for the Brazilian Amazon will permanently change the region's ecology with dire wildlife consequences; in addition, the indigenous people who live close to nature and depend on the undammed rivers for a livelihood will suffer the most—all in the name of economic development to provide electricity to growing populations.

The population issue is relatively clear. In the past few decades, great strides have been accomplished, and the many doomsday population scenarios have been brought into better focus. We are on a trajectory for a stable world population. But what quality of life can the world provide ten billion people, the expected population just forty years from now? There is a paradox: Higher living standards reduce family sizes and stabilize world population; however, we already consume more than the Earth can provide. And we are still embracing a cultural priority of further economic growth and consumption. How, then, can we provide more for everyone? The answer is simple: we cannot. In our new story, the following is true:

(3:7) "Seeing" is essential—the time of reckoning is arriving. We are knowledgeable enough to change course; change we will, either by choice or by imposition. The time for choice is limited. We cannot provide more stuff, more fossil-fuel cars, more second homes at the beach, more jet-airplane travel. What we can provide, upon changing our perspective, is a more meaningful life based on how we "see" the world. We can enjoy more relationships and intimacy; we can provide more spiritual connection. Nonpolluting alternative energy is a reality. Solar panels on the roof create electricity locally, without giant, polluting utilities.

In the future, high-speed electric trains will move us around, perhaps to fewer places than we are used to going, but we will get to know and love our local region better when we stay closer to home. In this case, less is more. Taking care of our neighbors and the Earth, simplifying our lifestyle, needing less stuff, and thereby having plenty—these are the qualities that create sustainable economies and a stabilized world population. This New Creation Story is meant to redefine our life purpose, recognize the Earth as sacred, and live in Natural Harmony—to "live simply so that others may simply live."

Nine or ten billion people can live together peaceably, as long as we make appropriate decisions about energy sources, pollution, and planetary wealth distribution. Our story shows us what the Earth can provide given today's remarkable technologies. The planet offers us tremendous recurring bounty, if we only use what can be restored. Many nonpolluting production methods are available, but we need courage to make changes and implement new ideas—to use our incredible genius to develop sustainable production that does not degrade our own nest, to share these life gifts equitably with others, and to discover satisfaction in relationships and profound experiences rather than in consuming and possessing.

Creation Stories emerge more from mystical experiences than from facts and information. Indigenous cultures have normally had shamans who are a reservoir for the community's mysteries and wisdom. The group's elders choose and initiate young people to become shamans based on the initiate's personality, skills, focus, discipline, and interest in the mystical. These young men and women are taught to *see* differently. There are modern-culture shamans as well; both men and women, they focus on Earth-honoring spiritual practice. They *see* and communicate the human-to-nature relationship, recognize our culture's "dis-ease," and attempt to heal our wounded planet.

Their thought process and communication methods are not necessarily scientific; they are more likely intuitive and metaphorical. Shamans are charged with protecting the people and the planet, guiding us on a middle path that benefits both and holds in heart and mind a vision for future generations' wellbeing. Our Creation Story is a shamanic approach to *seeing* the world. Shamanic wisdom and the evolution of human consciousness are partially a function of population density:

(3:8) There are thirty-five times as many people on the planet today as there were in Jesus's time. The Scientific Revolution was launched in 1600 CE, about four hundred years ago, when world population was around half a billion people. Perhaps half a billion people on the planet, for the first time ever, informed by the Renaissance, was a necessary critical mass needed to expand conscious awareness so that the systematic, logical thinking that we call the scientific method could take hold.

After several hundred more years had passed, these half a billion people propagated the first worldwide population totaling one billion people. This was a new critical mass that brought forth further consciousness evolution, producing the Industrial Revolution's many inventions: steam engines, mass-production factories, engineering technologies for bridges and buildings—all of these and much more blossomed to life. Although there was limited worldwide communication, in mysterious, interconnected ways this era's ingenious inventors were drawing from the intellectual and creative insights of the earth's entire one billion people.

From our story's shamanistic perspective, a billion-person popu-lation density was necessary to expand our planet-wide information "library" so that individual inventors could access the ideas needed to materialize their inventions. Intuition informs invention more than rational thought does. New creativity expanded and was stored in books and professional papers; it also accrued in nonmaterial forms, in cultural archetypes, and in amorphous planetary information clouds. Thus, it was necessary to have one billion humans on Earth to create "industry." Partially as a result of the success of the Industrial Revolution and the wealth it provided, human population began a further exponential expansion. By 1945, there were two and one half billion humans alive. That same year, during World War II, like the mythological heroes who stole fire from the gods, we built the atomic bomb using nuclear fission. We lost no time detonating this bomb in the densely populated Japanese city, Hiroshima—a watershed moment for the deteriorating human-to-nature relationship. Within a few decades, we reached, then exceeded, the earth's capacity to absorb our bomb testing and other industrious "insults"—the ongo-ing wounding that continues to damage the planet's living systems today: more bombs, more stuff, more people, more destruction.

When the planet's human density reached almost four billion, the earth's creative milieu brought forth new visionaries and proph-ets, including the author Aldous Huxley and others; Rachel Carson's book, *Silent Spring*, was published in 1962 and marked a new dimension in the human–nature relationship. In an effort to offset the ongoing social degeneration into production-and-consumption meaninglessness, these wise elders provided us with early warn-ings. Several more decades passed, and human population density continued to grow, thus providing an even greater creative, visionary base from which to draw. World population was a little more than six billion in the year 2000. As the millennium turned over, this popula-tion density was the critical mass needed for enough people to finally "see" the ongoing planetary damage and begin changing course. It took six billion people for our species to fully realize the current criti-cal necessity for a healthy relationship with the natural world.

The Ecological Epoch had arrived, and with it came thousands of environmental visionaries. Thomas Berry, a Catholic priest, wrote about Earth's sacred nature using concepts that are both accessible and inspi-rational. Brian Swimme provided awe-inspiring descriptions of humans' relationship to the cosmos. Lester Brown and his World Watch Institute published a series of "issues and solutions" manuscripts detailing the ecological problems and ways to solve each one. Al Gore swayed public opinion about the dangers of global warming and received the Nobel Prize for this work.

Currently, two cultural streams are on a parallel course. One is business as usual, blinded by greed and short-term profit; the other is a loosely knit coalition of artists, scientists, citizens, and even some businesspeople crying out for "a vision that all living things can share." Human population continues to expand. Planetary stress continues to grow. Our ingenuity will be tested severely in the coming decades. What population density is required to provide the creative genius necessary to rebalance life on Earth? The Earth can provide for nine or ten billion individuals but only if these are respectful human beings willing to be in humble relationship with nature.

Our greatest expression of love for our children is to deemphasize our addiction to *stuff* so that we can reclaim life's meaning and spiritual connections. It will take hard work for the next three or four decades, especially the onerous necessity to provide for ten billion or more people while we're learning not to degrade the planet further—but provide we can. We are once again witnessing Shiva's cosmic dance on Earth: death and rebirth, destruction and restoration. The older, consumption-diseased mindset is just beginning to fall away, yielding to the new consciousness. To live in Natural Harmony is to give priority to relationships and to increase intimacy with others and with nature. It means that we recognize a spiritual dimension in our everyday activities, thus realizing that the Earth is sacred essence.

CHAPTER 3

ECOLOGICAL EPOCH PHILOSOPHY

It is not clear that "time" exists; however, our solar system does have a definitive age. It is in midlife. Our story continues:

(3:9) Planet Earth is aging. In this process, it is building complexity. Human consciousness is one important example. We are coming to understand the world in more profound ways: how it was born, its geology, its life, and the regenerative systems that maintain all of its species in healthy balance. It functions as a holistic system—also a hierarchical one. Today's living species are built upon scaffolding provided by earlier life forms. Likewise, human consciousness has evolved from ancient forms.

The Earth is one fabric woven from interactive cycles: energy making matter then reverting to energy and repeating the process. All energy, all particles, and all bits are essential components. Nothing is excluded or superfluous. Beneath the material world, a quantum universe shimmers in vibrational excitement—an energy and matter matrix that sustains all material form. Complexity continues to evolve from this holism.

Existential challenges expand human consciousness because addressing these challenges creates deepened insight. Solving these survival problems eventually results in a new human consciousness stage—unique cultures are spawned as old epochs fall away, and new ones take their place. Spirituality takes on new forms. Worldviews become more comprehensive and pluralistic.

About four hundred years ago, the new, scientific-rational mindset began to analyze the world by reducing it to component parts. We have employed this working-parts knowledge to build skyscrapers, factory farms, airplanes, and nuclear missiles. This dissecting process created a fascination with components, and in the process we lost respect for the unified whole. Now our reductionist approach is tearing the fabric of Earth's living systems—a cloth that has been inexorably woven from minute threads to whole fabric over billions of years. Our shelter, our protection, our ecology have been diminished.

These insults have compelled the appearance of Ecological Epoch consciousness and with it a new spirituality based on scientific wholeness—seeing the Earth itself as a sacred manifestation of Creative Source. Our Creation Story is in alignment with recent developments in science and reveals that "form" and "emptiness," matter and energy, are different and yet the same—one unified matrix. This provides us with a scientifically based, Earth-honoring spirituality that has emerged from ecological consciousness and illuminates our numinous world.

Ecology

Creation stories attempt to explain life's meaning. In what respect is the term "Ecological Epoch" an appropriate moniker to represent the next step forward in human awareness? The word "ecology" is derived from a Greek word that combines "house" and "study." The Earth is our house, our home, our shelter, our sustainer, and our protector. Ecological study is based on systems—each part, no matter how small, is embedded in an inseparable whole that can perform properly only when playing in concert. The planet was formed about 4.57 billion years ago. Current life goes back about 3.8 billion years. Today's ecology *is* that first life, built upon, added to, and made more complex, evolving and enduring from then until now.

Just as our heart beats without our conscious attention, Earth's dynamic systems function with minimal human comprehension. Until recently, our society wasn't very concerned with ecological functioning. We were too busy dissecting the "working" parts to build our next invention. Now, out of necessity, the Ecological Epoch has arrived: the cars, the oil, the climate, the water, the air, our fellow species, the nuclear weapons and waste—all of these things are pushing back at us in ways that have changed how we perceive the world. They are providing a more comprehensive Creation Story:

(3:10) Earth's ecology houses ecosystems, which are complex, interdependent life processes that have developed together and adapted to one another over vast time frames. This results in mutually beneficial, community-sustaining relationships. Ecosystems are made up of both living beings and geological elements that interact to provide life support for the entire gestalt. They are biophysical systems. Life processes adapt; energy moves through these living communities in various ways to keep them healthy. Ecosystems are developed and sustained through incomprehensibly complex interactions.

The "biosphere" is the interactive sum total of all life contained in Earth's ecosystems. Chemical processes, geology, and biology interact in biogeochemical cycles that, over long time periods, create an interdependent system that balances itself in equilibrium, producing sustainable cycles lasting many millions of years. Minerals in the soil; rain; rivers, lakes, and oceans; gases in the atmosphere—these components and numerous others are the geochemical players that interpenetrate with living organisms—from bacteria to elephants to mountains to spiders, all living in delicate ecological balance.

Life is built from six elements that comprise the large molecules found in all living things: hydrogen, carbon, oxygen, nitrogen, phosphorus, and sulfur. Through mysterious biological intelligence, they are drawn from the chemical world into the living world. Chemical interaction underlies all geological processes and also creates all life, thus building interrelation within ecosystems. The life, the geology, and the chemistry work and play together. Thus, the biogeochemical cycles are born.

The Anthropocene

Our prehuman—that is to say *hominid*—ancestors branched from their primate relatives about seven million years ago. There have been ecological cycles, including various ice ages, during this time frame; however, planet-wide ecosystems have been in dynamic equilibrium. The Earth normally maintains geologic equilibrium that lasts for long time periods that are eventually followed by disruption and dramatic change. This transformative process eventually establishes a new and different equilibrium. The disruption often causes a large percentage of living species to disappear, thus opening new "niches" for different life forms to thrive. Human activity is beginning to cause such a disruption.

Some geologists, anthropologists, and other scientists propose we have entered into a new geological epoch called the "anthropocene." The name indicates that humans are affecting the planet's geology, atmosphere, hydrosphere, and biology to such an extent that our actions are now shaping Earth's physical form and function. The term "novel ecosystems" was recently introduced into professional ecological conversations. Unlike normal ecosystems, human activity often functions in parasitic fashion relative to the living Earth. This relating is nonreciprocal and therefore novel.

The term "technosphere" refers to the world's cumulative technological development and its effects on the planet's functioning, as well as its impacts on living beings. The technosphere is a human-created ecological system designed to provide comfort and prosperity for humans. It is not interactive with, nor supportive of, the earth's natural ecosystems. Therefore, it is considered to be novel. The consequences of the technosphere's unintended rapacious nature are damaging to practically all other living systems, producing unconsciously malicious behavior that causes climate change, destroyed animal and plant habitat, reduced biodiversity, inevitable mass extinctions, and various other deleterious consequences. The technosphere can create new life forms through genetic engineering;

however, there is little understanding about how this new life will interact with the existing planetary equilibrium. That is, there is insufficient concern for integration within nature's time-tested ecological niches that took many million years to emerge and perfect.

Humans live and work in various "anthropogentric biomes," which they create or modify for their own use: densely populated cities, rural villages, farmlands, grasslands, forests, and even oceans. There are few locations in which humans improve or maintain healthy, "natural" conditions in symbiotic interaction. In this respect, the technosphere is a parasitic, novel system that preys on other ecosystems.

Humans are not unnatural. We are children of the Earth and, because of our reflective consciousness, population density, and technology, we have become the dominant species. We are one animal within a vast system; however, for better or for worse, we have become the *keystone species* with life-and-death influence over all the earth's living communities.

Are we important? Yes, for our ability to support or collapse the ecological systems. Are we special? If we find our place within the system, survive, and become supportive of other life on Earth, we will have accomplished something special. If not, we will be shuffled off the planet, and in a few million years, another life form will be given the opportunity we now have—*a brief chance to advance consciousness toward intimacy with divine creation*. We do not yet know if we are special; our potential is built on the backs of our ancestors going back 3.8 billion years. Consciousness and spirit may advance through us humans, or it may find other avenues for its next, more complex expression. How we humans act in the near future is likely to decide this fate.

As mentioned earlier, there are two possible outcomes to our current destructive behavior: a proactive, graceful transition into an Earth-honoring sustainable way of life or economic collapse from the rising seas, weather anomalies, clean-water scarcity, and agricultural disruption—all creating innumerable environmental refugees, social chaos, and human death.

No matter which scenario eventual holds sway, the end result will be a worldwide society that has dramatically changed its appreciation for the earth's living systems and biological functioning. We will have completed the Ecological Epoch journey—changing our relationship with nature from ignorance to a reorientation based on respect and reverence. Will the transition needed to integrate this new consciousness into our culture be graceful or traumatic? That is *the* issue of our generation's short journey here on Earth.

Axial Age Wisdom Informs Our Creation Story

Ecological consciousness integrates all prior stages of human consciousness; however, it differs from Gene Gebser's *integral consciousness*. It is not the ultimate be-all, end-all stage; rather, it is the most advanced consciousness experienced thus far in Earth's evolution. There will be additional, future stages to come if we survive our current challenges. The next stage will absorb and integrate Ecological Epoch consciousness and will show up in ways we cannot yet conceive.

The Ecological Epoch requires a new worldview; nonetheless, it has been built on ancient wisdom. Some of the Axial Age sages who were discussed in *The New Creation Story's Book Two: Consciousness* also inform this segment of our new story. Today's advancing consciousness was grown from some of these brilliant, philosophical traditions. They are the intellectual and heartfelt core from which the Ecological Epoch emerged and are a foundation for our New Creation Story, as the following brief survey indicates:

(3:11) **Hesiod**'s Theogony proposed that the primeval Universe was Chaos. Out of Chaos was born Gaia, the Earth as deity—the Sacred Earth. The next quality to be born into existence was Eros; much more than erotic sexual encounter, Eros is attraction on all levels, including gravity, love, and all forms of relationship. Eros is the glue that bonds all living things.

There is an orderly, physical universe with exacting organizational qualities, conditions, and interactions. Discovering these qualities and living in coherence with them is the purpose of one's life. The Universe is self-regulated, without gods and goddesses; its relational nature supports an individual's concern for all life. One avoids killing anything whenever possible. Kindness in thoughts and deeds is a priority, as is a nonjudgmental outlook and respect toward others. Each soul is in a different relationship to higher consciousness, while striving in its own way for divine connection. These qualities define Eros.

Tao is the core of all things. Neither the human species nor an individual person is more important than any other of the many thousand things that compose the Tao. Humans have free will. The Tao is built from harmonious interrelationships that can be discovered and followed by a person, which is the epitome of a successful life on Earth. The Tao is a united interweaving of all diverse things, each with its unique existence and importance. "The Way" is the natural and harmonious state. "Wu wei" is the calming of desire and the epitome of correct behavior—the term is at once complex and paradoxical; it means both "nonaction" and "acting spontaneously within the moment's flow."

Confucian leaders are obligated to understand the people's needs and make decisions based on wellbeing for society. Each person is ethically obligated to work toward becoming virtuous and benefiting society. Confucius emphasized the "Golden Rule": Treat others as you wish to be treated. This requires compassionate understanding of the other person's circumstance. Li is a "given" standard of order to which an individual should strive to conform; each person can build Li through his skillful efforts and actions, all for the betterment of society. Li is not a fixed field but one that can be augmented from ethical actions. The term "Yi" represents behavior that is based on reciprocity and benevolence. Empathy is a guide for one's actions; it is better than reliance on government rules.

The core of **Buddha**'s message is this: One's mind creates suffering based on life's complications; suffering is caused from sensual craving, concern for status, recognition, importance, accomplishment, and fear of one's own death. Suffering can be ended by practices that discipline our thinking and behavior, resulting in an exemplary life of "right thought" and "right action." "Dukkha" is a normal state of human existence that includes anxiety, stress, frustration, discomfort, displeasure, anger, grief, and other forms of suffering. In actuality, neither "I" nor "mine" exists; we are fooled into thinking that the information we receive from our five senses is actually who we are, so we cling to these sensations. But they are not who we really are so they create Dukkha. The ultimate objective of Buddha's teaching is to show a person how to transcend suffering and thereby obtain total awareness and peacefulness. This is an ethical philosophy based on focusing one's mind by using meditative practices.

Heraclitus taught that fire is the basis for all things; through fire there is an ongoing rebirthing process and constant transformation occurring. Via fire, air is created. Air is transformed into water. This world was created neither by gods nor men, rather by fire, which with its creations has always existed as ever-ongoing phenomena. Fire gives rise to all things, and all things are eventually interchanged through fire. The stable state of an object is just an illusion because all objects are in constant flux between building up and tearing down. What we perceive as stable is a temporary state of harmony between the "strife" of the coming into existence and the going out, dissolving away. This tension between opposites provides temporary, provisional substance. All things are in constant flux, and the universe has a flowing nature. In this respect, everything is in the process of "becoming."

Socrates considered the essence of a thing to be its "Ideal Form." The physical object has some significance, but one's ethical and spiritual focus should be on the Ideal Form, not the substance. Knowledge and wisdom do not come from the study of substance but from "recollection" that illuminates the Ideal Forms. There is a transcendent, divine element to learning; it is not just observation of physical properties. Human custom is often at variance with nature; on the other hand, poetry is divinely inspired; the rapture of altered states, including alcohol, dreams, and sensuality, is to be appreciated because it helps provide divine connection.

Form Is No Other than Emptiness

To explore the forefront of human consciousness is to immerse oneself in a spiritual quest. To discover our Earth's most profound inner workings, its Natural Harmony, is to reveal its divine nature. There is a fundamental human urge to experience the Earth as sacred. Many threads weave our new epoch's fabric: cosmology, life origins, biological evolution, consciousness evolution, anthropology, psychology, spirituality, religion, civilizations, ecology, art, politics, economics, law, and science.

Ours is a story for the new millennium. In our old story, we were seen as isolated individuals, separated in time and space; our new story shows that we are interconnected with one another and the entire planet in ways that we are just beginning to discover. In the past, scientific reductionism, understanding the parts but not the whole, created scientific materialism. The Ecological Epoch embraces *scientific spiritualism*. Our saving grace is that we finally realize the havoc our actions have wrought on the planet, and now we care.

Our current origin myth could be called "scientific mythology." The "Big Bang" does not attempt to explain existence prior to that origin event or what might have been behind this beginning moment. Where did the "singularity" that exploded with such grandeur originate? What is the universe expanding into? Is it the vacuum of empty space? If so, what is this emptiness, what is it connected to, and where does it end? Assuming the physical events we call the Big Bang are scientifically accurate and did occur about thirteen and a half billion years ago, this still provides no explanation for our origin. The great creation mystery is still, as Lao Tzu characterized it 2,600 years ago, "Subtle wonder within mysterious darkness"; or, as expressed in the Buddhist Heart Sutra: "Form is no other than emptiness, emptiness no other than form."

Our story respects the divine origin as unknowable and concentrates on our human relationship with the sacred, natural world, which is creation's manifest form—allowing divinity to appear, providing opportunities for us to see and appreciate the sacred within each flower, person, bumblebee, and waterfall.

CHAPTER 4

MYSTICISM, SPIRIT, ECOLOGY

As mentioned, Ecological Epoch consciousness integrates all prior evolutionary stages. In the last chapter, we reviewed the Axial Age philosophies that formed a foundation for our newly arrived epoch. With this background, we are positioned to examine more recent philosophies that support our Creation Story and provide guidance to navigate today's dangerous rapids. Native Americans and other indigenous cultures had an Earth-honoring philosophical tradition. Some Western European and the Far Eastern philosophies also provide insight into solving our current challenges. The following pages identify important philosophies that will help lubricate our transition into the Ecological Epoch.

This new epoch is not only scientific; it is also mystical and spiritual. The Scientific Epoch became unbalanced, favoring the rational and the physical over the spiritual and metaphysical. In our story, balance is restored: scientists have come to realize science necessarily includes the mystical. In addition, metaphysical philosophies gain more influence. The following post-Axial Age philosophers helped build a worldview that has allowed today's ecological consciousness to emerge; these ideas are building blocks that help us to *see* the world in ways that can meet and solve our epoch's daunting challenges.

> **(3:12) Plotinus** was a third-century philosopher who understood "consciousness" to have its own existence, independent of humans: He believed in a concept that he called the "One," which was a non-dual, nontemporal unity existing beyond time and space. The One is the origin for all that followed; there is a "world soul" and a "human soul" emanating from the One. His outlook is similar to the way our new story describes "consciousness."
>
> In our story, the One could also be seen as a field of creative potential or the Creative Source. **Georg Hegel** was a European philosopher from the early nineteenth century. He wrote that human beings are vehicles for divine spirit to reveal itself through consciousness. In our story, there is an existential imperative that strives for deepening conscious and promotes this revelation process. **Henri Bergson** was a Frenchman who thought consciousness had its own separate existence and was using humans and evolution to express itself in the world.
>
> **Teilhard de Chardin**, a European writing in the twentieth century, suggested that consciousness uses human neurological complexity to attain greater freedom, drawing human consciousness toward a future merging with the "Omega Point," which is akin to a forward-attracting, dynamic essence. Per Teilhard, as future humans become more enlightened, they eventually will reach the Omega Point, an event that would be the culmination of this consciousness-attaining freedom process.

For now, human beings are Earth's most important animal species because we are the most advanced expression of evolving consciousness. On the other hand, if we fail to stabilize our relationship with nature, it is likely that the future will provide other life forms to carry forward the evolution of embodied consciousness. In this case, the next physical expression of advanced consciousness would have to wait for some future period, perhaps a few million years hence, to unfold. From this story's perspective, our current epoch is just one consciousness stage among many to come.

Ever more complex human consciousness emerges in stages as we evolve. Consciousness is not created by our evolution; rather, it is *revealed*. Our cells and brains and minds have evolved, but consciousness is not a product of our evolutionary process; rather, our advances in neurological complexity allow us to comprehend, integrate, and use more of what is *always-existent, ever-present consciousness*. When we move to a higher stage, we merely "get" more of what has always existed—thereby we are able to see the world through a new lens for the first time. Rather than creating consciousness, we are building a platform that provides a better perspective from which to see reality as it is and as it has always been. Our newest consciousness is providing the knowledge that can enable us to change our cultural and economic behavior and thereby avoid collapse and chaos.

Mysticism and the Ecological Epoch

I have traveled to about ninety countries during my adult years. Curiosity about both the external and internal worlds kept pushing me away from comfort and complacency and toward exploration of our fascinating, exotic world. Especially compelling in my travels were the temples, cathedrals, mosques, pyramids, stupas, standing stone circles, sacred caves, and mountaintop monasteries. Each place had its spiritual practice: meditations, repetitive prayer, sacred chanting, silent walking, and other such profound contemplations.

There seems to be intellectual dogma attached to each place—the mind attempting to explain philosophical beliefs and codify them into rules to control behavior; however, it's quite possible people in many spiritual traditions find more meaning in meditation and contemplation than in these various creeds and dogmas. Maintaining and enforcing rules provides control over church members. These boundaries are appealing to those who want to be in charge of the institutions. A few patriarchs are able to exercise authority, while the true contemplatives are deeply immersed in their divine communion.

People who practice mysticism—true mystics—have little need for those in authority. These mystics are able to make their own connection to the Great Mystery without a priest to act as an intermediary. This direct access can be challenging to those in charge, threatening their authority. Mysticism is always present in any successful religion, and, at the same time, it is usually marginalized by those in charge. At times, mystical religious practices have been declared heretical and then outlawed and persecuted, yet people within each religion have persisted because they find more meaning and connection in the mystical practice than they do in the dogma.

Christianity has attempted to contain mysticism within its dogmatic walls and to limit mystical practices; notwithstanding, important Christian mystics have emerged throughout each of the twenty centuries during which the religion has existed. Likewise, Sufism is a mystical branch of Islam, and the Kabala emphasizes mysticism in Judaism. The non-monotheistic traditions, including Hinduism and Buddhism, are inherently mystical, because they rely on meditation practices; however, dogma is still rampant.

Plotinus, the Philosopher and Spiritualist

As introduced earlier in this chapter, Plotinus was a Greek philosopher who taught during the third century CE. He serves as bridge between various religious and philosophical traditions. His writing demonstrates areas in which Plato's teachings are consistent with Christianity. Therefore, he provides our new story with a perspective that includes both existential philosophy and traditional religious teaching. These ideas support the Ecological Epoch's worldview.

Plotinus was born in Egypt about the year 205 and died in 270. He may have been from a Greek family. His student, Porphyry, in a series of books known as the Enneads, compiled Plotinus's writings into a comprehensive metaphysical philosophy that has inspired mystical traditions in all of the Western religions. Although Plotinus considered himself to be a follower of Plato, he had a large following of his own. The term "neo-Platonism" came into being in the nineteenth century to describe Plotinus and his influence.

At age twenty-seven, Plotinus began to study philosophy, spending the next eleven years in Alexandria, Egypt. He became interested in Indian and Persian philosophy (including Zoroastrianism and Mazdakism) and spent several difficult years in Persia before establishing himself in Rome at age forty. He spent most of his teaching years in Rome, where he influenced a number of Roman senators and held the respect of the Emperor Gallienus. He also taught a number of Rome's aristocratic women. During this period, the Christian Church was building a strong following; however, Christians were persecuted until the early fourth century.

Interestingly, Plotinus does not mention Christian theology in his writings—his teaching is more philosophical than religious. It combines mysticism with rationalism; it is both metaphysical and material. Matter was sacred.

Aristotle followed Socrates's and Plato's lead in recognizing Ideal Forms, but he was more intent on examining constituent parts to determine how things worked, an approach that was later referred to as "reductionism." Plotinus had access to the teachings of Plato, Aristotle, Jesus, and Christian literature, as well as ancient Persian beliefs and many Eastern philosophies, including the Vedas. He taught during a rich philosophical and spiritual period in which multiple religious traditions were available in Europe. Soon thereafter, the Western Roman Empire collapsed, the Christian Church became the state religion of the Holy Roman Empire, and Europe entered into a time of relative intellectual and philosophical stagnation from the fifth to the eleventh centuries—a time marked by declining population, a relative lack of architectural achievement, lost technology, and minimal philosophical innovation.

Plotinus had a wide-ranging philosophical exposure. His Six Enneads examine the human condition: ethics, cosmology and physical reality; the soul; knowledge and epistemology; and the One, which cannot be described but is behind all creation. These six books were writings inspired from lectures, essays, and notes that were compiled during Plotinus's last seventeen years of life. His own philosophical system blends Eastern and Western thought and is a valuable resource for our Ecological Epoch story:

> *Most philosophy is dependent on rational thinking; however, mystical philosophy is a door to spirituality. Blending philosophy and spirituality balances the logical and the intuitive, unifying each. Plotinus's "One" could not be described in words; it is a mystical concept that cannot be approached through the intellectual, rational process. The One has always existed: The world of objects came from the One but does not define the One, which is greater and more profound than the sum of its parts—it contains all potentiality, all possible things, including those now in existence and those to be manifest in the future. It is not a "thing" or a god. Perhaps it is pure essence with no describable qualities. It cannot be addressed by thought; it is infinite and transcendent, existing before any object or thought. Prior to manifestation all known phenomena are pure potentiality within the One. The universe is derived from the One, but not from any purposeful action, since the One is beyond purpose, action, thought, or decision. It is an infinite, immutable, pure essence without characterization.*

As in other mystical spiritual traditions, Plotinus taught that it is possible to experience the One through a non-rational merging with it—called "Henosis," an ecstatic unity. In such a state, someone is not "seeing" the One; rather, he is "being" the One. The individual's personal existence is dissolved.

The cosmos emanates from the One. *"Nous"* is divine mind. This is the first emanation. It includes rationality and the capacity for intellectual thought. Next comes the "World Soul," *anima mundi* in Latin, a life force that permeates all things; next, the individual Human Souls; and, finally, material objects. As did Socrates and Plato, Plotinus emphasized the "Ideal Form" from which physicality emanated. Objects were of lesser quality than the ideal form, a lower-value reproduction that could never obtain the ideal's perfection. This hierarchical ordering seems to contain value judgments; however, unlike the mystical Christian Gnostics, Plotinus's system considered all creation to be sacred because it emanated from the One.

He taught that happiness could not be achieved through success, power, or wealth; rather, it can come only from a connection to life's highest qualities—beauty and appreciation for the Ideal Forms. Happiness depends on one's level of personal consciousness. Even the condition of one's physical body has little to do with one's happiness. Happiness is beyond activities involving social convention. One's soul is the seat of reason and contemplation. This is where true contentment and joy reside in a timeless reality. Plotinus emphasized the importance of Henosis—unity, or "oneness," and connection. He was contemporary with the early Christian mystic, Origen, and both may have studied with the same teacher, providing a bridge between Platonism and Christian theology.

Kabala

Kabala means "receiving"; it is an esoteric branch of Judaism that was formalized from various mystical Jewish traditions, including written scriptures dating back more than one thousand years prior to Kabala's beginning. It coalesced into a more organized practice in Southern France and Spain in the eleventh to thirteenth centuries, eventually gaining popularity with Hassidic Judaism in the eighteenth century.

Kabala is a body of teachings that attempt to describe the relationship between an unknowable creator and the finite universe that came forth from this mysterious presence. The universe and everything it contains was brought into existence and will eventually die away; the creator is infinite, existing before time and space came to be and existing after all else is gone.

These teachings help define the nature of reality; they contemplate humanity's role within the universe and explore the purpose of life. The Zohar is Kabala's basic text. It was made public in the thirteenth century by a Jewish scholar in Spain named Moses de Leon, who claimed it was from an even more ancient oral tradition that had been written down in the second century CE, long after its origin. Most scholars today believe that, although certain scriptures are from antiquity, de Leon was the primary author; his second-century claims were an attempt to legitimize the writings.

The Zohar includes mystical elaboration of the Torah (the five books ascribed to Moses in the Hebrew Bible, which are also the first books of the Christian Old Testament). Its philosophy delves into cosmology, mysticism, and psychology, including the universe's origin, humans' relationship to God, human souls, God as "light," and the interaction between "universal energy" and humankind—all of which are visionary topics addressing the nature of reality. Kabala allows various new dimensions to be read into the Jewish scriptures, especially the Torah. It provides four levels of interpretation, including allegorical levels as well as mystical ones.

God is comprised of two aspects: One can be contemplated in thought; the other is endless and infinite—beyond rational conception. God is partially revealed through his creations, the manifest world. In this aspect, he interacts with humans and plays a role in preserving his creation. This aspect is partially accessible to logical thought processes; the endless and infinite aspect is transpersonal and transuniversal, entirely incomprehensible to the human mind.

Divine light is the central metaphor used to describe the interconnection among all things. This light flows from the creator and imbues all creation, providing existential significance to an individual's life. Through Kabalistic practices, a person is able to open to divine light and come closer to God. All existence manifests from God and contains his divinity.

The Serfirot are ten attributes with which God imbues his creation; He can be at least partially "seen" through recognizing these qualities that sustain the world—and is thus partially revealed. These ten revelations help describe humans' relationship to nature and to the divine. They include "Keter," which represents connection to divine light, accessible, yet above human consciousness; "Chochmah," which stands for the most accomplished potential for rational thought processes; "Chesed," representing loving-kindness (also a basic precept of Buddhism); and "Rachamin," which is the revealed quality of mercy. These divine aspects help humans partially comprehend one aspect of God but not the mysterious, indefinable, unknowable "other" aspect.

Christian Mysticism

Christianity's beginnings were highly mystical in character—that is, there were many occurrences that superseded normal events in everyday reality. Jesus performed miracles: changing water to wine, healing the sick, and walking on water. Jesus, the man, transcended his humanity, even while still alive on Earth; he became one within three aspects of God: Father, Son, and Holy Ghost. God's word was revealed to the New Testament prophets as infallible Holy Scripture, often coming directly from God himself—sometimes via communication with an angel. At other times, a prophet would hear God's voice in his mind.

The Christian church is replete with mysticism, especially in its early history; however, the church authorities scrutinized every instance so that, overall, these types of occurrences remained confined to singular events. In this way, the church could claim "ownership" of the events, and the resulting stories could be reinterpreted as church doctrine, cubbyholed, and categorized so that they served the leaders' needs.

Mysticism in all traditions involves a merging, union, or presence with God, even if only briefly. Jesus was thought to be God. Moses was in God's presence and spoke with him. The prophets received revelations from him. An audience with God usually transformed the individual—his life deepened, and his actions became more selfless. Consider these lines from John's gospel as Jesus speaks to his disciples:

> [18] *I will not leave you as orphans; I will come to you.* [19] *Before long, the world will not see me anymore, but you will see me. Because I live, you also will live.* [20] *On that day you will realize that I am in my Father, and you are in me, and I am in you.* [21] *Whoever has my commands and keeps them is the one who loves me. The one who loves me will be loved by my Father, and I too will love them and show myself to them."* (John 14:18–21, New International Version)

Jesus preached in the Aramaic language. Using an Aramaic interpretation, line 20 is a completely mystical statement. It is referring to those who comprehend unity with the divine ("Whosoever has my commands and keeps them...") and promises that these individuals will obtain union with God while still alive on Earth("...and you are in me and I am in you"). Jesus likely was saying that each person ("The one who loves me...") is capable of experiencing this divine union and thus was proposing a mystical way of being in the world. When you love Jesus through contemplation, mediation, and loving-kindness, then you come to understand the interrelational nature of all things: "You are in me."

Many Eastern spiritual practices, including Buddhism and Hinduism, encourage direct communion with the Creative Source. This is not so in the Christian church, where the Pope, bishops, and priests are the mediators between *their* flock and God. Indeed, in the Middle Ages, the church had difficulty discerning someone's experience of mystical union from possession by Satan. The authorities judged each episode in determining whether it was God or Satan who had visited the person.

Surrounded by the church's life-and-death authority, mystical possession was a dangerous predilection. The church alone decided whether one was communing with God or possessed by the devil. Nonetheless, revelations and mystical experiences were ongoing. In the Middle Ages, the Catholic Church was built on philosophy, creeds, dogma, and interpretation of the Holy Scriptures. Many mystical avatars appeared, some received adulation; others were burned at the stake.

Blessed Hildegard of Bingen was a German mystical theologian, philosopher, and composer born in 1098 into a large family with financial means. She began having visions at an early age and, perhaps as a result, her parents gave her over to the church. The visions continued, including ones in which she found herself in the presence of Jesus. At age forty-two, she heard a voice from heaven telling her to write down the things that were being revealed to her. After a great deal of soul searching, she did begin to write, eventually producing nine books, a hundred letters, seventy poems, and many ethereal songs. She claimed to have heard these things from heaven. She considered herself a scribe, recording revelations. Hildegard also founded two monasteries and was later declared a saint.

Jacob Boehme was a German from a peasant background. Born in 1575, he made a living as a shoemaker; at age twenty-five, he had a vision while transfixed on a beam of sunlight hitting a pewter dish. In this altered state, Boehme found answers to questions concerning the meaning of life, God's nature, and God's relationship to man and spirituality. He kept these revelations secret for many years but eventually began writing. His second book, *The Way to Christ*, caught the attention of the local pastor, who declared it heretical; Boehme was banished from the town. He continued to write and teach his theology, which contains some unique insights. For example, in Boehme's trinity, God is fire, Jesus is light, and the Holy Spirit is divinity within each person. Although his death came only a few years after his banishment, various noblemen supported his theological philosophies. He became widely published, and a multinational following developed after his death.

Saint John of the Cross was born to a poor Spanish family in 1542; he entered the Carmelite Order in 1563 and studied theology with some of the era's best teachers before joining with Teresa of Avila (later Saint Teresa) to institute a reform movement within the Carmelites. Local church leaders jailed John for nine months, during which time he wrote the "Spiritual Canticle," one of the most important mystical poems ever written in Spanish. It describes the soul's search for Christ using a bride and groom as the main metaphor. They are separated and experience ecstatic union upon their reuniting. The poem is known for its rich symbolism. His "Dark Night of the Soul" is equally brilliant, relating the soul's journey through the night as it overcomes adversity to find and merge with God. Later, he wrote expository texts discussing these poems, which were also important for their mystical, theological content, and his influence extends to many modern poets and writers, including T. S. Eliot.

Julian of Norwich was born in England in 1342; she came to be known through her writings as one of England's Christian mystics and was later exalted by the Anglican Church. She was not an important church leader and was little known during her lifetime. At age thirty, she contracted an illness and believed herself to be on her deathbed, whereupon a series of visions came to her. These lasted for months and did not abate until her surprising recovery from this near-death experience. The year was 1373; she wrote briefly about the visions, then put them aside for about twenty years, at which time they formed the basis for the book *Sixteen Revelations of Divine Love*.

During her lifetime, the Black Death visited Norwich on three separate occasions, killing a significant percentage of the population; Julian was familiar with extreme suffering. The theological authorities proclaimed that God was punishing people for their sins. Julian found a different message in her revelations: God was all-compassionate; he was not wrathful, angry, or retributive. Her visions showed her that these were human qualities and that God waited patiently for humans to mature to a point when they could pass beyond these dysfunctional emotions and attain divine unity.

> To Julian, sin was not evil, but just part of life, more like an error in judgment, a mistake that helps a person correct her course and grow toward intimacy with God. This outlook is similar to the Aramaic language's reconstruction of the word "sin," meaning life out of balance. There is no "good-verses-bad" moral judgment. There is no need for God to forgive sin because sin was not "wrong"; rather, it is part of a growth process—a disharmony that longs for correction so that intimacy can deepen.

God the father was a powerful image of the day, as it still is within the church. Julian's visions told a different story: She saw God as both father and mother, based on her appreciation of the bond between mother and child—a connection that is different than that with the father. This outlook ascribes a gender balance to the creator, respecting both feminine and masculine qualities in nature and in human nature. This is similar in outlook to the prepatriarchal "goddess" cultures described in our story's *Book Two*, albeit this prehistory was unknown to Julian's contemporaries. In a sense, she was rediscovering this past wisdom. In 1373, her theology likely would have been considered heretical, carrying a death sentence, had she been widely known. However, she was not a visible theologian and escaped church scrutiny, living until at least seventy-three years old. Her writings brought posthumous fame. Her revelations are in many respects consistent with Thomas's gospel that reveals a mystical Jesus (as elaborated in *Book Two*).

There are dozens of additional important Christian mystics who are now revered by the church. Origen wrote around 240 CE and turned some of Plato's philosophy into Christian theology, as did Augustine 150 years later. In the Middle Ages, the fourteenth century produced the mystical philosophers Meister Eckhart and Catherine of Siena. Ignatius of Loyola (sixteenth century) had several mystical experiences in which he "saw" God and found himself in the company of Jesus; he developed a wide church following.

As mentioned earlier, Christianity's Gnostic branch encouraged mystical practice for all of its members; however, they were considered to be heretical and were unrecognized by the official church. Connection to the Creative Source often includes divine mystical experiences. Although the authoritarian church fathers did not encourage such experiences, from a practical standpoint they were required to find ways to accommodate these phenomena. Thus, mysticism remained alive within the Christian religion.

Sufism

Sufism is Islam's mystical branch. Its spiritual practices attempt to open one's heart. Religious laws are based on rationality; however, pathways for accessing spirit are usually experiential. In Sufism, the institutional rules are only a necessary prerequisite—purification so that the individual might have an opportunity to enter into God's presence. Sufism knows God to be "essence"; his name is "Allah." One definition for Allah would be "essence without likeness." Sufism has been called a science to purify the body and, through the heart, allow one to travel into the presence of the divine. Purifying the body removes internal influences that do not love God, after which one is able to begin the mystical practice that opens one's heart to recognize Allah's presence in all creation.

Sufism is an esoteric, mystical form of Islam. In many respects, the Sufi philosophy predates Islam, with roots reaching back to early Hinduism and Buddhism. The term itself is probably a derivation of the ancient Greek word "Sophia," meaning wisdom. Sufism's adherents are called "Sufis" and, at times, "dervishes"; the term "whirling dervish" has entered the English lexicon, meaning something with boundless energy. This association is based on a Sufi spinning-dance that is practiced as a spiritual exercise to empty the mind and bring one's heart into communion with Allah.

Knowing God (gnosis) comes from purifying one's inner being and opening one's heart to God's love. It is important to obey, without fail, traditional Islamic law that dictates proper outward behavior. The various practices and techniques, such as whirling-dervish dances, chanting Allah's name, and doing esoteric breathing meditations, are not sufficient in and of themselves to enter into Allah's presence; however, if combined with appropriate selflessness and love for God, they create an opportunity from which a mystical experience might be born.

"Dhikr" is the practice of repeating God's name over and over for an extended period of time—a repetitive mediation on Allah that is used in classical Sufism. All Muslims hope to attain paradise in the afterlife; however, Sufis teach that one can experience God's presence while alive on Earth; it is possible to escape the dualism that creates "self" and "other" and to find unity with the divine. An accomplished teacher is essential to the seeker's success; the teaching must be transmitted from heart to heart through divine light, not from mind to mind through logic. Allegory and parable are often used to bypass the overly rational mind.

Only some people are mentally, emotionally, and psychologically prepared to enter into gnosis with the divine, so not everyone is qualified to receive these teachings. Humility, tolerance, and service to others must be cultivated before one begins the Sufi mystical practice, or else one might be overwhelmed and injured from the practice itself.

Islam flourished from the thirteenth through the sixteenth centuries; during this period Sufism was as a respected component, and Sufi practices were prominent throughout the Muslim world. Sufi influence has cycled in and out of prominence throughout the 1,400-year Islamic history. Perhaps the best-known Sufi in contemporary society is Jalal Rumi, a Persian poet, Islamic theologian, and Sufi mystic who lived from 1207 to 1273 CE. Today, he is said to be the world's most-read poet; English translations by Coleman Barks have made Rumi popular in North America.

Sophia's Tibetan Wisdom

(3:13) In 1982, before the Chinese government allowed tourists to enter Tibet, I was exploring Asia with a special interest in its various religious histories. The giant, ancient temple in Lasha, Tibet, called the Potala, was historically both the Dalai Lama's home and a major spiritual center. While the Chinese "cultural revolution" destroyed 90 percent of all Tibetan Buddhist temples, Mao Se Tung personally ordered the Potala spared. I was able to slip into Tibet through an outlying, peripheral Chinese Province. In Tibet, there were virtually no private vehicles. After a week in Lasha, my traveling companion and I traveled south toward Nepal, hitching rides on the backs of Chinese military trucks.

The road to Nepal passes through the Himalayas, near the base of Mt. Everest. At about 13,000 feet in elevation, it is one of the world's highest mountain roads. Oxygen is scarce. I felt disoriented from my normal, everyday reality. Traveling among these stark, glacier-covered peaks, Sophia's invitation to call on her for insight came to me.

Various questions arose: "Why am I here? How should I be using my life? What would give my life more meaning?" I heard this response: "Acknowledging Sacred Nature by paying attention to its beauty is sufficient—appreciating a special place, a whale's magnificence, the majestic mountain beside you, or another person's unique qualities. Allow all these presences to inspire awe; they are intricate designs manifesting the Creative Source. God, Great Spirit, or Tao—that is, whatever we call the essence that formed and informs our existence, this same source also informs you.

"Make yourself available to beauty. Some incredible process— far beyond your comprehension—has brought you into being and provides for your temporary survival. The Great Mystery is beyond thoughts, residing in incomprehensibly profound darkness. This unexplainable, creative flow is the source from which all wisdom, all science, all art, and all thought arise. It is revealed as Natural Harmony—the profound interrelationship that binds all things and reveals Earth's intelligence."

Sophia's voice faded from my mind into the mountain air. The bumpy truck ride continued. Eventually my Chinese soldier hosts dropped me near the Nepalese border on a forested trail that descended for miles and took me thousands of feet below the magi- cal Tibetan plateau. That high-altitude truck ride had been quite a journey.

CHAPTER 5

SCIENCE IN THE ECOLOGICAL EPOCH

"Whatever you see around is not outside of you. Whatever you want, want from yourself because you are everything. When a person reaches this level of humanity, the human meets the universe and the universe meets the human."
—Mevlana Rumi

In our Creation Story, the Scientific Epoch follows the Philosophical Epoch; all prior epochs are integrated and incorporated into this scientific period. Our story also shows how scientific thinking has recently evolved from the Scientific Epoch into the Ecological Epoch. For most of the Scientific Revolution, beginning about four hundred years ago, we emphasized reductionism—tearing apart the whole in an attempt to find the underlying functional mechanisms. We wanted to see the parts that made the clock tick. This is changing; we have moved into a new consciousness stage and realize that interrelationship is the universe's essential nature. Today's scientific methods are evolving to accommodate this new worldview.

Beneath the apparently stable surface, at existence's most profound depths, fundamental processes are constantly transforming energy to matter and back to energy again. This dance underlies life's holistic fabric. It includes Earth's atmosphere, its waters, and its geological composition. EE consciousness is producing science that reveals these innumerable, interpenetrating relationships.

All things are formed from oneness, unity, and singularity. Science originates with the Big Bang—its own creation myth. What came before? What will come after? The Ecological Epoch is generating new science, one that recognizes how energy and matter are both born from the whole. Energy becomes matter and soon becomes energy once again. $E = MC^2$ is entering our philosophical, cultural awareness almost one hundred years after Einstein first revealed the equation.

This same wisdom is expressed in the Buddhist *Maha Prajna Paramita Heart Sutra*, written around 350 CE. It says, "Form is no other than emptiness, emptiness no other than form." Ancient consciousness explorers used their own interiority, their subjective explorations, to discover the nature of reality. Heart wisdom, cellular intelligence, and emotional insight were the wisdom sources that spoke to them—no scientific evidence was required. In the Ecological Epoch, we are using this new wisdom to deepen our scientific understanding—a focus that will allow us, if given the will, to heal our Earth. Our New Creation Story is scientifically based. The following look at our scientific past, including the history and philosophy of science, will help us understand how science got to where it is today and where it is headed in the Ecological Epoch.

In some respects, the revolutionary science of Rene Descartes, Isaac Newton, and other Renaissance geniuses created a four hundred-year distraction from the Axial Age wisdom teachings (discussed in *Book Two*), eventually leading to environmental destruction and our current ecological crisis. Science became our god. Production and consumption became our cultural priority. However, there is an evolutionary pressure toward understanding the nature of reality in ever more profound ways. Scientific advances have recently joined the Ecological Epoch. Our story includes many holistic scientists with the awareness and courage to perceive reality anew.

> *"A knowledge of the existence of something we cannot penetrate, of the manifestations of the profoundest reason and the most radiant beauty—it is this knowledge and this emotion that constitute the truly religious attitude…. If something is in me which can be called religious then it is the unbounded admiration for the structure of the world so far as our science can reveal it."*
> —Albert Einstein, 1954

What Is Science?

Science started with philosopher-scientists, including Socrates, Plato, and Aristotle, who depended on intuition. "Metaphysical" literally means the "big picture" as it relates to the physical world. This was the beginning point for Plato and Aristotle. This classical science was partially lost during the following millennia, which included Europe's Dark Ages and ensuing Middle Ages. The Renaissance emerged from the late Middle Ages, reducing the vice grip that religion exercised on European culture. This circumstance opened the doors for scientific inquiry.

In the seventeenth century, there was a growing scientific perception that the world was mechanistic. Nature was thought to be like intricate clocks or other complex mechanisms, with various gears interacting and enabling the machine to fulfill its purpose. The scientific challenge in understanding these functions was to break down the mechanics into their constituent parts to analyze them, thereby explaining the material world.

To accomplish this objective, each function was reduced to its most basic components and looked at separately, thus minimizing the relationships involved. This mechanistic approach resulted in isolation of the human individual from the earth's natural systems. People were soon thought to be separate and different from the mechanical-like world.

Today's new science, including the recent Higgs Boson and Higgs Field discoveries, provide an alternative to this view: all matter is connected in the same underlying energetic field at the quantum level; human individuals exist in relationship to each other, other beings, and all matter—the entirety of which interacts at a subatomic-particle level.

Our story now examines how science evolved from its classical beginnings into today's new Ecological Epoch theories.

Roger Bacon was an English Franciscan monk who died near the end of the thirteenth century. Using scientific insights gained from the writings of Plato (who died 1,600 years earlier in 347 BCE) and his student Aristotle, Bacon was an early advocate for the "scientific method" in Europe. Aristotle defined science as a body of knowledge that could be rationally explained. This included knowledge about nonmaterial subjects, including philosophy. These two disciplines weren't split apart until the seventeenth century, CE. Philosophy became differentiated from science; the latter focused on "material" reality as distinct from subjective topics that could not be dissected and manipulated.

> *"As to science, we may well define it for our purpose as methodical thinking directed toward finding regulative connections between our sensual experiences."*
> —Albert Einstein, 1948

The *Oxford English Dictionary* says that scientific method is "a method of procedure that has characterized natural science since the seventeenth century, consisting in systematic observation, measurement, and experiment, and the formulation, testing, and modification of hypotheses." The Scientific Revolution began in Europe around the time that Nicolaus Copernicus published *De Revolutionibus Orbium Coelestium* in 1547. It continued for several hundred years, becoming an intellectual explosion that built a new edifice atop the thousand-year-old classical Greek foundation of modern Western thought.

This movement established today's modern scientific worldview. The primary objective was to systematically examine the laws of nature. Johannes Kepler (1571–1630) was a German astronomer and mathematician; Galileo Galilei (1564–1642) was an Italian physicist, astronomer, and philosopher. Each played a major role proving that we live in a solar system in which planets revolve around the sun; the Earth is not the center of the world. This realization and its cultural adoption had a major influence in opening the doors for the Scientific Revolution. Although Kepler and Galileo were able to scientifically determine through newly invented telescopes that the Earth revolved around the sun and had an understanding of our solar system, they had no concept of distant galaxies, the Big Bang, black holes, or the universe's age. It would be another three hundred years before some of this information became accessible to the human mind.

René Descartes was a French philosopher and mathematician who lived in the Dutch Republic (1596–1650). His writings are still used today in university philosophy departments, and Descartes's advances in the field of mathematics were essential to the Scientific Revolution. He bridged geometry and mathematics; he showed how a point located in space could be described in an equation and, thereby, he discovered analytical geometry.

Sir Isaac Newton (1642–1727) was an English physicist, astronomer, and theologian who some consider to be the most important scientist who ever lived. His most influential work was published in 1687 and establishes "classical mechanics" as science's foundation for the following 250 years. Newton developed what he called "laws of motion," from which evolved more disciplined studies of the earth's geology, biology, chemistry, and physics.

As the scientific method took hold, philosophy and other more subjective disciplines became known as "social sciences," while the term "natural science" was used for the disciplines that studied the material universe. With the rise of left-brain influence that created the Scientific Revolution, eventually, empirical science with replicable experiments became the only acceptable scientific approach. If an experiment could not be repeated, or the concept was not measurable, or if there was no material to be dissected or weighed, or if the results could not be replicated, then the entire idea was considered to be scientifically invalid; consequently, philosophy and spirituality were no longer considered to be scientific.

In the seventeenth century, classical Greek philosophy was resurrected and transformed into Cartesian and Newtonian science. The two hundred years that followed the beginning of Cartesian (so named for Descartes) and Newtonian physics realigned humanity's perception of the cosmos and had a major influence in defining the way all modern cultures perceive the world. These classical scientific ideas originated from within a particular ontological milieu—that is, a specific attitude about how and why we are here, alive on Earth.

Science is always changing—growing, deepening, and refining information, thereby becoming more profound. Any claim that new knowledge is no longer necessary would be tantamount to stating that science knows all there is to know. This can never be the case, and, naturally, no scientist with an inquiring mind would take such a position.

Cartesian physics successfully explained many phenomena; however, it left a lot of unanswered questions, especially concerning the very small (subatomic realm) and the very large (cosmic realm) phenomena. In the early twentieth century, new dimensions addressing these areas were appended to the scientific endeavor, including Albert Einstein's *Theory of Relativity* and, soon thereafter, quantum mechanics. These novel understandings enabled humans to develop sophisticated computing devices and walk on the moon. In time, quantum mechanics, through its abstract world of mathematical equations, discovered solutions to innumerable complex construction problems.

For the uninitiated person, quantum mechanics is very difficult to understand because it is counterintuitive; in many respects it just does not make sense—it is antithetical to our senses and our linear thought sequences. No matter how good quantum mechanics is at solving problems, it is still confusing to the man on the street when attempting to describe how or why its mathematical equations actually work. Unlike classical science, quantum physics is not logical to most high school and college-educated people; in addition, it is several steps removed from our normal lives. For these reasons, it is unable to provide ontological grounding—we do not get ethical guidance or any understanding of life's meaning from this modern science's precepts.

> *"Physics has changed from its earlier form, when it tried to explain things and give some physical picture. Now the essence is regarded as mathematical. It's felt [that] the truth is in the formulas."*
> —David Bohm[4]

Why is quantum mechanics so useful? This form of physics provides a more fundamental understanding of chemistry than did its predecessors; it is also essential in working with nuclear power. A large percentage, perhaps 40 to 50 percent, of the US economy relies on practical applications derived from quantum mechanics; this includes the electronic semiconductor industry; transistors; lasers; MRI (magnetic resonance imaging) medical scanning machines; nanophysics (information storage technology used in computers); neutrino and other "small particle" detectors; LEDs; all modern electronics; and superconductors. In addition, the next iteration

---

4. David Bohm, *On Quantum Mechanics, Wholeness, and the Implicate Order,* 1980.

of nanotechnology may produce a new generation of computing—more powerful "quantum" computers.

> *"Physics constitutes a logical system of thought, which is in a state of evolution…. We must always be ready to change these notions."*
> —Albert Einstein[5]

As mentioned, scientific research normally starts with an idea (hypothesis) that subsequently must be tested, proven, and replicated. The scientific method, which requires test results to be both material and replicable, has been the foundation of science since its introduction by Francis Bacon (1561–1626). Nonmeasurable insights have been relegated to pseudoscience at best and seen as ignorance at worst; however, times have changed. The scientific method, the foundation for claiming knowledge about the nature of reality, is now in question:

> *"All theories are insights, which are neither true nor false…. Man is continually developing new forms of insight, which are clear up to a point and then tend to become unclear. In this activity, there is evidently no reason to suppose that there is or will be a final form of insight (corresponding to absolute truth) or even a steady series of approximations to this. Rather, one may expect the unending development of new forms of insight…. Our theories are to be regarded primarily as ways of looking at the world as a whole rather than as 'absolute true knowledge of how things are.'"*
> —David Bohm, *Wholeness and the Implicate Order*, 1980

In the December 2010 issue of *New Yorker* magazine is an article titled "The Truth Wears Off: Is There Something Wrong with the Scientific

---

5. Albert Einstein, *Physics and Reality*, 1936.

74

Method?"[6] It addresses a phenomenon scientists recognize but rarely talk about. That is, proven scientific theories—ones replicated and accepted by scientists and scientific journals—often show a decline in their likelihood of replication as time goes forward. For example, an experiment that could be reproduced, with a 95 percent success rate months after the theory was published, often has an 80 percent success rate a year later and a 40 percent success rate several years after that. The phenomenon is called the "decline effect."

There are probably multiple reasons for this effect. A Canadian scientist, Richard Palmer, has studied the phenomenon. He concludes that at least part of this occurrence stems from unconscious, subjective bias in the scientists doing the studies and in those vetting the work for publication. Conclusions are "at best exaggerated in their biological significance and, at worst, a collective illusion nurtured by strong a priori beliefs often repeated..., subtle omission, and unconscious misperceptions." The decline effect shows that scientific results are not necessarily true. Beliefs and perceptions affect results even when the experimental method is meant to eliminate these biases. Science is much more about the individual scientist's consciousness and perception than most are willing to admit.

The pendulum is swinging. In the new Ecological Epoch, eco-science, which is focused on Earth's innumerable interrelationships, is so remarkably complex that experimental replication is often difficult. Do today's scientific priorities and industrial decisions lead to improved planetary heath and sustainability, or not? Given science's limitations, we are better served by using ecological philosophy (eco-philosophy) to measure our culture's ethical standards and behavior. Making choices that support Earth's health and wellbeing is the approach that best defines Ecological Epoch ethics.

---

6. Jonah Lehrer, "The Truth Wears Off: Is There Something Wrong with the Scientific Method?" *New Yorker*, December 2010.

Deepening Scientific Inquiry

"The notion that all these fragments [from subatomic particles to people] are separately existent is evidently an illusion, and this illusion cannot do other than lead to endless conflict and confusion. Indeed, the attempt to live according to the notion that the fragments are really separate is, in essence, what has led to the growing series of extremely urgent crises that is confronting us today.... This way of life has brought about pollution, destruction of the balance of nature, overpopulation, worldwide economic and political disorder, and the creation of an overall environment that is neither physically nor mentally healthy...."

—David Bohm[7]

There is growing evidence that an interconnected energy field permeates the cosmos and affects our lives and the planet in dramatic ways that are just beginning to be comprehended. Nature is not mechanistic, as Cartesian science would have us believe; rather, nature is intelligent, with information feedback loops capable of creating even more coherence and planetary intelligence. These mutual information systems apply to all life on Earth (the biosphere) and to the atmosphere, oceans, and mountains.

Biological evolution is sensitive to environmental factors. It is not just, as previously thought, random mutation combined with "natural selection" and survival of the fittest. This Darwinian model requires many generations before the superior traits' reproductive advantage can be fully expressed, resulting in significantly larger populations. Environmental factors also play a role in which mutations occur. As Rachel Carson comments in her book, *Silent Spring*, "The central problem of our age has therefore become the contamination of man's total environment with such

---

7. David Bohm, *Wholeness and the Implicate Order*, 1980. (Author's note: This prescient quote is from thirty-four years ago!)

substances of incredible potential for harm—substances that accumulate in the tissues of plants and animals and even penetrate the germ cells to shatter or alter the very material of heredity upon which the shape of the future depends."

New genetic research in a field called "epigenetics" confirms that toxins and other variables "turn on and turn off" various genes during a person's lifetime, thus affecting cells' genetic expression and consequent health. Diet, chemicals, toxins, and exercise all influence epigenetic modifications that determine which genes are expressed, that is, are allowed to affect a particular cell's function. The DNA code, encased in a cell's chromosomes, could be considered hardware, and the epigenetic chemical molecules, often attached to the chromosomes, could be thought of as software that affects cell function by shutting down some DNA sequences while allowing other sequences to express during cell reproduction. Whereas a cell's DNA is inherited, environmental influences often affect these epigenetic chemicals, explaining why exposure to toxins can cause a cell to malfunction and become cancerous.

Most surprisingly, some of these epigenetic-caused changes are passed on to offspring, not from modifying the DNA's genetic code but from the attached chemical molecules becoming imprinted, and consequently reproduced and inherited, in the next generation and future generations hereafter. The extent of these inheritable influences is as yet unknown. Cutting edge research is underway, as described in Michael Skinner's article, "A New Kind of Inheritance," published in the August 14th, 2014, *Scientific American* magazine. These feedback loops affect humans' biological evolution in both negative and positive ways. Likewise, many little-known interacting dynamics also affect human consciousness, often in short time frames.

"One is led to a new notion of unbroken wholeness which denies the classical idea of analyzability of the world into separately existing parts…. We have reversed the usual classical notion that the independent

> *'elementary parts' of the world are the fundamental reality and that the various systems are merely particular contingent forms and arrangements of these parts. Rather, we say that* **inseparable quantum interconnectedness of the whole universe is the fundamental reality** *[author's emphasis] and that relatively independent behaving parts are merely particular and contingent forms within this whole."*
> —David Bohm[8]

The "Cartesian" worldview was not able to explain how particles interacted at the subatomic level. Near the beginning of the twentieth century, scientific luminaries, including Erwin Schrödinger, Werner Heisenberg, Niels Bohr, and Wolfgang Pauli, developed quantum mechanics. Using this new physics, subatomic particles could be seen as energy "quanta," tiny energetic packages, rather than solid matter or separate objects. This led to revolutionary thinking and a plethora of inventions; however, these mind-bending concepts often flabbergasted even the experts. As Niels Bohr said, "Anyone who is not shocked by quantum theory has not understood it."

For example, in quantum mechanics, electrons (and other small entities) are theorized to behave like particles (matter) under some circumstances and like waves (energy) under other circumstances, depending on the type of experiment and the intervention of an observer during the experiment. Werner Heisenberg postulated the "uncertainty principle" in 1927 describing these phenomena. Heisenberg's uncertainty principle maintains that pairs of physical properties, such as position and momentum, cannot be determined simultaneously. The more one knows about a property that is paired with another, the less one is able to determine about the other property. Therefore, it is not possible to simultaneously

---

8. "On the Intuitive Understanding of Nonlocality as Implied by Quantum Theory," *Foundations of Physics*, Vol. 5, 1975.

know both the momentum and the position of an electron (or any other quantum particle) with certainty.

Only when a wave/particle is observed and one of the values is determined can a complementary value be calculated. The observer, therefore, becomes integral to the result—if there is no observer, momentum and position are indeterminate and can only be described as probabilities. Human experimenter and atomic entities had suddenly, in the eyes of this new science, become physically enmeshed. Both Albert Einstein and David Bohm were uncomfortable with many aspects of quantum mechanics; for example, this new physics was in some respects incompatible with Einstein's Theory of Relativity.

> *"The most radical change in the notion of order since Isaac Newton came with quantum mechanics. The quantum-mechanical idea of order contradicts coordinate order, because Heisenberg's uncertainty principle made a detailed ordering of space and time impossible. When you apply quantum theory to general relativity, at very short distances like ten to the minus thirty-three centimeters, the notion of the order of space and time breaks down."*
> —David Bohm[9]

According to Bohm, Einstein's relativity theory and other scientists' quantum theories are both valid within a certain sphere of influence. The apparent inconsistencies arise when the theories are generalized and applied to a larger range of phenomena than is appropriate for their theoretical accuracy. Thus, each theory can be successfully applied when used under particular interrelated conditions, but they become inconsistent with each other when attempting to explain all reality under all conditions. Therefore, both theoretical constructs are necessary, but neither is sufficient to provide a whole picture. In addition, Bohm argues that there

---

9. David Bohm, *On Quantum Mechanics*, 1987.

is a more all-inclusive structure of "undivided wholeness" underlying both disciplines that can be used to bridge the differences:

> *"In relativity, movement is continuous, causally determinate, and well defined, while in quantum mechanics it is discontinuous, not causally determinate, and not well defined. Each theory is committed to its own notions of essentially static and fragmentary modes of existence (relativity to that of separate events, connectable by signals, and quantum mechanics to a well-defined quantum state).…. A new kind of theory is needed which drops these basic commitments and at most recovers some essential features of the older theories as abstract forms derived from a deeper reality in which what prevails is unbroken wholeness."*
> —David Bohm[10]

Bohm proposed a new theory, bridging the inconsistencies between quantum mechanics and relativity:

> *"I came up with the causal interpretation (that the electron is a particle, but it also has a field around it. The particle is never separated from that field, and the field affects the movement of the particle in certain ways)."*
> —David Bohm[11]

The "connected field" concept is integral to quantum physics. It is an attempt to reconcile a number of inconsistencies between classical Cartesian/Newtonian science, quantum mechanics, and Einstein's Theory of Relativity. In the early 1900s, Max Planck, a German physicist, used mathematical equations to show that the space between atoms was not empty space—it contains energy. In 1913, Albert Einstein and Otto

---

10. David Bohm, *On Quantum Mechanics, Wholeness, and the Implicate Order*, 1980.
11. David Bohm, "Problems with Modern Physics," interview conducted by F. David Peat and John Briggs, published in Omni, January 1987.

Stern used Planck's discoveries and formulas to describe "zero-point energy."

The concept of a "zero-point field" was developed in later years. It maintains that all matter is connected to the same underlying energetic field at the quantum wave/particle level. Books have been written about this concept; however, it has remained more philosophical and subjective than scientific. Consequently, the zero-point field is not scientifically accepted. But science is changing quickly in this new epoch. A long-standing quantum particle theory called the "Higgs Field" has recently been more intricately elaborated based on the standard model of particle physics.

The Plasma Cosmos

Humankind first walked on the moon about forty-six years ago. We have never touched the vast universe beyond our solar system—past the boundary of our sun's influence, until now: Voyager 1 is, as I write, transitioning beyond the heliosphere—a sacred mystery that we are now probing. The sensors on board this spacecraft are intact after almost forty-four years in space and are still streaming information to us about cosmic rays (magnetic forces beyond our sun's influences), solar wind, and a "bubble envelope" the sun maintains. Is this outer region between our solar system and our closest solar neighbor, Alpha Centauri, just "space"? Is it an empty vacuum? What is the composition of the space between the several hundred billion stars of our galaxy, the Milky Way? Is it physically the same as the vast region that separates our Milky Way from the Magellanic Clouds, our closest galactic neighbor about two hundred thousand light-years away?

Albert Einstein's relativity theories assume that space–time curves. This outer space curvature is caused by gravity; therefore, his model of the cosmos is a gravity model. But what exactly is gravity? In Einstein's theory, matter is dead mass; it has no vitality. The mathematical equations that support his relativity theory help to explain the functioning of the observed universe; however, there are other issues that cannot be explained by treating the "mass" that exists in the universe as dead matter.

Other theoretical scientists are offering alternative explanations that may deepen our current understandings of how the universe functions—to the extent that we may now propose additional dimensions to Einstein's models. One alternative is perhaps that the cosmos is better explained as an "electric cosmos," not a gravity cosmos. Although we can't explain what gravity actually is, matter seems to create, and be affected by, this force, *and* matter has an electrical structure. New breeds of cosmologists are asking why this electrical force, immense when considering the entire universe, has not been factored into a working model of the cosmos. They claim it would explain many observed phenomena that currently stump the dead-matter-gravity model.

Magnetic fields seem to be threaded through space. These fields need a constant source of electricity to feed them. What is the source of this electrical input? Electrons move in ways that most readily equalize electrical charge. Perhaps electric currents are strung everywhere in space: between the Earth and the sun, throughout the space between our solar system and the next, and throughout the space between the Milky Way and each other galaxy.

The cosmos may be an electrical-plasma structure in which gravity plays a role, or it may be a gravity structure, as Einstein thought, in which influences from magnetic fields and electrical plasma play a role. Both these possibilities differ from our current scientifically accepted outlook. Electrical energy exists at the subatomic level as well as the atomic level of matter. Plasma contains electrically charged particles that are not bound to any structure, such as unbound electrons not tied to an atom. In a plasma universe, vast electrical filaments might exist anywhere in space. Indeed, many visible galactic forms mimic formations found in laboratory experiments that have created a plasma environment for study.

Energy in space can be measured by radio telescopes. Space may not be electrically neutral as is currently thought. If this is the case, "plasma cosmology" provides new and different explanations for various cosmological phenomena; for example, an electrical current connecting the sun to Earth would explain the Arctic's Aurora Borealis display. This outlook also provides new answers to many unexplained outer space issues: What causes a black hole's high-energy outbursts? What causes a pulsar to produce energetic pulses in strobe-light fashion many times per second? Is there such a thing as a neutron star that can rotate three hundred times per second, the currently accepted theory, or is this a physical impossibility—in which case the pulsating we observe may be better explained using a plasma cosmology model? Are all comets giant ice balls as we now teach, or might some be massive electrical bodies whose glowing tails indicate electrical discharge caused by the approach to a differently charged body?

The Voyager, just beginning to peek outside our solar system, will not answer these questions but may shed light toward the answers. This spacecraft is a metallic measuring device—a robotic sensor that deepens our relationship with existence itself. We are continually taking new steps; today we are not who we were yesterday. What we are learning from Voyager is helping to create the Ecological Epoch and a new stage for human consciousness.

How does a possible plasma-cosmos fit into our New Creation Story? Our story is founded on connections and relationship. The newly verified Higgs boson and its associated Higgs field are now scientifically accepted theories, showing that our planet is not isolated in empty space. There are vast distances between Earth and the sun, from one solar system to the next, and from galaxy to galaxy; however, this "space" is not empty. It is all one fabric that communicates throughout.

Like the Higgs field, the hypothesized plasma cosmos proposes underlying connections that explain some baffling physical phenomena. A plasma-cosmos model recognizes the vitality that is bound in matter at the subatomic level, a place where sacred creativity builds matter from energy—where material particles are constantly blinking in and out of existence. In a plasma-cosmos, we are not isolated; rather, everything is part of a continuous whole, and our expanding universe maintains its essential unity.

> *"The intellect has little to do on the road to discovery. There comes a leap in consciousness. Call it intuition or what you will, the solution comes to you and you don't know how or why."*
> —Albert Einstein

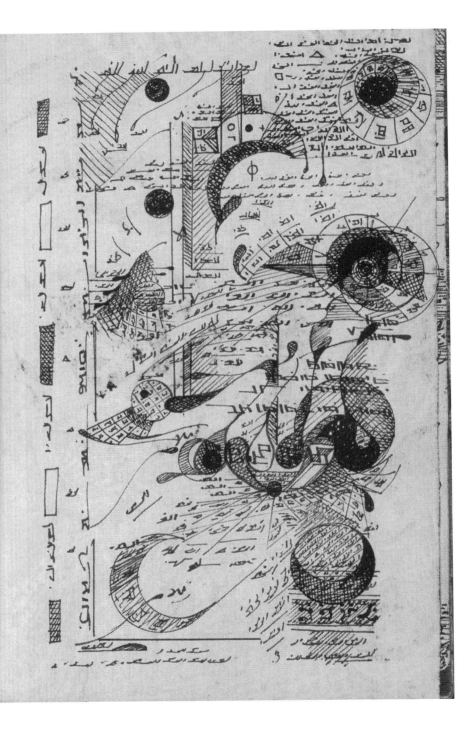

CHAPTER 6

LEADING-EDGE PHILOSOPHER-SCIENTISTS

The realization that air is composed of various gases and has significant substance is relatively new. At some point in human consciousness evolution, this idea took hold. The term "noosphere" is still quite abstract compared to atmosphere; however, the concept is gaining traction in philosophical theory. Noosphere represents the sphere of human thought—that is, everything we now know. The concept originated with several philosophers around 1920, including Vladimir Vernadsky and Edouard Le Roy, to indicate the emergence of a self-reflective universe—primarily resulting from the evolution of human consciousness.

The noosphere could be described metaphorically as an ephemeral membrane, akin to the Earth's atmosphere, encircling the planet and composed of all accumulated knowledge that humans have discovered since our origins. **Pierre Teilhard de Chardin**, a French philosopher-scientist who lived until 1955, elaborated this idea more than the others, and eventually became the best-known proponent of the philosophy. Teilhard's writings predated all but the most elementary computers. His philosophy originated before the term "cyberspace"; in fact, his thinking on the subject helped others to conceptualize cyberspace.

The noosphere is an interconnected information network that vastly exceeds all human-designed information processing and storage capacity. It includes all computer-stored information, all conscious knowledge to be found in the human mind, and all data and philosophy in libraries of any kind, anywhere. By definition, noosphere is all this, and more. Another analogy for this information repository is a planet-wide "organ" that is similar to a global brain.

When it was first described, the noosphere seemed to be a strange and radical concept. At present, the term cyberspace has been employed long enough that the average computer user takes it in stride. Cyberspace stands for the global network of interdependent information technology infrastructures, telecommunications networks, and computer processing systems. It includes the computer networks in which online communication takes place.

Similar to the noosphere, there is a cultural dimension to the term cyberspace that widens its application and includes all interactions catalyzed and inspired by the entire computing and storage network. Cyberspace also includes "virtual reality," a realm in which human avatars inhabit virtual worlds that include fantastic creatures. These worlds provide a participant with an alternative life in which he or she takes on an alter ego. None of this electronic and social media existed when Teilhard was elaborating his ideas about the noosphere; however, his concept incorporates all these dimensions. Teilhard proposed that our reflective thinking added more complexity and coherence to Earth's functioning; as such, the noosphere could be considered a new brain-like planetary organ.

"Reflection is the power acquired by a consciousness to turn in upon itself, to take possession of itself: no longer merely to know oneself; no longer merely to know, but to know that one knows."
—Pierre Teilhard de Chardin, *The Phenomenon of Man*

Teilhard envisioned an evolutionary progression from primordial elements (chemicals) and particles (geology) to ever more sophisticated life forms (biology), then to humans. The noosphere follows. Eventually there is an evolutionary pull toward a concept he calls the "omega point," where consciousness ultimately merges with God.

Noosphere implies an information and wisdom repository that is only partially dependent on human physiology. The noosphere is a global membrane organ with an independent existence, fed by the human intellect. Different researchers, with no interaction among them, sometimes concurrently discover the same invention or philosophical concept. When information exists in the noosphere, it is more accessible to others. Once a discovery has been made, it is more likely to be rediscovered. Naturally, this accessing requires preparation to create the intellectually fertile ground needed to comprehend the complex, abstract forms involved.

Teilhard advocated the importance of interrelationship and respect for ecology. As a "natural scientist," he studied both geology and anthropology. At times he was overwhelmed with the interconnections. He felt his own bodily connection with rocks, mountains, and other geological structures. He felt the pulsating life in supposedly inanimate matter, a quality that other scientists could not take seriously. He saw the Earth as a living entity, foreshadowing the Gaia Hypothesis by decades. To Teilhard, the earth's functioning geologic, hydrologic, atmospheric, and biologic processes were living systems. His philosophy presages the Ecological Epoch. Per Teilhard: "The Age of Nations is past. The task before us now, if we would not perish, is to build the earth.... The only truly natural and real human unity is the spirit of the earth."

Rupert Sheldrake, a biochemist and plant physiologist was born in 1942. His "morphic reasonance" theory, parapsychology research, and numerous publications have garnered a wide following—topics include animal and plant behavior, as well as mental telepathy and cognition. Focused on biochemistry and cell biology, Sheldrake studied at Harvard and was a research fellow at the Royal Society. Henri Bergson, a French philosopher, had an important influence on Sheldrake.

> *Sheldrake has proposed that memory is inherent to all organically formed structures and systems, arguing that bodily forms and instincts, while expressed through genes, do not have their primary origin in them. Instead, his hypothesis states, the organism develops under the influence of previous similar organisms, by a mechanism he has dubbed morphic resonance.*
> —John David Ebert[12]

The "morphic field" is an organizing principle for Sheldrake's theory. This field is created from repeated actions and thoughts of "morphic units," which are individual participants within the field. The more widely used biological term "morphogenetic field" predates Sheldrake's work and describes how a living thing is shaped—that is, how individual cells form organs and, more generally, how a living being develops from inception, and how it will behave. There is no implication of external influence.

> *The term [morphic fields] is more general in its meaning than morphogenetic fields and includes other kinds of organizing fields in addition to those of morphogenesis; the organizing fields of animal and human*

---

12. John David Ebert, "From Cellular Aging to the Physics of Angels: A Conversation with Rupert Sheldrake," *The Quest*, 86(2):14, February 1998.

behaviour, of social and cultural systems, and of mental activity can all be regarded as morphic fields which contain an inherent memory.
—Rupert Sheldrake[13]

Actions and thoughts set up and feed a morphic field, causing it to gain coherence and strength with additional input; the field is then able to inform an individual morphic unit—a person, for example, based on the accumulated knowledge of the entire field—thereby providing a loop of information-sharing back to the morphic unit and forward to the field and other units. In this way, similar morphic units (not necessarily located near one another) can communicate and share information nonlocally by "tuning into" the field. Morphic resonance is the term used to describe this communication and information flow.

An individual unit feeds the field, thereby strengthening it, and receives from the field, thereby gaining information. This communication and storage milieu includes transfers of information about bodily functions and personal experiences, as well as abstract creations, such as thoughts. For these reasons, Sheldrake proposes that memories are not stored primarily in the brain; rather, they reside in the morphic field and are accessed by morphic resonance. Similar forms generate more resonance than dissimilar ones—the greater the similarity, the stronger the connection to the field and, through reciprocation, back to other morphic units (individual participants). The feedback loop creates more coherence and a stronger field, thereby also enhancing and strengthening similar forms, such as the ideas and experiences of individual participants. As forms gain reinforcement and stability within their morphic field, they are able to evolve into more complex forms by building new morphic fields.

In his book, *Science and the Akashic Field: An Integral Theory of Everything,* **Ervin Laszlo** describes an ancient wisdom tradition from India called the

---

13. Rupert Sheldrake," *The Presence of the Past,* Chapter 6, 112.

Akashic Record.[14] The Akashic Record is based on ancient, prescientific insights, many obtained during meditative states. Laszlo compares this wisdom to newly emerging theories that postulate a universal energy field from which elementary particles are born and into which they are reabsorbed, similar to the Higgs field. In this respect, ancient wisdom intuited a great deal about what modern science is now rediscovering and verifying. These insights came thousands of years prior to their scientific validation.

Laszlo proposes that there is a "metaverse" that is all-encompassing, containing more than what we currently know about the universe. We are able to access only a small portion of its contents. This larger-reality metaverse is responsible for the phenomena we experience in our everyday world, including inexplicable, instantaneous information transfer, normally considered impossible. Indian lore describes "Akasha" as the birthing place that brings each thing into the physical world and that, thereafter, reabsorbs all things. The Akashic field is an underlying force that influences subatomic particles, rocks, bacteria, cells, human beings, thought forms, consciousness evolution, cosmic structures, and all other existing subjective and material things. This worldview provides building blocks for the Ecological Epoch's foundation; as such, Laszlo's following statements add a dimension to our Creation Story:

> (3:14) Could it be that our consciousness is linked with other consciousnesses through an interconnecting Akashic field, much as galaxies are linked in the cosmos, quanta in the microworld, and organisms in the world of the living?
>
> Hindu and Chinese cosmologies have always maintained that the things and beings that exist in the world are a concretization or distillation of the basic energy of the cosmos, descending from its original source. The physical world is a reflection of energy vibrations from more subtle energy fields.
>
> In Indian philosophy, the ultimate end of the physical world is a return to Akasha, its original subtle-energy womb. At the end of time

---

14. Ervin Laszlo, *Science and the Akashic Field: An Integral Theory of Everything* (Rochester, VT: Inner Traditions, 2004).

as we know it, the almost infinitely varied things and forms of the manifest world dissolve into formlessness…. In Akasha, all attributes of the manifest world merge into a state that is beyond attributes: the state of Brahman.

Although it is undifferentiated, Brahman is dynamic and creative. From its ultimate "being" comes the temporary "becoming" of the manifest world, with its attributes, functions, and relationships. The cycles of samsara [individual lifetimes]…are the Lila of Brahman: its play of ceaseless creation and dissolution…. The manifest world enjoys but a derived, secondary reality and mistaking it for the real is the illusion of maya.

Perhaps everything in our universe that has come into being in the past 13.8 billion years was seeded by the Big Bang. If so, this event contained the incipient expression for all things that have since manifest and for all things that will manifest in the universe's future. A giant oak tree's seed has in it the potential for creating a massive trunk, deep roots, thick branches, and delicate leaves. Similarly, the Akashic field is perhaps a seed that contains the blueprints that guide the unfolding universe.

David Bohm, whom was introduced earlier, was born in Wilkes-Barre, Pennsylvania, in 1917. He died in 1992. In 1947, Bohm became an assistant professor at Princeton University. While there, he wrote a classic, highly respected textbook titled *Quantum Theory* about the orthodox, Copernican interpretation of quantum physics. The book gained Albert Einstein's attention, and a series of conversations ensued between Bohm and Einstein.

Both scientists agreed they were not pleased with various aspects of quantum mechanics; for example, the theories were awkwardly counterintuitive. Neither was satisfied with the philosophical or theoretical coherency of this new physics. Bohm developed theories describing a new order of reality, including the "implicate order," wherein information is "enfolded" and is thus awaiting expression in the explicate order—the latter term meaning the visible or measurable world accessible to our senses.

He disagreed with the prevailing scientific worldview that assumed phenomena could be reduced to separate, isolated particles to be studied individually or that events could be separated in time or space. Bohm believed "continuous flow" is the underlying universal form. He disagreed with the scientific approaches most physicists followed and sought a grander vision. He called that vision the "enfolded order," in which elements have new and different relationships to time and space than those described in prevailing scientific thought.

Bohm describes one experiment like this: Start with an inner glass cylinder and a slightly larger outer glass cylinder. The space between them is filled with glycerin; black ink was added gently into the glycerin. Then the inner cylinder was rotated. The slow, circular movement elongated the ink into a spiral thread. The ink thread became so thin that it disappeared into the glycerin; then the cylinder was rotated back in the opposite direction, causing the ink to reconstruct into its original form. While not visible, the ink had existed in what Bohm calls the "implicate order" within the glycerin; it was enfolded. It was then precipitated out into the explicate order; it was unfolded.

According to Bohm, all science, including quantum mechanics, is restricted in its ability to describe reality. It covers one domain, yet much more is left unexpressed. A deeper reality connects all things, including matter, energy, force fields, mind, abstract thought forms, and all else in a grand wholeness without time or space separation. Bohm believed that "underlying order" is more than we are able to understand using the Cartesian worldview or quantum mechanics. These limitations also exist in classical physics and in Einstein's Theory of Relativity. Unlike conventional scientists, Bohm maintained it may not be possible to distinguish between thought and reality; in addition, it is beyond human capability to postulate scientific theories that fully describe the nature of reality.

Explaining the underlying structure of the universe, Bohm used a hologram as an analogy to describe implicate order: When we focus on any small part of a photographic plate containing a holographic image and project the image using only this part, we find that the entire image is still present, albeit in less focused contrast. The analogy indicates an implicit order existing in each location observed—both in time and space. "Implicate," from the word "implicit," means "folded inward" or enfolded. He proposed that an undivided wholeness is contained in the implicate order at any point throughout the universe, not individual particles spread out in space and time.

> *"The new form of insight can perhaps best be called Undivided Wholeness in Flowing Movement. This view implies that flow is, in some sense, prior to that of the "things" that can be seen to form and dissolve in this flow."*
> —David Bohm[15]

Using a flowing-stream analogy, the primary form is the moving water; however, eddies, vortexes, waves, and other water "forms" constantly appear and disappear. If the stream temporarily widens out into a river with a smooth bottom, the forms disappear; they could be said to be in the river's implicate order. The river itself is very sensitive to its environment; when its flowing water meets a narrowing, forms reappear, thereby coming into the explicate order. They are "fleeting forms."

The analogy holds true for "matter" temporarily unfolding from the implicate order and reverting back into it—be it a snowman, a person, or a stone. This also applies to abstract "things" like thoughts and new scientific ideas. They become explicate as they manifest from within the implicate order. Many ideas have long lives; they remain in the explicate order for extended periods. Likewise, a person's actions often have

---

15. David Bohm, *Wholeness and the Implicate Order* (London: Routledge & Kegan Paul, 1980), 11.

ramifications in the explicate order for much longer than the person's lifetime.

Moist air could also be used as an analogy: Until the moisture content reaches a certain level, the air seems clear and "empty" (implicate order). With sufficient moisture, clouds take "form," seemingly from nothing; rain begins to fall; perhaps the temperature declines and droplets become snowflakes, each with a fascinating, never-to-be-repeated unique structure. Snow blankets the ground, unique flake upon unique flake by the billions and trillions, merging in a new form in which each flake's individuality is hard to discern, hidden within the snow cover. They soon melt away into the implicate order once more, leaving emptiness behind.

In Bohm's underlying universal order of reality, both material things and consciousness are enfolded. Consciousness, memory, and thought processes are contained within the implicate order. Because matter and consciousness both reside in the implicate order, their separation is a temporary phenomenon that occurs only after unfoldment into the explicate order. They arise from the same source and eventually return to that same implicate-order source.

Memories provide a helpful analogy in understanding Bohm's point. Each memory is enfolded within the implicate order in the body (and perhaps also in other structures) until it is called forth to become a present-moment thought, at which point it becomes explicit. In a similar way, information is contained in the universal implicate order until it is retrieved, thereby becoming explicit. New insights are constantly becoming unfolded for the first time, emerging from the implicate order, and revealing the nature of reality.

We must learn to view everything as part of
Undivided Wholeness in Flowing Movement.
—David Bohm

Carl G. Jung (1875–1961) was a Swiss psychologist who deepened our understanding of the human psyche through profound personal and transpersonal inner exploration. He uncovered and identified universal images and culture-wide psychological influences. In addition to psychology and psychiatry, his insights shed light on mythology, religious symbols, and origin stories from many cultures.

Near the turn of the twentieth century, Dr. Sigmund Freud and Alfred Adler's psychoanalytical theories were revelatory. Many others further elaborated on Freud's work to create modern psychoanalysis. Freud was a mentor for Carl Jung but was disappointed when Jung would not fully adopt his theories. Jung believed the psyche was more complex and contained dimensions Freud had overlooked. Jung proposed such things as "archetypes" and "synronicities," in addition to other new, abstract concepts. Using these tools, Jung demonstrated how our dreams, imaginations, and fantasies affect our everyday activities, thereby impacting our lives. Two of Jung's numerous psychoanalytical insights are the most impactful to our Creation Story. These two are "unus mundus" and "archetypes."

Unus mundus is the term Jung used to express a radical, overarching theory, maintaining that the entire world is interconnected by underlying structures residing in a deeper reality than our day-to-day experiences. The "pulse of the universe" affects all beings. These structures are separate and unified at the same time. One's personal journey toward unification with this "pulse," if successfully traversed, will end in wholeness, wherein an individual finds harmony in his or her life. Unus mundus posits an underlying unity connecting all things. Like all the deepest mysteries, including creation and life itself, unus mundus can only be described, not explained. Positing its existence allowed Jung to draw valuable insights about interrelationships and psychological functioning.

Unus mundus includes Jung's "collective unconscious," a concept that encompasses spiritual, mythological, and mystical symbols—transpersonal information that feeds our folklore, origin stories, religious epiphanies, and other paranormal experiences. The collective unconscious is a non-personal, shared reservoir of information affecting all individuals. This "field" resides beyond the physical body but influences a person's psychological functioning and, therefore, behavior. Its influence impacts entire societies. The collective unconscious is distinct from "personal consciousness" and the "personal unconscious":

> *The collective unconscious is a part of the psyche, which can be negatively distinguished [differentiated] from a personal unconscious by the fact that it does not, like the latter, owe its existence to personal experience and, consequently, is not a personal acquisition. While the personal unconscious is made up essentially of contents which have at one time been conscious but which have disappeared from consciousness through having been forgotten or repressed, the contents of the collective unconscious have never been in consciousness, and therefore have never been individually acquired, but owe their existence exclusively to heredity. Whereas the personal unconscious consists for the most part of complexes, the content of the collective unconscious is made up essentially of archetypes...a second psychic system of a collective, universal, and impersonal nature, which is identical in all individuals. This collective unconscious...consists of preexistent forms, the archetypes, which can only become conscious secondarily and which give definite form to certain psychic contents.*
> —Carl Jung

The term "archetype" dates back to Platonic times, when it was used to describe a spiritually significant "perfect form," from which the less-than-perfect earthly counterpart was modeled. In English, the word derives from the Latin, meaning "beginning", "origin", or "first molded." Jung was not focused on explaining the origin of the archetypes; he was primarily concerned about how these energetic forms affect the psyche.

In earlier writings, Jung described archetypes as being images of instincts and considered them to be inherited; thus, there was a decidedly biological connection in the way archetypes were created from instincts and passed down from generation to generation through heredity. In his later writings, Jung moved closer to the Platonic description of "ideal forms" that were more than instinctual and hereditary—not just biological; they had an independent existence. Like Plato's Ideal Forms, archetypes were beyond time and space.

There are numerous archetypes, including several that are the most basic, all of which create an unlimited multiplicity of images. Dreams are a means for direct access to the unconscious psyche. Because they are not controlled by our conscious mind, they are a good source in which to find images that refer to a particular underlying archetype. If a person has numerous dream images that lead to the same archetype, this archetype is most likely influencing the individual's waking psyche and day-to-day behavior. Jung's primary archetypes follow.

- **The self** is the individual psyche's governing body and is in charge of one's individuation from parents and family and growth toward wholeness and personal transformation. Self is more than the person—in its completeness it represents spirit and the interconnected universe, unifying the world's conscious and unconscious components.
- **The shadow** consists of personal psychological material that has been acquired through conscious experience but has been submerged or repressed into the personal unconscious and is, therefore, inaccessible to everyday conscious functioning.
- **The anima** is the feminine aspect (qualities) of a man, which is often unexpressed in the man's personality, having been subsumed and repressed by his "manliness."

- **The animus** is the masculine aspect (qualities) of a woman, which is often unexpressed in the woman's personality, having been subsumed and repressed by her femininity. Both anima and animus are elements that must be integrated into the psyche to find wholeness, which is critical in becoming a complete human being. This integration process is also necessary in finding one's connection to spirit. Anima and animus are both important components of one's "soul" and "spirit":

Every man carries within him the eternal image of woman…. This image is fundamentally unconscious, a hereditary factor of primordial origin…an imprint or 'archetype' of all the ancestral experiences of the female, a deposit, as it were, of all the impressions ever made by woman.
—Carl Jung[16]

- **The Syzygy (Divine Couple)** represents wholeness, a coming together of disparate parts and reintegration into one; for an individual it means finding one's soul and merging with it. When referring to couples, this is often called "becoming one with a soul mate."
- **The Persona** is the façade we each use in presenting ourselves to the world at large. The word is derived from "mask," indicating an artificial construct, sometimes referred to as the ego. It is designed to protect the individual from painful emotional experiences and to provide boundaries, enabling him or her to control the emotional and psychic environment.

It could be said that when related to a particular individual, each basic archetype provides an energetic structure that pertains to that individual's relevant psychological experiences and emotional memories; each one is

16. Carl Jung, *Collected Works*, 17:338.

associated with its archetype. Dreams, fantasies, associations, and neurotic and psychotic states often create images or behavior that, through careful analysis, can be assigned to a particular archetype. This enables an analyst to recognize which archetype is causing the patient's unhealthy behaviors. These images also appear in creation myths and fairytales. Sometimes they arise in differing cultures that are not geographically close or even accessible. They appear independently in various physical locations because they are universal forms that are independent of time and place.

> *There are as many archetypes as there are typical situations in life. Endless repetition has engraved these experiences into our psychic constitution, not in the form of images filled with content, but at first only as forms without content, representing merely the possibility of a certain type of perception and action. When a situation occurs which corresponds to a given archetype, that archetype becomes activated and a compulsiveness appears, which, like an instinctual drive, gains its way [controls behavior] against all reason and will, or else produces a conflict of pathological dimensions, that is to say, a neurosis…. There is no lunacy [that] people, under the domination of an archetype, will not fall prey to.*
> —Carl Jung

Although the images are innumerable, some recur often:

- **The hero**: notable in US culture as "superheroes" in films that have recently become more and more popular.
- **The devil** (Satan): whose image has an impactful social influence through media and church teachings.
- **The child**: as adults, we never truly transcend our childhood influences.
- **The trickster**: a potentially destructive prankster, exemplified by costumed Halloween characters using the term "trick or treat."

101

The trickster isn't kidding and can cause significant psychic or physical damage if not paid (paid attention to).

- **The Great Mother**: seen in the Bible's Mother Mary and many other religious icons around the world. This archetype represents resolute mother love that perseveres in protecting her offspring, even in dire circumstances.

- **The Wise Old Man**: an image that recurs frequently in stories, including the Yoda character in the movie *Star Wars*, and in contemporary "gurus" (religious teachers), who are sought after by acolytes in an attempt to find spirituality and wholeness.

The above images are also categories—that is, containers for many individual examples. **The Hero**, as expressed in multiple forms from Superman to Batman to Lancelot, is the rescuer and champion. *Grimm's Fairy Tales* are a compilation of European children's stories containing hundreds of archetypal images that have survived many generations, while wending their way down to our children. Still used today, they contain archetypal images that garner their power through connection to universal archetypes. **The Maiden** is a character representing purity and innocence. **The Magician** appears in many stories and exercises mystical powers.

Another common image is the **Wise Old Woman,** which prompted a Catholic Church backlash against Earth-honoring religions and was therefore recast by the church as an evil witch, prominent in European folklore. **Earth Mother** images represent a connection to nature. Archetypes are transpersonal, containing forms that are accessible to a person's psyche. As containers, they hold personal images, not language. More associated with soul and spirit, they bypass the rational. This is one reason there is such power in mythological images and religious icons.

Like the collective unconscious and archetypes, another basic concept supporting the existence of unus mundus is "synchronicity." The term describes occurrences that are more than coincidence and unbounded by time and space. Coincidences can be understood by statistical percentages and fall into a causal arena that is rationally explainable—not so with synchronicity. According to these understandings, subjective activity can affect the outer, material world. This implies that there is a connective tissue between subjective and objective realities.

It is probably a coincidence if you bump into your college roommate in London ten years after graduation, and there is nothing more to the encounter; however, it is more than coincidence (synchronicity) if two medical researchers in different countries make the same discovery within days. It is likely that both people have studied the leading-edge research in their field, thereby comprehending the essential variables needed to make a new breakthrough. However, a major discovery within such close proximity points to profound processes at play in which both researchers have access to similar transpersonal information.

Following is one of Jung's true-life examples: Without knowing that his sister had died of a heart attack in Boston at noon on Tuesday, the brother suffered from a sharp chest pain in New York at precisely the same time. These are "a-causal" events, connected, but without rational explanation for their cause. They cannot be scientifically explained. They are beyond space–time causality and provide evidence that there is an underlying interconnection affecting the occurrences.

Psyche and matter exist in one and the same world, and each partakes of the other, otherwise any reciprocal action would be impossible.
—Carl Jung

Are Sheldrake's morphic reasonance theories or Bohm's implicate order hypothesis or Jung's archetypes ingenious new scientific insights to be integrated into fully accepted scientific theory—or are they pseudoscience, founded only in philosophy and intuition? This is an ongoing question; however, new scientific discoveries, including the Higgs field, indicate that "hard" science is beginning to correspond with these more subjective theories in its efforts to explain various phenomena that have been inexplicable until now.

The assimilative power of the human intellect is and remains strictly limited.... It is just as important to make knowledge live and to keep it alive as to solve specific problems.... All our knowledge is but the knowledge of schoolchildren. Possibly we shall know a little more than we do now, but the real nature of things, that we shall never know, never.
—Albert Einstein[17]

"Implicate order," "noosphere," "morphic fields," and "archetypes" are all philosophical products of the Scientific Epoch, and they are more. Each new human-consciousness epoch emerges from, and incorporates, its predecessor epoch. These scientific philosophers are innovators who presage the Ecological Epoch while going beyond the confines of hard science. Our Creation Story describes how the world is more relational and interdependent than our society's current scientific perspective presupposes. Bohm, Tielhart, Sheldrake, and Jung provide glimpses of how these underlying interactions function.

Each of these four scientist-philosophers cracks open our four hundred-year-old scientific worldview, one that has held us hostage to its myopic restrictions. This same science has also produced these forward thinking geniuses that are expanding our comprehension of reality. In this respect, they provide a foundation from which to construct our newest perspective. Humans are coming to realize that prioritizing our species' interaction with nature is paramount for our future success and for the earth's health. During the Scientific Epoch, the more subjective

---

17. Albert Einstein, *The Expanded Quotable Einstein* (Princeton, NJ: Princeton University Press, 2000), 208.

intellectual insights, such as philosophy and mental-health theory, were segregated out from hard science, which was based exclusively on objective experimentation. It was a materialistic period. Times have changed. We have come full circle.

The Ecological Epoch is once again breaking down the boundaries between hard and soft science because even rigorous, hard science experiments are pointing us in this new direction. A good example, as discussed in the following chapter, is the newly verified, all-pervading Higgs field. This and other Ecological Epoch insights, combined with the scientist-philosophers discussed, enable us to better integrate our physical and metaphysical universe. In our new story, science is not only tied to matter and the old scientific method; rather, it also embraces consciousness and creative intuition to bring about changing worldviews. In this new science, ontology has a place, as it did in Socrates's time, and the earth's living systems become a priority. In our continuing story, Sophia comes to visit in Fiji.

(3:15) About eight years ago, I traveled to Fiji to join the research ship Infinity, whose crew was studying the declining health of coral reefs. The world's oceans are absorbing excess atmospheric CO_2, thus creating a more acidic environment for sea life. Coral reefs are early victims. My friends on the hundred-foot-long sailing vessel were gathering data and publicizing the ongoing damage to shine a spotlight on this situation. All the crew members were divers; it was exciting for me to join them in the crystal-clear waters. The ocean was teeming with sea creatures.

Fiji is a country with 332 islands; two-thirds are unsuitable for habitation. We were anchored off an island with several villages. The authority of the local chieftain extends out into the ocean where we were working, so it was necessary for us to ask permission to be there. I was invited to join the delegation going ashore for this purpose. The village was in an exquisite, natural setting. There were no cars—tropical flowers, bananas, and coconuts were growing everywhere. Most of the men were small-boat fishermen.

We were directed to the chief's home, a small cinderblock building. He quickly gathered together a "council" group—all men—to assess our request. Their tradition for this process was quite different from my expectations. Our group from "Infinity" was composed of four people. We all sat in a circle on the floor with the six villagers. A local plant, kava, was brewed into a mildly psychoactive, relaxation-inducing tea and served to everyone. No questions were asked; we all just talked about anything that came to mind—the weather, the sea, the children, the village. There was little, if any, discussion about where we had come from, our boat, or our reasons for being there. In effect, this was an interview to determine who we were as individual people, man to man. They were not interested in what we were doing; rather, they were assessing our energetic presence.

This long council exchange was fertile ground. I admired their dignity and self-sufficiency. The village seemed to have a sustainable lifestyle—causing no harm to their surroundings or their neighbors. There was no pollution. Although primitive by our standards, everything was maintained nicely. During a quiet moment in the conversation, a kava-induced question came to mind: Wasn't the entire Earth like this before all the cities; isn't this village situation better than the life we have now? What happened?

Sitting still on the floor, legs crossed, the circle was quiet while several minutes passed. Then Sophia's voice entered my inner thoughts: "More than seven billion enterprising humans are sharing the planet with Earth's many million other species. Humans have become dis-integrated. As human population expands and industry churns out ever more "stuff" to satisfy indulgences, Earth's remaining life is relegated to smaller and smaller habitats until, like expiring candles, these lives are snuffed out one by one. Incessant consumption is a thief in the night, stealing the future from your children's children.

"Humans arrived on Earth only recently. Earth's grand life-community evolved long before that time and created the conditions that have allowed people to flourish. Reciprocity within nature is fundamental to any species' success. Human freedom of choice is an evolutionary experiment. Humans belong to the natural world, as do flowers and giant sequoia trees, but reflective intelligence comes with burdens, including existential angst that is often expressed in destructive ways. The suffering that people create in the world is a symptom pain. It stems from the human species' current isolation and lost intimacy—disconnection from nature's community.

"Earth's resplendent life was not created to serve human's artificial needs and unlimited economic expansion. On the contrary, reintegration with the natural world is the solution to the current human dilemma. Relationship creates intimacy; with intimacy comes love; with love comes heightened concern for that which is loved. The wisdom is at hand for reparation—but the courage has not yet appeared."

With that message, the inner voice faded away. My awareness returned to the council circle. Hours had passed. Our hosts were finally ending the interview. Our anchorage was never specifically addressed. They did not say we could stay, but somehow we knew it was all right. A few days later, we had a cultural exchange; they came out to our boat, where our entire ten-person crew sang and danced for them. They did the same for us—two different cultures but one common gathering.

CHAPTER 7

THE HIGGS-LIKE FIELD

The Higgs Boson

Relationship and interdependence sustain life on Earth; realizing this, we humans can mend our torn ecological fabric. How does this interconnection actually work? The existence of a universal, omnipresent energy field is one answer to this scientific/philosophical question. If it can be proven that everything, everywhere, is actually interactive, then the idea that we are all "one" would become more valid. Recently, a quantum particle called the "Higgs boson" has appeared in newspaper headlines. Also called the "God particle" in the popular press, its recent scientific verification could help change our culture's worldview.

The year 2013 was an exciting time for theoretical physics. Peter Higgs is a Scottish physicist. Approximately fifty years ago, Higgs and five other notable physicists proposed that an energy field pervaded all space (our story calls this the "Higgs energy field"). They described it using a molasses metaphor. The field was proposed to be energetically alive. As subatomic particles move through this energized molasses field, it creates resistance to their movement, which slows them down. Without this resistance, these particles would fly about at the speed of light and would be unable to coalesce into matter. This slowing process imbues the particle with mass; as such, a particle is able to interact with other particles to form atoms. The field creates different resistance levels for different particle types; therefore, a particle's mass varies by type.

Peter Higgs took the theory a step further; he proposed that this energy field would contain its own unique particle, in addition to quarks, neutrinos, and other known quantum particles. This theoretical particle became known as the "Higgs boson" (the term "boson" is an alternative for "particle"). Physicists theorized that, if the Higgs energy field was subjected to sufficient perturbation—that is, struck with enough energetic force—the Higgs boson (particle) would appear and would be visible to research equipment.

This research is done using particle accelerators that cause particles, usually protons, to collide at enormous speeds. One or more protons are present in each atom's nucleus. A proton is composed of quarks. The high-energy collisions cause protons to break down into their constituent subparts, albeit for just an instant in most cases. The process is recorded and analyzed. Subatomic particles are identified in this way.

The problem was that no particle accelerator existed that was powerful enough to "strike" the Higgs field sufficiently hard to produce the Higgs boson, a unique particle that had never been "seen"—until recently. The Large Hadron Collider, much larger and more powerful than any previous research facility, began operations in 2010 near Geneva, Switzerland. By early 2012, enough research had been completed and analyzed to confirm that the Higgs boson actually existed. Thus, Higgs's theory was finally verified and accepted by mainstream science.

This development is important to theoretical physics. The so-called Standard Model of particle physics is a comprehensive set of mathematical equations; it was constructed during the past thirty-five years and is used to describe the cosmos and how it functions. Because the Standard Model predicts a Higgs field, and the Higgs boson is the only physical evidence with which to demonstrate the field's existence, finding this particle was critical in verifying the Standard Model.

Without this particle's existence, the model cannot be proven and, therefore, many scientists would consider it to be invalid. A new theoretical construct would be needed to explain how the cosmos behaves. The Higgs boson is a bridge that connects theoretical particle physics with empirical experiments, thereby validating Standard Model theories, showing them to be consistent with the observable physical world. With this discovery, the Standard Model has been upheld.

The Higgs field also provides possible explanations for vexing, seemingly "unreal" occurrences. Although it does seem to have all the requisite characteristics Higgs proposed, the newly verified Higgs boson could be an even more exotic particle that will require the Standard Model to be further refined. For this reason, some scientists are calling the discovery the "Higgs-like particle."[18] Similarly, the Higgs field may not be precisely as Higgs describes it. For our discussion, I refer to it as the "Higgs-like field," or HLF for short. Our New Creation Story has more to say about this fascinating phenomenon, but first let's look at two inexplicable scientific realities.

---

18. One measure of a subatomic particle is its apparent weight, or mass. A particle can be described by using its energy, as measured in "billions of electron volts." A photon seems to move unimpeded through the Higgs field; therefore, it is weightless and has no mass. Finding the Higgs boson was difficult because its mass was unknown. A proton weighs one billion electron volts; the newly discovered Higgs boson turns out to be a heavy subatomic particle, 126 times heavier than a proton when measured in billions of electron volts; the W boson and Z boson, carriers of the weak force, weigh 100 billion electron volts, a similar mass to that of the Higgs boson. Electrons are tiny in comparison, with one proton weighing two thousand times more than one electron; therefore, the Higgs particle is 250,000 times as massive as an electron.

Entanglement and Nonlocality

In quantum mechanics, "entanglement" and "nonlocality" are two qualities that have been shown to be empirically real and, at the same time, inexplicable. Quantum entanglement occurs when particles, such as photons, existing in a connected system are linked in such a fashion that the quantum state of one cannot be explained without reference to all others. In classical physics, the *principle of locality* holds that an object can only be influenced by its immediate surrounding—that is, some sort of contact is necessary with the thing that is doing the influencing.

Nonlocality means one or more objects are influencing an object at a distance—there is no direct contact. Remarkably, with no physical connection, a change in one can instantaneously affect the other(s). This change seems to occur faster than the speed of light, which is not supposed to be possible.

Nonlocality and entanglement are not the same thing; however, in quantum physics, entanglement of objects is a necessary precondition for nonlocal influences to occur. Entanglement is a defining quality that separates quantum mechanics from classical scientific thought. Entanglement has no place in the older science; however, entanglement and nonlocality are key elements in postulating the existence of a connecting field. Without such a field, or some alternative formulation not yet forthcoming, there is no acceptable explanation for these physical occurrences.

Our Creation Story stresses nonlocality and entanglement because they are scientifically proven phenomena within quantum physics' Standard Model. These phenomena occur and recur, yet have no explainable basis to exist. Ecological Epoch science is rational, and it is more. Profoundly coherent imagination is needed so that we are able to expand our current worldview to accommodate these nonrational, yet scientifically accepted, phenomena. The Higgs-like field is a scientific beginning point from which we are able to perceive the world in more relational ways. Mystics have known for millennia that the earth's living beings are inextricably entangled. Now scientists are beginning to show how this occurs.

> *"Entanglement is a strange feature of quantum physics, the science of the very small. It's possible to link together two quantum particles—photons of light, or atoms, for example—in a special way that makes them effectively two parts of the same entity. You can then separate them as far as you like, and a change in one is instantly reflected in the other. This odd, faster-than-light link is a fundamental aspect of quantum science. Erwin Schrödinger, who came up with the name 'entanglement,' called it 'the characteristic trait' of quantum mechanics."*
> —Brian Clegg[19]

John Bell was a quantum physicist who devised a theorem that, as a necessary component, includes nonlocality within quantum systems (Bell's Theorem). To illustrate this theorem by example: when particles decay into constituent parts, the resulting new particles must obey various conservation laws—even when these particles separate from each other, their states remain entangled. Consider spin, which is a property of particles such as electrons. In one well-known quantum mechanics experiment, the spins (up or down orientations, for example) of a pair of electrons are initially unknown—that is, the possible values can be represented only by probability equations until they are observed. When the spin of one electron is observed, the spin becomes known and its value becomes fixed. The entangled "partner" electron then immediately takes on a fixed value for its spin, commensurate with the conservation laws, even though the two electrons can be arbitrarily far away from each other—thus, nonlocal interaction at a distance between the electrons appears to happen.

---

19. *California Literary Review*, Interview with Brian Clegg, author of *The God Effect: Quantum Entanglement, Science's Strangest Phenomenon.*

"Entanglement doesn't throw away the concept of cause and effect. But it does underline the fact that quantum particles really do only have a range of probabilities on the values of their properties, rather than fixed values. And while it seems to contradict Einstein's special relativity, which says nothing can travel faster than light, it's more likely that entanglement challenges our ideas of what distance and time really mean. Similarly, entanglement is no challenge to the scientific method. We need to use a different kind of math, but this is still the same science."
—Brian Clegg[20]

Nonlocal influence is not supposed to happen in classical physics—yet it is proven to happen in quantum mechanics. There is still a mystery surrounding the transition that exists between classical behavior, which is dominant at the scale in which we make routine observations, and quantum behavior, which is observed in the microscopic realm. With the Higgs boson and corresponding field confirmed, we might be able to explain many enigmatic idiosyncrasies and provide a missing bridge between the two views of reality. The Higgs-like field does not depend on space and time. Entanglement and nonlocality require the suspension of space and time to work. Perhaps the term "suspension" is inadequate; rather, "irrelevance" may be more useful.[21]

---

20. Ibid.

21. Ken Hennacy, PhD, a science researcher, described to the author the following scientific commentary regarding nonlocal influence: First, there are different interpretations of quantum mechanics, so some people would say nonlocality isn't necessarily observed (that is, nonlocal influence at a distance doesn't actually occur). For example, in a purely statistical interpretation, the states of the entangled particles are determined during their interaction, but given that the observer doesn't know the initial states to begin with, the outcome is uncertain until a measurement is made. Hence, the measurement result may suggest "instant" communication when nothing of the sort happened. In this at least, Bell's theorem is correct if by using the term "nonlocality" it is meant that no classical "communication" mechanisms are involved. Second, in the standard interpretation of quantum mechanics, the entangled state can freely extend over space and time—that is, as the particles travel farther apart, they never lose their quantum description (let's call it a "wavefunction"). This wavefunction is not physically measureable and so does not have any direct physical limitation to its ability to characterize the evolution of a system. That's not to

The perception of time by the human mind and our bodily senses is a way to order the multiplicity of stimuli bombarding us at any moment. Each present moment is the only actual point of existence. Everything else is past or future. Once passed, the memory merges with all other memories and is susceptible to "order confusion" as memories blend into one another. Time is an illusion based on all of these memories and on thoughts of future activities, none of which are precisely accurate. They are totally subjective; for example, even with honest witnesses, a trial judge often hears conflicting eyewitness testimony; some testimony is similar, some totally at odds. What is real, and what is erroneous perception?

With an interconnected field, actions can affect one another instantaneously—faster than the speed at which light travels. This concept requires space and distance to be understood differently; it is as though space and distance collapse into a different dimension, perhaps a singularity—a single point. The Big Bang theory of the universe's origin starts with a singularity; perhaps that singularity, in some timeless, not-yet-understood way, still contains our universe. Maybe our universe will collapse back into that singular point and start again.

The HLF could be the basis for quantum-mechanics phenomena that seem logically impossible, such as *nonlocal influence at a distance*. I'm not proposing an actual theoretical explanation for the collapse of space and time; rather, I'm pointing out that there are many possible explanations to be explored, some of which will, when today's future becomes tomorrow's present moment, prove to be more accurate descriptions of reality than

---

say there shouldn't be a physical model for it; it's just that none are known at this time. Third, the Higgs field specifically addresses the acquisition of mass from a constant field. It doesn't concern itself with conservation of angular momentum—for example, "spin," which is the typical entangled property that people talk about. That isn't to say, though, that the Higgs field couldn't be some property of a more general field (or concept) that characterizes the evolution of a system. Physicists are ultimately looking for a description of a system where "all is one," but getting that description is difficult. Maybe the Higgs field has some connection to the nonlocality of quantum mechanics, but that connection would be weaker than some other mechanism, which unifies all the actors in physics (fields, matter, and dimensions).

those in use today. Quantum entanglement and nonlocality are examples. Extrasensory perception, in which a person can access another's thoughts, also defies scientific explanation, as does "psychokinesis," wherein a person's mind can move material objects.

There are many other phenomena that are inexplicable using today's science. "Remote viewing" allows a person to observe, mentally, something occurring at a distant place. Taken together, these strange abilities are referred to as "psi," which is the first letter of the Greek word "psyche," meaning *mind* or *soul*, phenomena. Any such activity is in violation of the principle of locality and therefore inconsistent with classical physics.

We now understand that we inhabit one planet in one solar system in one galaxy among many billions of galaxies. The brightest scientist five hundred years ago was unaware that our planet exists on an outer spiral arm of a galaxy we call the Milky Way, which is one among several hundred billion other galaxies, each with hundreds of billions of stars and planets. In Copernicus's time, this was not-yet-available information. We are continually deepening our human perception. The HLF is a new scientific way of seeing reality.

Dark Matter and Dark Energy

Today's best scientific theories predict that the universe is composed of 70 percent dark energy, 25 percent dark matter, and just 5 percent "normal matter." The latter 5 percent is material that, given the proper investigative tools, could be "seen" in the conventional sense. This normal matter makes up the earth, the planets, the moons, the stars, the comets, and the cosmic dust—all the material we humans have been able to identify in the universe. This includes everything we see as our telescopes look across the sky and all we extrapolate from the evidence we have obtained.

What is dark matter? What is dark energy? Those questions cannot yet be answered; when they are, a Nobel Prize will be forthcoming. So, what can we say about these concepts? There exists in the universe an energy field that is altogether foreign to our understanding, as is the matter within it. As mentioned, all the known material from the Big Bang event makes up only 5 percent of the universe. The remaining 95 percent is a mystery. We know dark matter and dark energy exist by observing how the universe behaves; for example, the galaxies are moving away from each other at an accelerating rate. This was proven just a little more than one decade ago by measuring exploding stars in the distant regions of the universe.

It has been about 13.8 billion years since the Big Bang conceived our universe. Light takes time to travel to us. When we observe the universe's outlying regions with telescopes, we are seeing light that has reached us after billions of years traveling through space. The images we observe are showing us what happened at their origin when these light particles first started their journey, thus, we are looking back in time! The most recent past, the last four billion years, indicates accelerating expansion, while earlier periods—for example, ten billion years ago—show decelerating expansion. These observations mean that mysterious forces are at work.

The Big Bang was an inconceivably powerful event that initiated this outward expansion. Early in the universe's life, before much expansion had occurred, all matter was contained in a more confined "space" than would be the case after additional expansion billions of years later. This more densely confined matter provided strong gravitational attraction that tended to hold the early universe together. Yet the universe continued to expand, albeit at a decelerating rate. Why? Dark (that is, invisible) energy is the answer. It was, and is, pushing the galaxies farther apart—a universal galactic push and pull exists between gravity and dark energy.

The farther apart the galaxies travel, the less gravitational influence they have on each other. However, assuming that the mysterious dark energy does exist, and *if* it remains constant, it would be able to push the galaxies apart faster (that is, at an accelerating rate) as their gravitational attraction is weakened from the additional space between them. Einstein initially included a concept similar to dark energy in his equations describing the cosmos. It was represented by what he called the "cosmological constant"; he later retracted the idea based on his own incorrect assumptions regarding the universe's expansion. We now realize Einstein's concept was fundamentally sound: there is energy in the universe we cannot see.

As recently as 2004, observations from the Hubble telescope in outer space confirmed the change from a decelerating expansion in the early universe to an accelerating expansion more recently. This galactic behavior verified the dark matter and dark energy predictions, but it did not explain what dark matter or dark energy actually is—just that it exerts an influence and therefore must exist.

Dark matter's gravitational attraction has been discussed in theoretical physics since the 1970s. For example, galaxies seem to have more mass than their visible matter could contain, unless we assume dark matter's existence; to explain the gravitational effects we see, stars' rotational movement within distant galaxies would require that they contain more mass than the amount we are able ascertain from observation. This additional mass would be explained *if* something more than the universe's known visible matter is restraining the galaxies' outward momentum and holding them together.

What can be said about dark matter? The most compelling idea describes it as "weakly interacting massive particles," or *wimps*—that is, subatomic particles created in the Big Bang 13.8 billion years ago that have not been incorporated into visible matter and move freely throughout the universe, perhaps in higher concentrations near galaxies. In quantum-size spaces—that is, the space between atoms and between the particles that constitute atoms—distances are vast relative to particles size. Dark matter, *wimps*, can pass right through a human body, or the entire Earth, without touching another particle.

As for dark energy, which is thought to compose 70 percent of the universe, we have no understanding of it whatsoever, except to say that there is a force that counteracts gravity and causes the universe to expand. There are currently four known forces: electromagnetism, gravity, the weak force, and the strong force. Dark energy may turn out to be a fifth force, or its existence may be integral to these currently known forces, each of which has a particle to "carry" them: the photon for electromagnetism, the graviton for gravity, the W and Z bosons for the weak force, and the gluon for the strong force.

The most up-to-the-moment scientific research provides evidence that helps build the foundation for the Ecological Epoch's New Creation Story. What we are currently coming to know is as much an acknowledgement of what we don't know as it is a compendium of what is known. Paradoxically, this is a step forward—acknowledging what we don't know leads us to realize the sacred nature of our personal existence and, therefore, to feel awe, respect, and appreciation for the miraculous Earth and its many beings. In this humility, we will be less likely to mistreat nature. The cosmos, the earth, and all life exist in holistic interconnection. Paying more attention to these innumerable relationships could be our saving grace.

Higgs Boson and the Ecological Epoch

As mentioned, not all physicists agree that the newly observed boson is the same particle that Higgs predicted. Although it does seem to have the requisite characteristics, many are calling the discovery the "Higgs-like particle." However, this Higgs-like boson is important in our discussion, not only because it is a newly discovered particle, or because it further verifies the Standard Model, but because it also validates theories that a pervasive, universal energetic field does exist—like the theoretical Higgs field mentioned earlier. As with the particle, this field may or may not be precisely as Higgs and other renowned physicists originally describe it; however, we are now coming to accept that a mysterious force field does exist. For our New Creation Story, as mentioned, I am calling this the Higgs-like-field (HLF). The HLF furthers our Creation Story.

(3:16) Visualize "empty space" as not empty; rather, as filled with vibrant energy, which in mysterious ways causes particles to dance continually in and out of existence. Different particle types obtain apparent mass by moving through the HLF; some of these interact with each other to build the universe's visible matter, which is only 5 percent of all the universe's energy and matter. Other particles that we call dark matter stay hidden behind the curtain of human awareness, still in the Great Mystery realm. Although currently thought to be "weakly interacting massive particles," we are not yet able to prove what these particles are or how they may interact with the HLF. They remain closer to the Creative Source than our imaginations are accurately able to go.

The Higgs-like particle validates the HLF's existence. It is everywhere—a vast energetic symmetry through which all elementary particles swim. The field slows these particles, making them appear to have weight or mass. Slowing the particles breaks the all-pervading symmetry. Slowed sufficiently, they are attracted together to form atoms. The HLF's primordial, subatomic particle soup is a container that allows visible matter to exist: so that atoms can form, so that molecules can come together, so that stars can ignite, so that elements can build planets, so that planetary chemicals can interact, so that spirit can imbue matter with life, so that life can "see" this process and reflect upon its profundity.

In scientific terms, the HLF is an energized force field containing the potential to manifest physical particles, which, in turn, construct all material things and provide the scaffolding for life itself. In philosophical terms, the HLF is the "energy of being" from which the "ground of being" is manifest. In spiritual terms, the HLF is an expression of the Creative Source, and all humanly known things arise from within this field.

These viewpoints describe the nature of reality from different perspectives. Scientifically, philosophically, and spiritually, there is coherence in what we are and how we arose. There is symmetry from which we came and to which we return. All matter, all things, all beings are temporary phenomena, arising from the same source and returning again to that beginning. People have a short "hour upon the stage"; suns and planets are longer lived but also fleeting in cosmic terms. We are diversity within unity, each a temporary manifestation held within holistic union. We exist within one huge, woven energy fabric; to know ourselves, to find meaning in life, is to know Natural Harmony and live life with guidance from this sacred structure.

Describing the HLF

The HLF offers potential answers to real-world anomalies that have, until now, had no scientific explanations. As such, its existence can support the leading-edge philosophical and scientific concepts discussed in these pages. Carl Jung was very familiar with the new physics of his time called quantum mechanics. He sometimes worked closely with the renowned physicist Wolfgang Pauli. Jung suggested that archetypes and, similarly, the tiniest physical particles were what he called "irrepresentables"— that is, both categories were too subtle and unknowable to be described adequately.

Archetypes, synchronicities, and small-particle physics each provide evidence for Jung's unus mundus, which proposes "that the multiplicity of the empirical world rests on an underlying unity...."[22] To what extent does matter interact with consciousness? Is "mind" composed of matter and consciousness? Is there such a thing as unification of mind and matter? All of these interrelationships are possible within a fabric that connects everything, everywhere. The HLF is such a fabric—its recent validation invites additional philosophical speculation: ESP phenomena, such as remote viewing and psychokinesis, might now have a scientific basis for their existence. In addition, similar to Teilhard's "noosphere" discussed earlier, the HLF might be an information-storage mechanism for both present and past data, acting as a medium and facilitating information transfer.

The HLF may also be the energy source that creates the known universe—perhaps all physical matter comes into being from the field's generative vitality. Perhaps it is the energy matrix that has created all material forms that have ever existed. If so, it also contains the implicit

---

22. Carl G. Jung, *The Collected Works of C. G. Jung* (Princeton, NJ: Princeton University Press, 1958).

potential to create all future matter—everything that will come to be. In any case, the HLF concept helps establish a scientific worldview that shows that interrelationship and interdependence form the scaffolding that underlies everything from quantum particles to complex life.[23] In our Creation Story:

> (3:17) Material objects have a "perceived" surface and solidity; however, within this substance lays the proton–neutron–electron atomic structure, and further within we observe the smallest subatomic entities, including quarks, leptons, and bosons—flitting in and out of existence in a seething energetic sea of creativity. These are among the fundamental objects in quantum field theory's Standard Model. They have all been experimentally observed, including the Higgs boson. By analogy, the earth's oceans have many names, but they are all connected to each other; they are all one ocean. The whitecaps far out to sea, the surfers' waves roiling to shore are perturbations within the one sea, temporary forms made of sea stuff, emerging from the vast body in unpredictable shape and size, then, just as quickly, losing their separate form and merging back into their source. Is there a trace left behind? Yes and no.

---

23. In quantum physics, the quantum vacuum is defined as the lowest energy state of a system of which the equations obey wave mechanics and special relativity. It is the locus of a vast energy field that is neither classically electromagnetic nor gravitational, nor yet nuclear in nature. Instead, *it is the originating source of the known electromagnetic, gravitational, and nuclear forces and fields. It is the originating source of matter itself.* From Ervin Laszlo, The International Society for the Systems Sciences and The Club of Budapest, as referenced from *Consciousness and Physical World*, CISE-VENT, Moscow 1995 (in Russian, with English summaries).

The view that space is empty and passive, and not even real, is in complete opposition to the view we get from contemporary physics. It is clear that what they describe as the unified vacuum—the seat of all the fields and forces of the physical world—is, in fact, the primary reality of the universe. What we think of as matter is but the quantized semistable bundling of the energies that spring from the vacuum. In the last count, matter is but a waveform disturbance in the nearly infinite energy sea that is the fundamental medium—and hence the primary reality—of this universe. (Ervin Laszlo, The International Society for the Systems Sciences and The Club of Budapest, as quoted from Mary Desaulniers, *Ervin Laszlo's Metaverse and Cosmic Consciousness*, October 18, 2008.)

The following pages provide some exciting scientific and philosophical possibilities that the HLF may eventually explain. There are several intriguing theories. One proposes an electromagnetic basis for the universe's structure—that is, the energy within the HLF may be electromagnetic radiation that is uniform throughout the universe and provides interconnecting scaffolding for all physical phenomena, as opposed to the currently accepted theory that gravity is the controlling force. Such a universal electromagnetic field would be difficult to observe because of its uniformity. As such, we do not yet know the universe's underlying composition. Our Creation Story is new and evolving; we are still coming of age.

The HLF theory can be employed to explain classical physics in addition to quantum physics. Normal classical physics combined with the HLF's existence is sufficient to explain all observed physical phenomena. An omnipresent HLF could explain Newton's concepts of *inertia* and *mass* in a new light. As mentioned in prior paragraphs, the field itself would provide resistance to acceleration of an object moving through it. Newton thought that mass was necessary to explain inertia; however, the laws of electrodynamics, when combined with effects from the HLF, eliminate the need for Newtonian inertia and mass as the basis to explain physical reality.

The HLF also helps bridge classical physics with elements of quantum mechanics that have been irreconcilable until now. Using this field theory eliminates the need to rely on quantum mechanical principles, such as the Heisenberg Principle, that disturbed even Einstein.

HLF, Interconnection, and Real-World Phenomena

Let's examine some phenomena that might be explained by the HLF's existence. For example, it could be the basis for an information-storage milieu, similar to that proposed by Teilhard de Chardin's noosphere, which allows information to be accessed remotely and instantaneously.

This would be a decentralized, yet unified reservoir, that, under the right conditions, anyone could access. This could explain mental telepathy, channeling, remote viewing, and other anomalous occurrences.

The evolution of human consciousness is a process in which nature continually creates more coherence and complexity. This phenomenon is neither positive nor negative. Its current cutting edge is the evolution of *Homo sapiens'* consciousness, a process that may lead to either human enlightenment or to massive ecological degradation. As an individual delves further into more profound awareness, she or he is given greater access to information contained within the HLF. That person will typically gain more clarity, deeper intuition, and greater creativity. Ingenious human discoveries become more likely with access to this universal information library.

Individual perception invents time and space. Perhaps time-and-space perception is necessary for our minds to sort out the otherwise overwhelming visual and mental stimuli accosting us in each moment. Our personal survival requires us to cope with each immediate circumstance using a linear sorting-out mentality. This approach accentuates isolation, promoting the illusion of separateness. Given our current challenges, our species' survival demands that we perceive the world less in linear ways and more in holistic ways.

The HLF is not subject to time and space. According to Albert Einstein, "Time and space are modes by which we think and not conditions in which we live." Einstein also states that we should "entirely shun the vague word 'space' of which we must honestly acknowledge we cannot form the slightest conception."[24]

When time and space are set aside, memory merges with the present moment. This altered state can be experienced through various practices, including deep meditation, hypnosis, ingesting psychoactive plants, and other such activities. Shamans, gurus, and other wise men and women

---

24. Ibid.

have purposefully accessed these transpersonal states for many thousands of years. Perhaps the HLF will provide scientific validation for these perennial, wisdom-seeking practices.

Conventional science, for the most part, maintains that memories reside in one's personal thinking-organ called the brain. Some theorists take the position that memories are stored outside the body and, when needed, are accessed by the brain and other sensing mechanisms. In this respect, creativity would be a more an "opening to the field" and retrieval process rather than a personal invention. With proper preparation and focus in a particular area, the individual mind might be able to access an "all-inclusive mind" residing within the HLF, gaining knowledge while concurrently cycling new insights back into the field. Perhaps this reciprocal cycle is the essence of creativity.

Many discoveries have been made almost simultaneously—more than one person "was given" the idea. For example, Charles Darwin and Alfred Russell Wallace came up with similar evolution theories within months. These ideas were ingenious and profoundly insightful; it is likely there was more than coincidence at work. The Nobel Prize for science is often shared. Different scientists have won the award in tandem while working on the same problem. They have access to the same research that has paved the way; thus, each has cultivated fertile ground, but they have taken additional new, ingenious steps without any collusion. We've all heard the term "an idea whose time has come."

A scientist often works on an issue for years, then voilà! Perhaps while lying in bed, or in silent mediation, or while on a daily jog, without "trying" or thinking, the problem resolves itself. In our Creation Story, the solution to a problem might already exist in the HLF, which is being "fed" by individuals throughout the world and is storing this cumulative intelligence. Preparing the ground is critical; only an expert who is immersed in the issue at hand is able to find and retrieve a problem's solution from the HLF.

In addition to intellectual pursuits, the HLF feeds other creative endeavors that require intuitive connection. In some cases, normal time is suspended, as though the event were occurring in slow motion and the physical activity in process becomes more creative and harmonious. That is, it becomes more connected to a greater whole, like a masterful dance or a deeply meaningful poem that seems to "come through" the poet while she writes without effort. Elite athletes refer to entering "the zone" when performing physical feats that would normally defy success. In the zone, time seems to slow down, and movement is perceived in slow motion.

How is it that a quarterback in football's Super Bowl championship game can complete 75 percent of his passes against the best defensive players in the world (with a very small statistical probability of success)? This occurs only if he is able to access an altered state that orchestrates his movements. Just a little too much thinking will take him out of this awareness and impede his success. A sixteen-year-old Olympic gymnast or a fifty-year-old ballerina might also find this zone and put on her life's best performance.

The HLF may also store memories or even the holographic history of deceased individuals. If so, access to this information pool could explain our beliefs in ghosts, "channeling deceased individuals," and "clairvoyance." Belief in reincarnation would be accentuated because a living person could, under the right conditions, tap into a deceased person's life-experiences or memories. This would also seem to be evidence, albeit mistaken, for seemingly experiencing one's own "past life."

In addition to remote viewing and mental telepathy, another ESP phenomenon, "remote healing," has sometimes succeeded in helping an ill person recover. At times there have been large groups in remote locations focused on a particular individual's health. Positive results indicate a real, yet unexplainable, connection to the ailing person. The HLF is a possible basis for this interconnection. An individual illness is a breakdown in the body's coherence. Using the HLF, healthier bodies could possibly transmit their own coherence to the ill person, making this form of healing possible. A person does not exist in isolation; seeing the world in ways that are receptive to life's infinite relationships helps one stay healthy.

The HLF functions using subtle processes, creating and exchanging energy with the tiniest subatomic particles. The field operates at these minute levels; therefore, it requires coherence in materially dense objects, including human bodies, to produce an unusual result, such as a new invention or an ESP experience. Without this coherence, these special events are blocked out; for example, mental barriers formed by an erroneous worldview often create illusions that limit access to the HLF. A person is re-created as his perception of reality changes. Young children have fewer blockages than adults, explaining why they seem more innocently connected to spirit. A child of five years old or younger is often in a state of openness; perhaps his or her brain has more access to the HLF because it is more often functioning in an alpha state, similar to meditating adults who become more emotionally and psychologically open.

An individual human mind, no matter how accomplished, is a far cry from humankind's vast knowledge library. Insights, inventions, and other discoveries are more likely to occur while tapping into the collective. This is not to say fully developed solutions to all problems are just waiting to be downloaded to an individual's brain. Human knowledge is accumulated in tiny increments, as is the evolution of human consciousness—billions of ideas are needed to build the knowledge base that eventually creates a breakthrough to new wisdom. Human consciousness is changing, as it always has. Wisdom is built over millennia, creating the cultural epochs described our story. In more recent eras, changes in consciousness have cycled faster because the accumulated information stored in the HLF, or a similar "cloud" or noosphere-like structure, is expanding exponentially.

Some important discoveries throughout human history have been scientific, others ethical, and still others have been philosophical. Newton's discoveries helped us understand how nature functions; Buddha's insights about human suffering deepened our introspective capabilities; Jesus's teachings enhanced compassion and conscience in human culture. All of these discoveries emerged from evolving human consciousness. Important insights are retrieved from accumulated wisdom, become integrated, and eventually result in cultural change. New values become part of the social fabric with each new consciousness stage.

Currently, our species is in a dangerous circumstance, and we are endangering most other planetary life forms. Fortunately, a new epoch has arrived, bringing with it wisdom about relationship and intimacy. We have been given a chance to reform how we interact with one another and with creation itself.

Science not only purifies the religious impulse of the dross of its anthro-pomorphism but also contributes to a religious spiritualization of our understanding of life.
—Albert Einstein

An open mind that includes 'all possibilities' is infinite in scope and, therefore, connects mind to Creation.
—Sophia

CHAPTER 8

SOLUTIONS

Science is providing both physical evidence and, surprisingly, a philosophical underpinning for the new Ecological Epoch. As our culture continues to transform, all of the professional disciplines will use ecology as their touchstone and guide.

Ecological economics will show us how to build sustainable economies. Ecological energy policy will be more focused on preventing climate change. Ecological social policy will consider worldwide policies as much or more than national priorities; for example, the redistribution of wealth will help lower planetary population growth. Ecological agriculture will place more value on food quality, soil health, and reduced farm-created pollution. Ecological architecture will make beauty, efficiency, and conservation the priority. Ecological medicine is beginning to find allies in the body's own beneficial bacteria. Ecological religion is imbued with participatory spirituality that includes nature mysticism.

Ecological education makes ecology the underlying principle for all coursework. Ecological art acknowledges nature as its primary focus and inspiration. Ecological philosophy, as in this Creation Story, begins with nature as its foundation. Ecological psychology recognizes the emotional ties between each person and nature, and so it goes with *every other* professional and intellectual discipline. We are on the path to realizing this fundamental premise: ecology is the bond that integrates all things within one another.

Ecology and Business Practices

Stakeholders from various social and economic sectors are combining their creativity to envision and implement ecologically sound business operations. For example, Ceres is a Boston-based nonprofit organization advocating for "sustainability" leadership. Its consortium of investor, labor, social-justice, religious, and environmental groups developed the Ceres Principles in recent years. The strategies they promote apply to industry, agriculture, and other forms of business. They provide a format that measures a company's effectiveness at operating with fairness and with a reduced ecological footprint. Various corporations and other businesses have signed on to the principles and have used them to design their own operations. Naturally, environmental protection and concern for human rights are front and center in the Ceres Principles. This includes protection of resources such as water, air, soils, forests, and the Earth's minerals.

The principles require that today's uses support the Earth's health so that future generations will inherit a healthy planet. Eliminating waste is one principle; recycling and reusing are also guiding principles, as would be expected. Energy reduction not only helps the global ecological picture; it has tremendous potential for cost savings and increased profit margins. Ceres also includes principles that are concerned with employee safety and welfare. Additionally, there is a focus on a business's relationship with the surrounding communities.

These and similar practical guidelines are available now for any business operation to plug into. I earned an MBA in finance at the Wharton Business School in 1971. At that time, the Ceres Principles and other such endeavors had not been started. With these new initiatives, we are making progress in defining ethical commerce; however, a great deal of consciousness-changing work remains before these ethics are successfully integrated into our economy's industrial operations.

Naturally, all-out growth without limits is not sustainable; in fact, we are well past the point where economic growth can be used as a measure of the health and welfare for the planet and its human population. It is Earth that has always met our human needs; its health must be maintained so that our children's needs are also met. On an individual level, one's personal health requires sustainability—by the same principle, so does the planet's health. As the Ecological Epoch gains traction, we will learn to make all economic and social decisions using a sustainability prism as our guide. From an Ecological Epoch perspective, the term "standard of living" is redefined so that it applies to a more meaningful, spiritual, and happy life, rather than one's yearly income or net worth.

There is a current rigidity in world economies that makes change difficult. Behemoth international corporations control much of the world's transnational commerce. These companies, in addition to large and medium-sized US business operations, provide the extensive campaign funding necessary to gain high office in the United States. As a result, elected politicians often create laws and regulations that favor big business. It's no wonder that ongoing street protests, starting with the 1999 "battle for Seattle" against the World Trade Organization and continuing with today's climate-change protests, typically have labor, educators, and environmentalists on one side in conflict with big business and government on the other.

Fortunately, individual corporations are changing because they see new opportunities in "green" policies and products; some are even changing for ethical reasons. Our job as Ecological Epoch citizens is to bring pressure to accelerate these changes. The work of a membership group called the Sustainability Consortium is described in the December 2012 issue of *Scientific American* magazine. The group includes representatives from ten leading universities, many not-for-profit organizations, and more than eighty international companies.

The consortium is designing a sustainability index for products, including food production, appliances, autos, home building, and many other categories. Each input in a product's supply chain is to be tracked based on such variables as carbon emissions, labor practices, water usage, and waste. This index can be used to inform consumers about the environmental impacts of product they are considering; in addition, the consortium's reports and recommendations can help businesses reduce expenses by identifying new opportunities and eliminating inefficiencies.

International Initiatives

In May 2011, the Third Nobel Laureate Symposium on global sustainability was held in Sweden. Among other business, the symposium held a demonstration—a judicial trial in which the Earth was the plaintiff and the human species the defendant. In an effort to harness the wisdom of our times, Nobel Prize winners were invited to act as jurists; their published report from the meetings is called the Stockholm Memorandum. It offers conclusions and "court orders" stating that the Earth is an extremely complex system and that human "progress" has come at a very high ecological price, creating new global risks and unsustainable economic systems.

The planet is no longer able to absorb all the abuses of current human activities and still remain healthy. Irreversible consequences for human communities and ecological systems are now beginning to overwhelm the Earth's healing capability. There is a false dichotomy occurring in which economic activity and planetary health are seen to be in opposition—looking at long-term benefits, successful economic development and environmental health are in alignment, not opposition. We cannot attain social justice and raise living standards without environmental sustainability.

The Stockholm jury called for "fundamental transformation and innovation in all spheres" to reverse environmental degradation. It ordered changes in policies, frameworks, and institutions. Its conclusions state that the entire world, including the wealthy industrialized countries, will benefit from helping developing countries' economies to reduce poverty, initiate climate stabilization policies, and enhance ecological stewardship. The jury calls for CO_2 emissions to be reduced and for global warming to be held to no more than two degrees Centigrade. This can be accomplished by phasing out fossil-fuel subsidies, taxing fossil-fuel use, and using the tax proceeds to develop alternative energy.

Overconsumption is to be eliminated; the throw-away mentality is to be replaced with "circular material flows" in which autos, appliances, and other large products are returned to factories for renewal and resold as new. Strict resource-efficiency standards are needed to change relationships between production and resource use—that is, new business systems are to be instituted using currently available technology with radically more efficient energy and material inputs. Entire new industries will spring up to accomplish these efficiencies, providing more jobs with living wages.

The report points to human population growth as a problem and acknowledges a lack of attention to basic human needs, including the environmental vulnerability of the poor. The goal is to create a sustainable and equitable worldwide Earth community. Population growth can be reduced and the global population eventually stabilized by providing better public health services and contraception to the fast-growing developing nations; women need better education and employment opportunities—conditions that have been proven to lower birth rates.

In broad terms, it is necessary to transform humanity's relationship with the planet. It is important to create and support new institutions that are focused on this purpose. Science has a critical role, as the report recommends: There should be a major worldwide research initiative to determine the most effective solutions for sustainability problems, similar to the scientific attention given space exploration, national defense, and public health.

The Stockholm Memorandum states that we need new policy frameworks to address overall resource use and to encourage a new "industrial metabolism." In its conclusion, the document includes this passage: "We are the first generation facing the evidence of global change. It therefore falls upon us to change our relationship with the planet, in order to tip the scales toward a sustainable world for future generations." Perhaps these Nobel Prize winners, our wise elders, will be given the respect they have earned so that they are able to change the world's business-as-usual model into a more responsible one.

The report focused not only on industrial products but also on the need to reform agricultural production. Industrialized farming is a major cause of ecological degradation. Less than 2 percent of America's population is employed to produce food for the entire population, therefore, this reform can only be accomplished by changing corporate-controlled factory farming techniques. Most of the remaining 98 percent of the population does not know much about where their food comes from, what's in it, or how it is grown. Industrial agriculture often destroys small farms and rural communities.

Corporations have pushed family farmers off the land and into the cities because families cannot compete with these large companies' economies-of-scale operations and their willingness (including their obligations to their shareholders) to externalize all the costs they can. Managers prefer today's profits when compared to profits obtained in the next decade, hence their willingness to grow and market less-nutritious food and degrade the land's health.

Large-scale agriculture has provided very low-cost food to consumers in the United States but with huge environmental and public health costs. Food production is currently wasteful and unsustainable; it uses too much oil and phosphorus. Growing crops on marginally fertile land accentuates topsoil loss and desertification. Massive-scale deforestation from planting crops changes land cover, affecting the planet's ability to absorb and radiate heat. This creates more CO_2 buildup and changes weather patterns. It is likely that climate change will have major negative impacts on agricultural production in the near future. There has been a critical loss of biodiversity and a reduction in carbon-sink capacity because so much forest and so many grasslands have been converted for crops and for biofuel production.

As in many industries, these ecological-degradation costs are hidden. The public loses its clean air and water and suffers health problems. The giant corporations that control food production profit because their products' selling prices do not include hidden social costs: the depletion of nutrients in soil that had been built up over many hundred years, polluted water from pesticides and herbicides, topsoil loss, and more. In cattle raising, fresh-water usage and contamination is remarkably high, while cows produce a significant amount of CO_2 by continually excreting methane gas, thereby exacerbating global warming.

Off-season foods that are marketed around the globe require long and costly shipments of produce from the Southern Hemisphere to the north and vice versa, exacerbating fossil-fuel use and causing additional marine and atmospheric pollution. If the pollution costs were added to the product's selling price, many companies would be forced to change their business models; society would benefit by becoming more sustainable.

Rio's Earth Summit

Many attendees at the 1992 Earth Summit took on the task to develop guiding principles for future development—ones that delineated how and why it was important to include ecology in local and global business decisions and why both rich and poor people were to be included. The document was finally finished in the year 2000, stating in part: "We must recognize that in the midst of a magnificent diversity of cultures and life forms, we are one human family and one Earth community with a common destiny. We must join together to bring forth a sustainable global society founded on respect for nature, universal human rights, economic justice, and a culture of peace." Another section continues: "This requires a change of mind and heart. It requires a new sense of global interdependence and universal responsibility. We must imaginatively develop and apply the vision of a sustainable way of life locally, nationally, regionally, and globally." Although a great deal has been done to delineate how these objectives can be met, there has been little progress in actually implementing the overall vision. Our economies are not sustainable.

If there is one word that best defines the Ecological Epoch, it's sustainability. We often hear this term in reference to individual industries and entire economic systems; in addition, sustainability is important in personal relationships and in forging international agreements. Sustainability requires an understanding that economics, human social organization, and ecology are so intertwined that decisions within one area must include concern for healthy functioning within all areas. These are ethical and spiritual issues in addition to practical ones.

At the United Nation's request, Gro Brundtland, Norway's former Prime Minister, led a commission that produced the Brundtland Report in 1987. The document states, "Sustainable development is development that meets the needs of the present without compromising the ability of future generations to meet their own needs." Although an accepted concept now, it was novel in 1987. The report was referenced extensively at the1992 Rio Earth Summit environmental conference and the follow-up summit conferences since that initial one, including the 2002 Rio+20 conference.

Sustainability requires that today's development does not "take from" future generations' ability to fend for themselves and their children. This concept is founded in equity and fairness from one generation to the next. Sustainability also requires more equality in today's distribution of wealth. On September 16, 2013, the *Los Angeles Times* reported that a UC Berkeley study "found that the top 10 percent of US earners captured 50.4 percent of the total income in 2012." This may not surprise everyone because we often read about astronomical corporate salaries and top athletes' contracts that exceed $10 million per year; what is more relevant to our sustainability discussion is the sentence's conclusion: the 50.4 percent of total income taken by the top 10 percent is the highest percentage since 1917.

We have been going in the wrong direction; however, Seattle has a new program to redress the imbalance and tilt the scale a little further in the direction of the lowest paid workers. On June 2, 2014, the city council voted to raise the minimum wage to $15 per hour, which will be the highest in the nation. The federal minimum wage is $7.25. About 25 percent of the city's residents currently earn $15 or less per hour. The new minimum will lower Seattle's 14 percent poverty rate and also reduce the number of families that require public assistance. There will be wealth redistribution from corporate profits to each worker's housing and food budgets, without making any structural changes to the existing free enterprise system.

Today's poorest people are not able to live with comfort, health, and dignity; therefore, the ways we currently do business lack sustainability. When a large percentage of the world's seven billion-plus population is living in poverty, it is difficult to prioritize ecological health. As we move into the Ecological Epoch, social justice is a necessary step in creating the worldwide sustainability and wealth redistribution that are important for our ecological initiatives to succeed. Seattle's community-first approach is a good starting point. The new ordinance refers to the city as, "a community dedicated to democratic principles and economic advancement and opportunity."

Andres Edwards's book, *The Sustainability Revolution*, provides an overview of numerous international conferences, decrees, government policies, and expert philosophies that are available to solve our sustainability challenges. We know the solutions to most of these social and economic issues. Finding the common desire, the public-will, to implement the required changes is now the most pressing challenge.

Sustainable Community

For several months each year, I am involved in a small community in British Columbia called Salt Spring Island, with a population of about twelve thousand year-round residents. There is ample farmland to serve the island and to export some surplus. There are no traffic lights and no fast-food franchises because the community has made a conscious choice that these things would be detrimental to the island's lifestyle. No Walmart-like big box stores are permitted; as a result, there are many mom-and-pop businesses. Customers know the stores' owners. Trust is part of the local commerce—neighbors support one another and their day-to-day business activities.

This environment has nurtured a local currency—the community created its own money, which is imprinted with a Salt Spring logo, printed on the island, and accepted in many stores and businesses. Using this currency means the transactions stay local because the money would not be accepted "off island." It builds community spirit, as does the locally grown and branded wine and many other island products. People take pride in the things they grow and make. Lives are enriched. This local feeling has attracted many musicians and artists as residents, which adds to community spirit and is another reason why, in addition to its remarkable natural beauty, Salt Spring has become a tourist destination.

Small communities often have fewer problems to deal with than do larger cities. Vancouver, the largest city in British Columbia, has focused on solving both ecologic and social problems with equal priority. The current mayor, Gregor Robertson, inherited a large homeless population in addition to numerous drug addicts who were living on the public streets. In recent years, rents have skyrocketed beyond the reach of many local residents. Young people and artists were forced to move out of the city, which consequently lost diversity.

Robertson's administration put people and community first: The drug problem was addressed in novel and effective ways; housing was made available to reduce homelessness; new programs were implemented to help those living on the street; zoning was changed to allow artists to live and work in their studios; bicycle lanes and a new subway train system were installed to reduce downtown auto traffic; a private company, Car2Go, was permitted to provide shared, short-term car rentals that currently serve 23,000 customers, further reducing private auto congestion on city streets; and public parks, where residents could gather and play, were made a priority.

National and international issues affect local government. Concern for the planet's health and fear of oil spills led Vancouver City to oppose the expansion of Alberta's tar-sands oil. Although the oil companies and the provincial government want ship-docking facilities in the city's heart, the municipal government is doing everything possible to prevent that from happening. In addition, knowing the harm that oil, coal, and nuclear power cause—both for its citizens' health and for the earth's ecology—the city is expanding renewable energy sources for its own use.

Recycling and reusing resources is another priority for the city's managers. All of these foci and more have given Vancouver the opportunity to claim to be the world's "greenest" city; naturally, a few other cities think they deserve the honor. This attitude fosters a friendly, Earth-honoring competition that also promotes civic pride. It takes a village to raise a child well and to lovingly care for the village idiot. That village can be small, like Salt Spring, or large like Vancouver. In either case, heartfelt community is necessary for the Ecological Epoch to become firmly rooted.

Sustainable Business

Corporations that trade on the New York Stock Exchange and other such public trading platforms have a major impact on society and the environment. Innumerable small business and numerous intermediate-sized commercial enterprises also impact our culture's ethics and healthy functioning. We do our daily work and exchange our work products through this commerce. The US economy is based on "free enterprise" principles; however, many necessary controls govern what we are allowed to do. Monopolies are not allowed. Minimum wages must be paid. Safety regulations must be followed. Labor unions have an important voice in many industries—and on and on. Government can and should be sure that particular business activities are good for everyone and that corporations do not have unfair advantage—for example, by profiting from shifting their production costs onto society and getting away with causing social harm. This often occurs in pollution-causing industries, especially with fossil-fuel-energy companies.

The Securities and Exchange Commission (SEC) is a government agency that oversees publicly traded companies. The February 21, 2013, issue of the *Los Angeles Times* newspaper reported that "The SEC issued guidance saying corporations should disclose to shareholders the potential effect of climate change on their business and their strategies for dealing with the risks." This directive has opened the door for numerous shareholder resolutions attempting to introduce new company policies that will make their operations more ecologically friendly, which is an encouraging trend because proposed changes will be coming from the investors; it is insider pressure and can be more effective than opposition from the outside.

Planned Obsolescence or Cradle-to-Cradle Design

In earlier chapters, I have referred several times to "two rivers of cultural influence" as a metaphor to distinguish business as usual from

142

sustainable economics. On a functional level, "planned obsolescence" compared to "cradle-to-cradle design" represents this contrast. Planned obsolescence is a business strategy that was initially proposed in 1932 to help companies recover from the Depression. Engineers purposefully created products they expected to have a relatively short lifetime, much shorter than the life that a different design could have provided.

The automobile and clothing industries are good examples: To sell the same product more frequently, marketing executives used nonfunctional, yearly style changes and advertising campaigns to manipulate consumers into thinking they needed the latest model. Because consumers were expected to repurchase the product within a few years, it was built shoddily and had a short shelf life. For example, my experience with 1950s and '60s automobiles was that they had a reliable life of less than forty thousand miles. In addition, cosmetic changes each year clearly announced to my neighbors whether or not I was driving an "old" car—there was peer pressure to be up to date. Both function and psychological desirability were manipulated to artificially buoy up manufacturing. Although less in vogue in today's globally competitive economies, this waste-and-exploitation strategy bodes badly for Earth's health. Planned obsolescence is one reason we now find ourselves suffering from overproduction and industrial toxicity.

The antithesis to planned obsolescence is cradle-to-cradle design in manufacturing a product, characterized by minimizing resources used in making the product, using recycled materials whenever possible, providing design durability to ensure a long life, and ensuring that the product's component parts can be readily reused and recycled when its useful life is complete. The objective is to be as efficient and waste-free as possible. Each product's entire life cycle is examined from an eco-friendly perspective, and its potential toxicity is eliminated or minimized.

Walter Stahel first used the term "cradle-to-cradle" in the 1970s. Decades later, the Association of Home Appliance Manufacturers has adopted the concept in a policy meant to encourage appliance efficiency: Manufacturers, including GE, Whirlpool, and Viking, have signed onto the agreement, along with environmental groups like Earthjustice. These stakeholders expect the policy to create more jobs in addition to huge energy savings. This approach includes dishwashers, clothes washers and dryers, air conditioners, and refrigerators. The agreement promotes new, efficient energy standards and encourages government tax credits to accomplish these goals.

Some companies are able to model sustainability for an entire industry. Once these innovative leaders introduce methods that provide a competitive advantage, their operating principles are likely to be applied in other firms. The entire society will benefit, so it makes sense for government to provide incentives for innovation, as it is doing for the electric-car industry.

Cradle-to-cradle design is a subset of a broader design concept called "biomimicry," stemming from the ancient Greek words "bios" (life) and "mimesis" (to imitate). The term first appeared in English in 1982. Nature has been developing today's life forms for 3.8 billion years. Through biological integration, the Earth has created sustainable solutions to most problems. Nature provides creative inspiration in addition to practical solutions. Biomimicry applies nature's design solutions to human industrial design and manufacturing challenges. Using biomimicry strategies in manufacturing demonstrates our respect for conservation and the ways of nature. In addition to industry, this approach also can be used for agricultural production, city planning, community building, economics, and other social systems; as such, it is a valuable tool for the Ecological Epoch.

Sustainable Agriculture

World population currently exceeds seven billion and is likely to reach nine billion by midcentury. That's a two billion-person increase in about thirty-five years. How can all these new humans be fed without further compromising the Earth's health and vitality? There are solutions in Ecological Epoch agriculture; however, as in all professional disciplines, just knowing how to solve problems is a long cry from implementing the needed changes. Transforming our way of seeing the problem is also essential; this requires a whole-planet perspective that balances peoples' nutritional needs with Earth's ability to maintain its health so that forests, oceans, grasslands, humans, and other animals can all support and sustain one another.

As mentioned previously, industrial agriculture has degraded grasslands, caused topsoil loss, depleted soil nutrition, reduced biodiversity, polluted water resources with pesticides and herbicides, increased fossil fuel use, and forced families off the rural landscape and into cities. However, the news is not all bad. We know how to produce healthy food in sustainable ways.

Our story's new worldview provides a twofold solution to the current agricultural dilemma—how to feed the inevitable human population increase without further damaging Earth's healthy functioning: *first, eating further down on the food chain will help wealthy people improve their health; second, more efficient food production, especially in the local regions where the food is consumed, will provide the necessary calories to feed the world's poor.* As with other eco-business models, we have the knowhow to achieve these goals and, with appropriate regulation, our objectives can be met within the economic parameters of today's agro-business model, profits and all.

What does it mean to eat lower on the food chain? A pound of corn provides a lot of calories for a cow or a person when consumed directly; however, a cow must be fed 100 calories worth of grain to provide three calories for a person who eats the beef. Chicken is much more efficient. One hundred grain calories fed to a chicken provides twelve calories when the chicken is consumed. Chickens must be fed about two pounds of grain to yield one pound of human body mass, compared to seven pounds of grain for cows. In this respect, chicken is a much more efficient human food; it is further down the food chain than beef or pork.

Seafood is even better. Fish can convert one pound of food into one pound of fish body mass. Shellfish are near the ocean food chain's bottom. For example, unlike ocean fish farms, oysters can be grown without supplemental feed, antibiotics, or hormones that are often used in fish farming. Staying closer to the food chain's beginning keeps us humans closer to the earth; in addition, it vastly reduces the negative environmental impacts caused from cattle rearing.

Agriculture is the most extensive human endeavor on the planet. Throughout human history our approach to expanding food supplies has been to add more territory to the land used for food production. Our population has grown so large that we have penetrated into lands that are ecologically fragile, including rainforests and delicate grasslands. Most of this intrusion produces food for cattle, not people. In the process, agriculture produces more global warming gases than the world's entire transportation industry. Cattle emit vast quantities of methane gas, which is much more potent than CO_2 as a greenhouse gas. Fertilizers for crops give off nitrous oxide. Deforestation—burning the forests for cattle ranches and palm oil farms—adds massive amounts of CO_2 to the atmosphere.

Corn and soybeans that are grown for cattle and ethanol fuel are major consumers of clean water resources, as is cattle rearing. Fertilizer runoff and from crops and manure from cattle are major polluters of streams, lakes, and coastal ecosystems. Cutting forests also eliminates wildlife habitat and accelerates species' extinctions. Alternatively, Ecological Epoch consciousness provides a multifold strategy to produce enough food while sustaining the planet's health. Starting in May 2014, the *National Geographic* magazine ran a series of articles that address food security issues. These are a valuable contribution in understanding the challenges the world is facing in order to produce more food with less ecological degradation.

According to the *Nation Geographic* articles, 36 percent of the crops grown worldwide are used to feed livestock. From an environmental perspective, perhaps the most important goal is to reduce agriculture's footprint, that is, to pull back from the use of ecologically sensitive land so nature can nurse these degraded habitats back to vitality. The rainforest and marginal prairie lands used to feed cattle are not needed when operating from a new equation in which the world's beef consumption is reduced by 50 percent. Chicken can help to make up the reduced beef protein, and fish can supply the remaining nutrition. We can ill afford more tropical forest being destroyed for cattle, corn, soy and palm oil.

Existing farms can be made more productive. As mentioned previously, there is an imbalance of small, local family farms when compared to corporate agricultural production. Farmers' markets are expanding rapidly throughout America, providing small farmers with distribution outlets in their own bioregions. This eliminates the middleman and makes the endeavor more profitable for family farmers. Their produce is typically more nutritious because it is fresher, and the crop choices and varieties are not dictated by such factors as durability for long haul shipping. In recent decades the average age of farmers has move steadily upward; there has been no place for young farmers. Transformed attitudes toward food and health can change this trend and facilitate family farming once more.

In our story's planet-wide food formula, there is still a place for agribusiness with its efficient economies of scale, especially in vast regions without sufficient population centers to sustain local markets; however, these large land tracts, even though privately owned, should be considered to be part of the public's commons and regulated as such. For example, France has a free-enterprise economy that is regulated so that the agricultural sector functions with small farms, nutritious food, and public health in mind.

Comparing continents, Africa's population is expected to grow faster than any other in the coming decades. In Africa most food is still grown by small farmers; however, the methods used and technology available has been less than efficient. Farm machinery is too expensive to purchase, and fertilizers are typically too dear to use; production per acre is about one-fourth that of US farms. If currently available techniques for organic, therefore affordable, fertilizers are used, and training is made available, small farms can readily double and triple production.

Africa has huge tracts of nonproductive, potential farmlands. Large-scale investment by businesses can efficiently employ Africa's underutilized growing regions. Care must be taken not to take land from the small farmers; in addition, it is essential to use environmentally friendly techniques, especially when starting these massive agricultural projects from scratch. Organic production methods that include cover crops and mulches can be used as substitutes for chemical fertilizers, even on large projects. When chemical fertilizers are required, taking great care with fertilizer blends that minimize the amounts used will decrease costs and increase profits. Drip irrigation systems can also improve efficiency while lowering water use.

Lots of food calories are currently wasted. In the wealthy countries, the waste occurs when meals at home go unfinished, restaurants serve in excess, and grocery stores dump outdated produce. In the less developed countries, food often spoils due to lack of transportation and storage facilities. Perhaps as much as half the food that is produced is not consumed. As world population increases, it is likely that creative ideas will come into play so this waste can be reduced. For example, supermarket produce will be used to feed hungry people before its useful life expires; more creative distribution systems in the developing world will help to feed locals before the produce spoils.

Should the wealthy-world pay to reduce and eventually eliminate rainforest destruction? Yes, indeed. The burden cannot be borne solely by the counties where the destruction is occurring. Brazilian rainforest beef feeds European and American stomachs; it will take an international effort to design sustainable food programs that can feed nine billion people, but that's what the Ecological Epoch is all about—cooperation and relationship.

Red meat from beef has proven to be less healthy for the human diet than poultry, and cattle ranches extract a much higher ecological cost than chicken farms. Fish is a more healthy way to get the body's needed protein; it also provides essential omega-3 oils not found in red meat. Because fish are cold blooded and buoyant, they need a fraction of the calories required by cows, pigs, or chickens; as mentioned, farmed fish require only one pound of feed to produce a pound of fish, compared to almost two pounds for chickens and seven pounds for beef.

Fish farming has its own environmental challenges. In the ocean, fish pens have historically been big polluters. There are so many fish in the pens that antibiotics are needed to deal with diseases; excrement fouls the area with nitrates, phosphorus and other byproducts, and diseases spread to the wild fish populations. Land-based operations also have important negative impacts. In the open ocean, wild cobia, salmon, and other favorite varieties consume smaller fish. To supply enough nutrition, the fish farm industry buys foraging fish like anchovies, sardines, and krill from open-ocean fisherman to make fishmeal for their farms. This practice is currently having a serious impact on the lower end of the oceans' food chain.

There are solutions. The more progressive fish farms are supplying their fish with nutrition from vegetarian diets and showing that very little ocean-caught fishmeal is needed. There are also "poly-culture" ecological models for producing seafood in the ocean. One such operation raises cod in pens and places shellfish in nearby baskets so that the fish excrement provides the shellfish with nutrition. Edible kelp is grown next to the pens, which helps to cleanse the nitrates and other chemicals that the fish produce. Using ecology-protecting strategies, fish farms can supply the lion's share of protein and nutrition needed for the inexorably expanding human population. Naturally, reducing population growth, and eventually lowering the number of people on the planet, is a major Ecological Epoch objective, as discussed elsewhere in our story.

The Ecological Epoch's plan is to use existing farmland more efficiently while enhancing the land's vitality. There are farming systems that can improve production and provide significant yield increases, especially on small farms in developing countries. These methods improve the soil's health and eliminate toxic by-products. A more detailed look at one of these systems provides an example. A Japanese farmer and philosopher, Masanobu Fukuoka, practiced "ecological farming" for many decades before his death in 2008. His techniques use biomimicry garnered from carefully observing natural ecosystems. His ultimate objective was to meld the farmer with the land in a spiritual relationship.

The healthiest way to farm is to observe how nature functions and follow suit. Biomimicry does just that—it employs natural systems in which the relationships among each element become apparent and are respected. Interaction among the farmer, the soil, the plants, the water, the animals, the buildings, the machinery, and all of the other inputs is factored into an equation that supports the land and its produce. Agribusiness has different values and priorities—profit comes first; however, many biomimicry techniques could be incorporated into large-scale farming; for example, reducing fossil fuel use and pesticides can actually increase profitability using this system. With the need to develop local economies in the future, these techniques can be applied in the United States to restore farmland's vitality and reduce toxic by-products. International shipments would also decline.

Fukuoka inspired biologist Bill Mollison to develop a new philosophy he called "permaculture." The term combines the words "permanent" and "agriculture." This lifestyle approach has numerous dimensions that supersede normal farming. It also includes ecological architecture and building, agroforestry, organic gardening, and much more. The term stands for sustainable development in general. The first priority for permaculture is to care for the earth—always augmenting, never depleting—using nature as a guide.

Following this design system allows fuel and labor inputs to be minimized because nature is helping the farmer. There is no struggling against nature; rather, the farmer's cooperative relationship with nature is emphasized. Mollison dedicated his professional life to practicing permaculture, learning from his experiences, and writing books that refined this philosophy. These publications have influenced thousands of adherents throughout the world in what is now an ongoing, growing philosophical movement.

Permaculture employs various techniques. One is an integrated system called "agroforestry" that combines reforestation with raising crops and animal rearing, thereby increasing production and profitability. Another is called "food forests," which combines trees, shrubs, animals, and crops using interrelated layers, each one benefiting the whole system. Yet another technique is "natural building," using locally available materials that are readily renewable and need minimal transport.

When we use permaculture techniques, nature helps us heat and cool our buildings. For example, my home is a passive solar design with windows facing the south to capture the winter sunshine; it has thick walls for insulation and flooring material designed to absorb the sun's warmth. In summertime, the building can be opened up so that air flows through and circulates to every corner; my family does not require air conditioning.

Ecological Epoch agriculture reprioritizes family farms and hands-on gardening; there is more mind, heart, and love in the food produced. Local food growing supports local economies and provides more nutritious food because the produce does not have to stand up to strenuous shipping, handling, and big-box retailing. Family farmers live where they work; they also eat the food they produce. They are concerned about toxicity in their surroundings and about minimizing the use of expensive fossil fuels. Some farms have been in the same family for many generations, in which case preserving the health of the soil for the benefit of the children is an ongoing goal. These farmers are much more likely, when the knowledge is available, to partner with nature. They realize that the soil, the plants, the water, and the animals are nature's gifts and are to be respected and enhanced.

In the world's poorest communities, more radical approaches are needed to mitigate poverty and biological degradation. Marc Barasch founded Green World Campaign (GWC) in 2006 as a project of EarthWays Foundation. As Barasch states in a recent report about the project: "tree planting is a way to restore degraded soil, increase arable land and crops, feed livestock, provide building materials and firewood, increase rural employment, reestablish biodiversity, protect watersheds, adapt to climate change, and even absorb excess atmospheric CO_2."

Barasch is currently focused on one species that he considers a super-tree: "The moringa tree's leaves are 30% protein with an astonishing array of vitamins and minerals, while its pressed seeds yielded ultra-high quality oil. Moringa could be a keystone species for restoring the ecology and economy of the world's poorest places, providing communities that struggle to live on degraded land a new source of food security and income. Villagers add the moringa leaves into delicious local recipes, ensuring that no village that grows this super-food tree will ever starve. Local women are now using GWC-provided hand-presses to produce seed-oil for cooking and body care, saving 25% of scarce family income that can be repurposed for food and school fees."

Government Intervention

Both the Canadian and US public is beginning to pressure government to force polluting companies to clean up their acts. For example, creating

electricity from coal produces toxins that cause major public health problems, in addition to being significant contributing factors to climate chaos.
Barry Saxifrage writes in the Oct 19, 2012, issue of *Vancouver Observer* news
magazine that coal plants are being phased out for economic reasons. If
coal power plants are forced to clean up even a fraction of their toxic
emissions, including CO_2, sulfur, mercury, soot, smog, and acid rain, then
natural gas, wind power, geothermal, and solar energy become compara-
tively less expensive to produce.

The US government has passed legislation that will restrict CO_2 emissions in coming years. Coal-plant owners are likely to face huge equity
losses as coal production becomes even less competitive with alternative
energy sources. Knowing the damage that coal plants cause, insurance
companies are becoming afraid to cover them. The stock prices of US
coal companies have fallen dramatically in the past few years, including
Peabody Coal, Alpha Natural Resources, and Arch Coal. Per Saxifrage's
article: "The Sierra Club's Beyond Coal campaign says that plans for over
150 proposed coal-fired power plants in the USA have been cancelled. In
addition, a quarter of the existing coal plants in America have recently
announced firm dates for retirement."

American and foreign auto companies selling cars in the US marketplace
are cooperating with new regulations that require doubling the average vehicle's
performance to fifty-four miles per gallon by the year 2025. Bill Vlasic wrote
in the July 28, 2011, issue of *The New York Times*: "The new standards are seen
by the Obama administration as critical to reducing oil consumption and cutting consumer expenses at the pump, and the White House made it clear to
Detroit executives that the changes were coming and they needed to cooperate."
New technology is helping auto manufacturers meet these standards, including
hybrid cars that incorporate gasoline and electric motor propulsion, "plug in"
all-electric car engines, and better batteries that make these electric vehicles viable. Most auto companies are producing more efficient, smaller engine designs.
Better efficiency and more miles per gallon will reduce toxic emissions.

President Obama was originally elected on a platform that included reducing CO_2 emissions from all industrial sources as well as from autos and from the entire transportation industry. Although the US Congress has done little to create new environmental legislation, the Supreme Court has upheld the existing Clean Air Act, and Obama has begun to use the Environmental Protection Agency (EPA) to enforce those regulations. This can be done without congressional support. Starting now, the agency has plans to regulate, during the next ten years, all sources that produce significant greenhouse gases. It has authority to require efficiency standards and emission restrictions on industry throughout the country. In the spring of 2014, the EPA announced requirements that power plant emissions be reduced 30 percent by 2030 from 2005 levels, at a cost of almost $9 billion. The same announcement estimated health and social benefits totaling $55 billion from the cleaner air.

Environmentalists had great hope for progress under the Obama presidency; however, after almost six years in office, his visionary rhetoric has mostly turned into frustrating inaction. Obama's successes have included increased auto fuel mileage standards, resistance to the Keystone XL oil pipeline that, if constructed, will help to expand Alberta's environmentally disastrous tar sand oil production, and the EPA's actions mentioned above. Notwithstanding these achievements, the current president has opened massive new territories to oil drilling and coal mining, failed in an effort to impose a pollution cap-and-trade program for industry, and has been unable to pass any major new energy legislation.

Symbolically, Obama recently installed a solar system to produce electricity for a portion of the White House; ironically, it took him six years to implement this improvement—one that he promised when he first moved into the building. It's a positive step, but the scenario demonstrates how difficult it is for even a well-meaning chief executive to make things happen.

We desperately need more visionary leaders in government. Jerry Brown is California's current governor. During his multi-decade political career, he has always valued the long-term view. California currently has the most ambitious atmospheric CO_2 reduction policies in the nation. Brown wants half of the state's energy to come from renewable sources within twenty years. He has several specific purposes for these regulations; one is to "encourage other states, the federal government, and other countries to act." To this end, he met with other governors at a Washington conference in early 2013 in an attempt to convince them to follow his lead. His policies, although costly, will produce "green jobs" and improve public health, among other advantages; however, if other states fail to enact similar legislation, California will be at a competitive disadvantage because its businesses will be paying more for energy.

Although there will not be income parity in the near term, sustainability requires changes, such as more equitable wealth sharing between the developed world and the developing countries; the education of girls and women; the creation of job opportunities for women (which has proven to lower birth rates and population increases); and good food, housing, health care, and clean water for everyone on the planet. As mentioned, in wealthy countries, sustainability includes a reduced level of income disparity—we have to learn to share better, just as we were taught in preschool. For the sake of today's preschoolers, the time is now.

People go one by one and you say goodbye and goodbye, until the time comes when it's your turn to go and they say goodbye. I guess the important thing is Carpe Diem—seize the day—and then let it go.
—Isaac Asimov, *It's Been a Good Life*

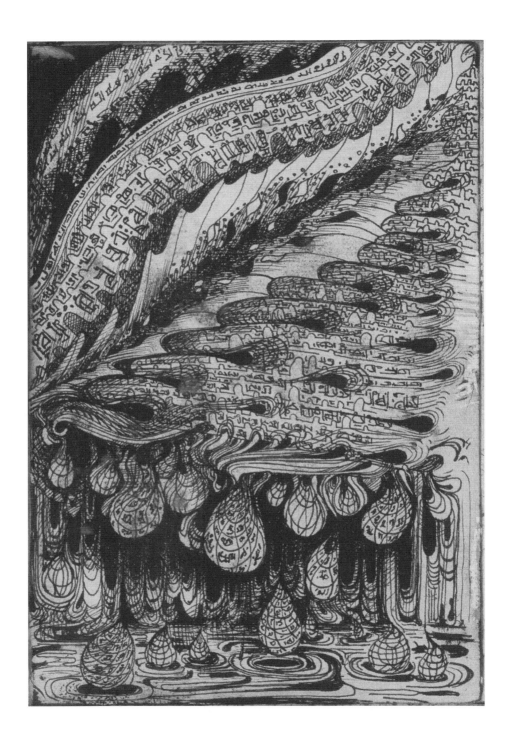

CHAPTER 9

ALTERNATIVES TO FOSSIL FUELS

Our Story Continues

(3:18) As hominids evolved toward modern humans, using fire was a milestone—an essential step that helped our prehuman ancestors along the road to becoming fully human. Controlled fire use likely came about when people learned to capture hot embers from lightening fires. Before we discovered how to start fires with flint or friction, hot coals were transported from one campsite to another; this "captured lightening" was perhaps a hominid group's most valued asset. Fire provided warmth from the night air and protection from predators; it greatly expanded our diet because cooking breaks down otherwise indigestible foods; it helped us produce sharper spears, and its heat aided in making more effective flaked-stone tools. Lightning fire became our friend and protector; eons passed; hominid's mental capacity expanded, and a special moment arrived, beginning the era when our ancestors, perhaps while "flaking" stone tools, discovered that sparks can start fires. We came to own fire in a new way—not captured lightning fire; rather, fire that could be produced anywhere at any time.

More eons passed. For innumerable human generations, our fires were fueled primarily from dead plants. Things changed. The Industrial Revolution invented ingenious machinery with an appetite for more efficiently packaged fire fuel. Coal served this hunger so well that steam engines multiplied, manufacturing plants became ubiquitous, steam locomotives opened new territories for development, and economic activity multiplied. Starting in the late 1800s, England and other industrial nations built the first large factories to mass-produce industrial equipment and household goods; most were coal-powered. Entire cities were engulfed with coal soot and its by-product chemicals, including sulfur dioxide, mercury, arsenic, lead, and other particulates. Mixed with precipitation, these chemicals created "acid rain." This bad air was dangerous but localized. World population was about one and a half billion people; time passed.

Spurred by further invention, another sudden change occurred—repackaged fire came onto the scene—liquid gold. The thick, black pools of oil, remnants of ancient carbon forests and massive animals, which sometimes seeped to the surface, had been prized for several thousand years—known but little used. That changed quickly as the Industrial Revolution continued to unfold; its momentum would not be denied. Oil made possible the newly invented internal combustion engine. New technology began to produce millions of engines with voracious appetites. Fossil fuels feed the beast, heating our homes and workplaces, powering our industry, and producing electricity for thousands of other uses.

Populations expanded fivefold; human ingenuity coaxed oil from deep within the earth, miles below the seas, and even from tar sands that require immense processing at high costs. Economic activity multiplied exponentially based on fossil-fuel energy. The waste-carbon from these activities was dumped into the atmosphere, caused the climate to warm, and disrupted all life on Earth. As the second Great War raged, we delved further into nature's sacred workings, splitting uranium's nucleus for bombs and nuclear power plants, thus enslaving yet another fire to serve our growing appetite for transportation, warm buildings, space exploration, and more "stuff." Uranium's toxicity and radioactive waste has now begun to haunt humanity.

As the Scientific Epoch came to a close, coal, oil, and natural gas produced most of the energy that fueled our modern life, but momentous transformation continues. Nature's photosynthetic processes create the carbon needed for the planet's biosphere to function; plants capture energy and sequester carbon in their growth. Recently, human inventiveness has begun to mimic biology, creating photovoltaic panels that produce electricity from the sun's ever-present photons. Once again our gift, our fire, has changed. This time, because we are paying attention to nature, this new fire is more subtle; it is more efficient, neither wasteful nor destructive. By entering the Ecological Epoch and following nature's lead, we have found a fire that will serve us without destroying all we hold dear— our surroundings, our children, and our future on Earth.

As I write in late 2014, many Eurozone economies are financially stressed. Greece almost fell into bankruptcy and was rescued by the stronger member groups, including Germany. The Greek economy has been in recession for five years, and many Western economies have suffered contractions. What is the reaction? The January 14, 2013, issue of *The New York Times* reports that environmental regulations installed as safeguards in better economic times are now being watered down or disregarded in pursuit of more economic growth. Oil exploration is being initiated in delicate environments. In uncertain economic times, gold increases in value. As a result, at least one Canadian company is resuming marginally profitable gold mining in an ecologically sensitive area.

The article goes on to say that regulations to protect water, air, and land use are being ignored. More coal use is planned; therefore, more pollution will result; in Greece, a billion-dollar environmental fund for energy efficiency and ecological preservation is being hijacked to pay the government's bills. The Athens environmentalist Theodota Nantsou, was quoted as saying: "We see laws changing, policies changing.... We see things getting rolled back under the guise of eliminating impediments to investment. But over the long run, all these things will have a heavy cost." A local hotel operator, Christos Adamidis, is leery: "The dust this will create will be killing off the leaves. There will be no goats or olives or bees here."

An article in the *Los Angeles Times* on the same day discusses air pollution in Beijing, China, referring to it as "airpocalyse"—the worst air pollution ever recorded—in a city that is notorious for bad air. A three hundred to five hundred reading for air quality defines the dangerous level; the article notes that Beijing was off the chart with a seven hundred score and had been for some time. The government was asking people to wear masks and telling children to avoid exercise; nine hundred young people were treated at hospitals on January 12, 2013, for respiratory problems. Dai Qing, a democracy activist, was quoted as saying, "If there is social unrest in China, it will happen not because of the gap between the rich and the poor...but because of the environment."

To put both the Greek and the Beijing examples into context, unsustainable economies provide growth for some period but result in economic hardship when that period has ended. That endpoint is here, now! A downward cycle has begun. China is the world's number two economy; having grown thirtyfold since 1989, 70 percent of China's energy comes from dirty coal. In 2012, twenty million vehicles were sold in China, leading all countries. In 2013, many of the world's most polluted cities were in China. In Beijing, authorities announced that factories were shutting down as an emergency measure, and low visibility was causing cancellation of airline flights. The smog even shut down highways. Jobs were being lost. Public health costs were rising. The quality of life was declining as blue skies became hidden behind the pea-soup haze. The World Bank estimates that pollution-related reduction in economic activity and additional public health expenses caused a decline in China's economic activity by $100 billion in 2012.

Until about 1945, the Earth absorbed our industrial insults. The world population was 2.5 billion. We now have more than seven billion people. Notwithstanding the country of origin, polluting the air, defiling the water, or damaging delicate open lands will result in social costs that far outweigh financial gains. We should anticipate climate chaos, poor public health, and social unrest. In our story:

(3:19) Just as a junkie is addicted to heroin, the developed nations have become addicted to fossil fuels. Derived from underground

160

pools, these fuels are extraordinarily cheap—there for the taking. So we take it—mainline it—running carbon molecules through millions of engines for transportation, heat, cooling, industry, and electric power plants. Then we send the waste into the air. Of course, nothing is really wasted in nature. Over thousands of years, the Earth will "scrub out" the excess CO_2 and do something useful with it; however, that will be too late for our welfare. We now know CO_2 and other greenhouse gases are making the Earth sick and are even capable of severely damaging the biosphere. The heroin addict knows his habit is sickening and potentially lethal. We are unable to change our fossil-fuel habit for the same reasons a heroin addict does not quit. The immediate gratification feels so good that long-term health is ignored.

Cheap fossil fuels have given us wealth; we have become addicted to our comfortable lifestyle. Consequently, economic growth and personal income have become the new religion. We have a minimal spiritual life and try to find meaning in our "stuff" and creature comforts. If we lose this low-cost fuel, we will have fewer cars, televisions, second homes, and "free time." Just like heroin, our overindulgence is too enticing to allow us to face up to the damage that climate change will cause to our future and our children. We would feel lost without our personal assets because our spiritual lives have been deflated.

Do you personally know an addict? What justification does he use for that next "fix"? Life seems meaningless when he's "straight," or he's depressed unless he's using. Perhaps he has a list of problems and issues in his life that he can escape from only when he's high. There are many more cigarette smokers than heroin users. Everyone in our culture knows about the long-term health hazards that smoking causes; however, cigarette sales continue to grow. A brush with lung cancer usually convinces a smoker to stop. What weather-caused calamity will it take for us to face up to climate-change dangers?

We create myopic justifications, like economic growth statistics, to continue using fossil fuels and excreting CO_2 into the air. The heroin guy can list ten good reasons why he can't stop; of course, none of the addict's arguments make sense to a health professional. It is up to Ecological

Epoch professionals in all disciplines to intervene and provide health care for our addicted culture. Fortunately, these experts know many viable alternatives.

(3:20) Transforming an entire society is hard to do; it's not easy to give up a comfortable lifestyle to which we've become accustomed. I know from personal experience that changing one's lifelong habits is difficult, even when not doing so is likely to shorten one's own life. I'm a sugar addict; this is a problem for me. Cancer feeds on excess sugar. Three years ago, I was diagnosed with prostate cancer. It was in an early stage and was not yet dangerous; however, to increase the odds that I could keep it from becoming life-threatening required me to change my diet significantly—no more sugar, minimal meat consumption, many fewer calories, limited grains. I also needed to add some prostate-healing foods and supplements to my diet each day and double my exercise.

I did a good job researching what my case needed and under-standing my cancer's level of progression. I attended conferences and found the right doctors and technology for my particular case. Using this research, I developed my own protocol: no sugar, juiced spinach in the morning along with nine supplements, antioxidant foods with alkalinizing potential for my body's chemistry, and only one significant meal in the late afternoon. I believe changing my life-style in these ways is keeping me from developing more cancer and adding years to my life. Knowing this, am I following the protocol completely? Some days yes, some days no. I could do much better.

My personal health situation provides an analogy in which the Earth is a living body. The Ecological Epoch has arrived. We know how to behave so that our planet's illnesses can be treated. If we fol-low the earth-healing protocols that we know will work—eliminating toxins and developing sustainable economies—the Earth will even-tually recover and will, therefore, be able support our children in the future. Knowing how to heal the planet is one thing; being impec-cable in implementing this knowledge is another. I work at curing my cancer every day; I also work at improving my discipline. I know that I am not impeccable; my failure to be more disciplined may be short-ening my own life. Therefore, I certainly cannot judge our society for its slowness to change.

As a species, we have not yet acknowledged the earth's illness. "Death is the only wise adviser that we have.... Ask advice from your death." This statement is a directive from the shaman Don Juan to Carlos Castaneda in Carlos' 1972 book *Journey to Ixtlan*. I read this statement forty years ago but did not really know how to apply it to my own life—that is, until after my cancer diagnosis. The Earth is also ill and partially dying—we can let the ongoing species extinctions advise us. Only if we all do our best will we have chance to succeed in bringing our Earth-body back to health. Only the planet's health will allow my nine-year-old AnaSophia and eleven-year-old Leonardo to fulfill their own life's destiny in beautiful ways.

Wind Energy Makes Dollars and Sense

President Obama avoided the climate-change issue while campaigning for a second term, as did his rival, Mitt Romney. However, in his inauguration address, Obama made the issue as important as his other current priorities: gun control, immigration, health care, and fiscal reform. Producing electricity creates about 40 percent of all greenhouse gas emissions; so cleaning up power plants is a necessity. Although Congress has been politically paralyzed and unable to pass new environmental legislation, there are enough laws already on the books to begin the required changes. The EPA is charged with enforcing existing laws, but the president has to lead the way, which he intends to do.

The EPA could also block the Keystone pipeline that will transport dirty oil from the Alberta tar sands to refineries and ports in the United States. If the pipeline is allowed to be built through the United States, it will facilitate more tar-sands oil production and the associated pollution. This Canadian project is as detrimental as any in the world. Business-as-usual lawmakers in Washington have attempted to block any legislation they think will increase fuel costs for US business. They believe such legislation will lower profits, reduce economic growth, and slow down job formation. This shortsighted viewpoint ignores the vast growth potential that will occur by creating new jobs and profits in the alternative-fuels sector.

Alternative energy can compete with fossil fuels; for example, Denver billionaire and accomplished business tycoon Philip Anschutz is planning to build a massive wind farm in Wyoming to bring electricity to California homes within a few years. His plan requires a major investment in high-power transmission lines across Wyoming, Utah, and Nevada to get the power to California's grid. His company intends to invest $9 billion—good for jobs and economic growth.

These wind-farm investments are helped by state law because California has mandated that 33 percent of its electricity be produced from clean alternatives by the year 2020, providing incentives to create green energy resources. This mandate creates new jobs while retaining the US economy's much-revered "free competition" among the solar, wind, hydro, geothermal, and other potentially clean alternatives. Competition promotes efficiency when the playing field is level; so far, it has been tilted in fossil fuel's favor—younger, more skillful competitors have been kept on the sidelines.

Chinese citizens aspire to what most Americans already have: nice houses, one or two cars per family, modern appliances to reduce house-work, shorter work hours, and vacations to foreign places. Citizens of India have similar aspirations. Combined, these two countries contain more than one-third of the planet's population. China has become an economic behemoth; its pollution and climate-change emissions are rapidly expanding. Interestingly, China is taking the lead in developing low-cost solar power, for both environmental reasons and for economically competitive ones.

The Chinese government is providing a clear path for its industry to develop alternative energy, giving its companies a competitive advantage compared to US companies that do not have government assistance. The Chinese are good entrepreneurs who have become the world's number one supplier of solar panels, wind turbines, solar water heaters, and other helpful environmental products—not to save the environment, but to capitalize on worldwide demand for these products.

What can American business do? Promote more enterprise in this burgeoning financial arena. Be creative, be inventive, be efficient, and thereby develop alternatives that outcompete the Chinese. China has a goal to produce almost 10 percent of its energy from renewable sources by 2015. In the North, the Green Wall of China is a project that intends to reforest one and a half million acres. Let's encourage more of the same. If US businesspeople can implement solutions that are more efficient and cost-effective, China will happily follow suit. Competitive business innovations, combined with concerns in China for public health and social unrest, will help put numerous Chinese coal-burning power plants out of business.

In Los Angeles UCLA is researching alternatives energy sources that can substitute for fossil fuels, including various synthetic fuels, algae-based materials, and molecularly engineered sources. The university has also been a leader in power conversion and storage technology, creating systems that use batteries in electric cars to store solar energy in the daytime, and then use it to power homes at night—a substitute for centralized power plants.

Climate-Change Partners

Hope and momentum are building for international cooperation based on a series of yearly meetings called The United Nations Climate Change Conference. In 2010, the conference was held in Cancun, Mexico. At the last minute, when it appeared the conference would fail to reach any accords, the Mexican delegation was able to garner forward-thinking agreements among all the attending national committees. In 2011, the Durban Conference advanced the cause further with the Durban Platform, "forcing countries for the first time to admit that their current policies are inadequate and must be strengthened by 2015.... It has reestablished the principle that climate change should be tackled through international law, not national volunteerism."[25]

In 2012, the United Nations held its eighteenth climate-oriented conference since the 1992 Kyoto Climate Change Conference. It took place in Qatar. It reaffirmed the Durban Platform and extended the expiring Kyoto Protocol until 2020, calling for a successor protocol to be developed by 2015 and put in place by 2020. The ground breaking concept called "loss and damage" was included for the first time, in which countries with large, climate-changing industries would be accountable to small countries. International agreements would hold wealthy, polluting nations financially responsible for damage to less developed, nonpolluting countries, in the case that these wealthy countries do not reduce their carbon emissions.

The delegations at these conferences include young people, businesspeople, military leaders, financial investors, and representatives from nongovernmental organizations (NGOs), among others. This broad participation itself is reason for optimism that change can occur in time to hold global warming to a manageable two degrees centigrade increase, compared to the disastrous four-degree increase we are currently heading toward.

At the Cancun conference, numerous youth delegations represented the next generation, including the China–US Youth Climate Exchange, young people who worked together in strategy sessions and produced joint Internet blog posts read by youth groups worldwide. Another participating group, Kids Versus Global Warming, has the objective of mobilizing a million young people in the United States to work on the climate-change issue. Many businesses are consciously working to reduce their carbon footprints, motivated both by saving expenses and a desire to help reduce

---

25. Elizabeth May, Green Party of Canada blog, attributing this quote to Michael Jacobs, visiting professor at the Grantham Research Institute on Climate Change and the Environment in London, UK, http://www.greenparty.ca/blogs/7/2012-01-18/durban-and-road-ahead.

global warming. One participating watchdog group, Climate Counts, has been rating businesses' performance since 2009. Highlighting individual companies' improvements by publicizing their progress provides good public relations, both for retail businesses and production-oriented companies.

Somewhat surprisingly, the US military is also on the low-carbon-footprint bandwagon, at least to some extent. In Cancun, Admiral David Titley stated that the Marine Corps plans to reduce its energy use 30 percent by 2015 and to increase its use of renewable electricity sources to 25 percent by 2025. Other military chiefs have recognized the fact that energy dependence that relies on foreign suppliers is the number one issue likely to cause future wars. Energy independence in the military makes sense for national security and provides a model for other government agencies.

Alternative energy investments are becoming hot. In the past, US investors have been slow to support solar and wind-energy innovations. They allowed Europe to get out of the blocks first with new, cost-effective wind generators and stood by while China took over the photovoltaic (solar panel) markets. However, the savvy US financial community has finally recognized the immense opportunities for profits and, consequently, it is off the sidelines and in full stride. Even though the fossil-fuel industry continues to be heavily subsidized, alternatives are becoming more cost-competitive and are beginning to take away part of the fossil-fuel companies' market share. Investors realize there are numerous opportunities for growth and profits as transportation converts to hybrid and electric vehicles and as the electric grid is reconfigured to include solar and wind. Wind power is currently cost-competitive with fossil fuel in many regions and is expected to make up 12 percent of global energy needs by 2020, which is a huge increase.

NGOs like 350.org have been formed to work directly on climate-change issues; in addition, numerous citizen groups with many different primary missions are now adding climate change to their priorities.

For example, the partnership umbrella organization called TckTckTck has more than 350 partner groups representing in excess of one hundred million individual members. It is a growing, worldwide alliance to create awareness about CO_2 emissions and promote public support for changes that will reduce atmospheric concentrations to safe levels. TckTckTck includes environmental groups as well as organizations that work to alleviate hunger, reduce poverty, and deal with other humanitarian concerns. Labor unions, church groups, the YMCA, and the Boy Scouts are also participating in TckTckTck to help solve climate change's many daunting challenges.

Fuel Solutions

All of this ecological damage has occurred over the past 150 years—a blip in time sufficient to change the world forever. Fossil fuels are causing the most destruction: public health suffers; terrorist acts are emboldened and funded from oil income; national security is endangered by foreign-oil dependence; "oil wars" rage one after another; centralized oil refineries are targets; and the elephant in the living room, climate chaos, has begun to impress, and even convert, many former "climate deniers."

Is it possible to fuel our economies in nondestructive ways? Not only do experts say "yes", they also provide specific blueprints for how to accomplish a transition to safe, healthy alternative fuels in the relatively near future. We do not lack the skill, expertise, or technology; however, we have lacked the will—until now, that is. The Ecological Epoch is revealing pathways that can solve our dilemma, provided we can find the intestinal fortitude to implement the changes. Are they too costly to afford? Will investment in alternative-energy sources overly burden our economy? On the contrary—the new technologies and required capital investments are likely to provide economic stimulus that will provide more jobs and more economic growth than would be the case if we do not make the necessary transition.

It is way too late for business as usual and the status quo. Alternatives are available and can be competitive now, without additional new laws or more government subsidies. Yes, there is a need for massive, new investment in existing technology to transform how we operate cars, heat buildings, run factories, and produce electricity. The good news is we know how to do these things—and the capital resource investments needed for this transition to occur more than pay for themselves. The new energy infrastructure will be noncentralized, clean, safe, healthy, renewable, and fully sustainable for an indefinite time into the future. We are faced with the need for determination, creative implementation, resolve, and far-sighted vision—not with extreme hardship.

Business executives and politicians have their hands and minds full doing what they do. There is little time for self-reflection or other personal growth work that can lead to awakened awareness about the current ecological crisis. Yes, the information is available to them, but without an ecological perspective, without a heart connection to this extreme situation, why would they change their policies and behavior?

Thankfully, it is possible for visionary solution-finders to effect economic and political decision-making. This outcome is much more likely if the proposed programs and policies are in alignment with the objectives of those who are controlling the decisions. For business, this usually means bottom-line profits; for politicians, it means benefiting their constituents and staying in office. Consequently, economic and social transformation can occur when visionary experts are clever enough to focus solutions in ways that benefit the corporations, when at all possible.

This was the approach taken by the many coauthors from the Rocky Mountain Institute in their book, *Reinventing Fire*, whose foreword was written by a major oil company's chief executive.[26] The approach provides

---

26. Amory Lovins, Reinventing fire, The Rocky Mountain Institute, September 2011.

industry buy-in from the first pages. This book and others offer specific solutions that will facilitate a transition from our current fossil-fuel-energy model into an array of alternative energy sources. In the following pages, I use *Reinventing Fire*'s structural approach in analyzing the US fossil-fuel-energy production and utilization cycle.

Four economic sectors are responsible for almost all fossil-fuel consumption: transportation, buildings, and industry use fossil fuel directly and also use electricity that has been produced from fossil fuel. The fourth sector is electricity production, which primarily uses fossil fuel but is also expanding production methods to include alternative, ecologically friendly, primary energy sources. Let's briefly examine each area in determining how to best transition away from fossil fuels and substitute clean alternatives. I am in debt to *Reinventing Fire* and its many authors at the Rocky Mountain Institute for providing ideas, solutions, and visionary thinking, some of which are incorporated in the following pages.

Transportation

Substituting alternative fuels for fossil fuels requires major investment; however, the economic stimulation and the overall savings from fossil fuels "not used" can more than pay for the transition. These changes require a systemic approach. Lighter-weight materials will allow more efficient fuel use; new-generation motors will provide more miles per gallon. The materials, motors, and transition fuels will come from technology that we already have available; these technologies need only be refined and scaled up for mass-production cost savings. Cars that can operate on electricity generated from clean sources, including photovoltaic cells on rooftops, are already available from most auto companies. I drive a "plug-in" Prius powered by my home's solar system.

Sustainable biofuels produced from farm and municipal waste streams can provide ethanol fuel, and because this system uses waste to produce these fuels, it is not necessary to divert agricultural land from the production of food crops, as is the case with biofuels. Autos running on hydrogen fuel cells may soon become competitive with electric cars; hydrogen combines with oxygen to generate electricity with only water as a by-product. There is no pollution. Fuel cells can provide a much longer driving range than today's electric cars. This is a competitive advantage that may soon give this technology the edge.

Electric and hydrogen cars are only as clean as the source of their electricity. Hydrogen must be manufactured using primary energy resources; as such, it is a carrier of energy, not a primary source. Recharging your car from an electric grid that is making its electricity by burning coal is not a solution, although plugging into your home photovoltaic solar system is. Ethanol refineries primarily produce biofuels; the processes are often polluting. In addition, vast amounts of agricultural land are taken way from food production in biofuel producing locations such as Brazil. The poor then suffer higher food costs.

Natural gas is a source of primary energy that, although it is a fossil fuel, will be used in the transition from dirty fuels to alternative fuels. It is less climate polluting than other fossil fuels. Although the newly popular "fracking" process for producing natural gas is experiencing explosive growth, it is causing ground-water pollution that requires immediate and comprehensive regulation. This industrial technique is currently becoming a public health problem.

California once again leads the way, as reported in the *Los Angeles Times*: "The nation's toughest restrictions on a controversial oil drilling technique known as fracking were signed into law by Governor Jerry Brown on Friday, September 20, 2013. Hotly opposed by the oil industry, the measure establishes strong environmental protections…." Although natural gas is a fossil fuel and therefore not a long-term solution, it will help bridge the gap to sustainable alternatives over the next several decades.

Research done by The Rocky Mountain Institute shows that integrating lighter materials with better auto designs and next-generation motors will result in vehicles that get 150 miles per gallon and more. Costs associated with ramping up these new technologies to "economies of scale," in addition to developing alternative fuels, will amount to about $2 trillion between now and 2050. The good news is that the savings will amount to more than $5 trillion. All of this is feasible with today's technology, given resolve and willingness to change—that is, unless entrenched interests in the fossil-fuel industry impede the transition.

This challenge is perfectly suited for our current competitive economic system. We are good at creativity. What's needed is more efficiency: less material use; innovation and design that are already incubated; and alternative, sustainable fuels. The transition period may need some encouragement from government regulation, but not a lot. For example, if fossil fuels had to pay for their external costs, including pollution, then alternatives would be cost-competitive now. To be fair, all fuels should be required to pay for the pollution they cause: photovoltaic electricity would have no tax; natural gas some tax, and gasoline from oil would have the highest tax.

Although these few paragraphs have focused on autos, the same principles apply to the trucking and airline industries.

Buildings

Homes, office buildings, malls, warehouses, main-street shops, and other buildings are the largest energy users in our economy; it's estimated that they consume more than 40 percent of all energy use and more than 70 percent of all electricity that is produced. For the most part, they are extremely inefficient. Dramatic savings can be obtained immediately from insulating older buildings, replacing poorly sealed windows, providing windows that open to the fresh air where air cooling is not essential, and other simple and low-cost approaches. In almost every case, the return on investment is high relative to other business expenditures, often exceeding a 30 percent return per year. In addition, lighting with LED bulbs can reduce electric use in lighting fixtures by as much as 70 percent. In large buildings, these changes quickly amount to important savings. Better air and lighting in the workplace also add to worker productivity and reduce absenteeism.

New buildings can incorporate these and other forward-thinking design elements beginning with the drawing-board phase. Cookie-cutter architectural plans for large and small buildings can be replaced with more site-specific designs—for example, ones that take advantage of passive solar heating in winter and landscaping for cooling shade in summer. Climate-specific design becomes important: Heating and cooling plans can use natural elements more and depend less on artificial lighting, heating, and air cooling. Some government programs are already in place to encourage these savings. Local utility companies are finding these remodeling changes to be more cost-effective for their operations than attempting to produce or purchase more energy for their customers; hence, they, too, are offering incentives. This is an example where the corporate objectives are in alignment with conservation and sustainability and, therefore, the programs are more likely to succeed.

The Rocky Mountain Institute research team estimates that retrofitting old buildings and designing efficiency into new structures can reduce building energy use 38 percent on average during the next four decades. The demand for additional new buildings is expected to add 70 percent more floor space to the current building stock during those four decades. This more efficient new construction and plans to retrofit many older buildings could result in total energy usage that will be about 20 percent less than that used for all US buildings today.

How can these changes be instituted? My local building code requires smoke detectors and metal-strap-secured water heaters before a house can transfer ownership. These regulations could be extended to an energy audit for each sale. Even if the upgrades were voluntary, the information alone about the available savings would educate the new buyer and encourage retrofits. Using a similar policy, my electric utility company is currently doing free energy audits for any homeowner who requests one.

Investment in a building's energy-use efficiency is cost-effective because the investment is low compared to the potential return. Government regulations can help; in addition, banks should be willing to provide financing for these improvements because the retrofits make sense from a financial return-on-investment perspective. It is estimated that an expenditure of an additional $500 billion (over and above the business-as-usual model) invested in superior design and efficiency during the next four decades will produce savings amounting to four times the investment—that's $2 trillion.

Although these solutions are available, their implementation will not come easily. Making the changes requires concerted effort, knowledge that the savings are possible, and demands that the government encourage efficiency and cooperation among utility providers, builders, and investor-owners. Working together, we can create integrated designs that will produce these massive savings and investment returns. Ecological Epoch solutions call for interactive relationships among parties, the way that nature functions.

Industry

How *does* nature function? Examine the forest. It is continually producing interactive, living systems—biological beings—as well as ongoing geologic transformation. Each tree's leaves graciously receive the sun's energy-providing photons. Using CO_2 from the air and water from the ground, carbon molecules build its woody trunk while oxygen powers the tree's cellular activities. High temperatures are not necessary; nothing is wasted. As the earth's processes unfold by the trillions, the death of one being provides food to sustain another.

Nature produces living things, each with a lifecycle; by analogy, these processes can be tangentially compared to the products that human industry makes. Until recently, we, too, wasted nothing as we gathered food and hunted other animals; we were both predators and prey. When carnivores ate us, we helped support nature's cycles. Upon death from other causes, our bodies dissolved into the Earth to be consumed by other animals. Times have changed. The world's wealthy humans have become wasteful creatures, using much more than we need and discarding still-useful materials. Each product has a lifecycle. Until now, the least expensive production methods have been used; important cost categories are ignored, including toxic pollution that is dumped into our landfills, atmosphere, and oceans. In addition, little concern is paid to a product's disposal after its useful life is over.

The Ecological Epoch is teaching us to pay attention to the forest— indeed, to nature's entire interactive way of functioning. Mimicking nature, the biomimicry concept mentioned earlier, can help our industries produce things by using more efficient inputs with less waste and much less pollution—for example, heat from manufacturing processes is a valuable by-product that is usually wasted. Following nature's lead, this heat could be used in a complementary production process for another product. Today's technology is much more sophisticated than our current industry standards. By using the up-to-date technology that is already available, we can improve our manufacturing processes.

The Clean Water Act was passed by the US legislature in 1972; The Clean Air Act was passed in 1963 with major changes in 1990. Both Acts establish detailed rules about how we are allowed to treat our "commons." This legislation did not hamper industry; on the contrary, it provided opportunities for creative businessmen and engineers to tackle problems that had been intractable. The same applies today. We have many new technologies; some require new legislation to serve as a catalyst so that the entrenched interests are given more competition and greater efficiency is achieved. This is the way that effective free enterprise works—better competition leads to creativity, which leads to efficiency and lower prices.

As we know from experience, free enterprise is not free of rules. Business competition is often an efficient means of production; however, just like boxing or football, rules are needed to protect the players' health and wellbeing. Let's implement regulations that will allow us to set sail on the best course for our children's future. Cleaner industry using alternative fuels will result in improved public health. Reusing materials means that we don't have to continually mine the Earth for dwindling supplies of raw materials.

We know how to manufacture renewable products such as appliances; many European countries are requiring refrigerators, stoves, and dishwashers to be made with this renewal as part of the plan, sending the product back to the factory in old age instead of the landfill. For example, several European and American companies are now selling refrigerators that are designed to be returned to the factory after their useful life is over. Each component is to be recycled: the metals, the electric motors, and even the insulation. Nothing will go to the dump. Autos, too, could be designed so that they are returned for restoration after a planned useful life of ten or fifteen years.

Industry uses heat and pressure to transform materials. Many of these processes are decades old. Today's technology could make them more efficient. Using chemical interactions at room temperature could replace some high-heat processes, adding efficiency. Energy-input savings would be the reward. Another area of potential savings is that motors in industrial plants can be made more efficient. This is akin to the auto industry's successful efforts to wring out more miles per gallon from gasoline.

Government is mandating auto efficiency. Although initially resistant, auto companies now support the regulations. Their bottom line is being helped, not hurt; the same applies to motors that power industrial operations in manufacturing plants. With some creativity, we can find regulations that improve competition while encouraging sustainability. If all participants are treated equally and regulations are applied fairly, industry eventually will benefit from the new requirements.

Due to product replacement, increasing population, growing demand, and changing tastes, in four decades US industry is expected to produce perhaps 100 percent more products than today. To meet this demand and still operate in sustainable ways may not be possible; in any case, much more efficient processes are needed to utilize all industrial by-products, including heat. New plants can be designed to accomplish these goals, especially those that involve energy use for production. When Ecological Epoch policies are adopted, efficiencies will be implemented, consumer demand for products will be less urgent, and more attention will be paid to emotional wellbeing and public health.

Making these changes happen is not an easy task. In addition to business and engineering ingenuity, it requires thoughtful regulation based on concern for the public, reduced raw material input, and minimized pollution. Incorporating new and existing state-of-the-art technologies is essential, and it makes financial sense. The Rocky Mountain Institute's research estimates that an investment over and above business-as-usual will cost about $300 billion in today's dollars over the next forty years; however, the savings will be worth more than $600 billion.

Electricity

Electricity is an energy carrier. In the United States, we produce electricity in various ways. The electrical "grid" is a system that connects producers and consumers, spanning the nation; it gets its electricity from many sources, ranging from huge centralized plants to small household-mounted photovoltaic panels. Large plants use "primary source" energy to make electricity: coal, oil, natural gas, biomass gases, hydro energy from dams, uranium from nuclear power plants, and, in recent years, a few large-production alternative sources. In the last two decades, wind power and electricity generated directly from the sun's photons have become primary energy sources that are being used to feed the country's electric grid.

Some power-generating facilities in outlying regions do not have access to the grid and are built for a particular local use, such as an isolated small town or large factory. The primary power for these smaller facilities is likely to be oil, coal, natural gas, and, more recently, wind or solar power. Nuclear power is too capital-intensive for these outlying applications. As such, our electric system has both centralized and dispersed elements.

Electricity is now being employed for more and more uses. We have entered an electronic age, powered by electricity. As recently as this new millennium's beginning in the year 2000, most information was stored in photographs, tapes, books, and other paper documents; now more than 90 percent is stored electronically. Electricity has become more important in powering autos and other transportation modes; it is reducing the role of oil and gas for heating buildings, and electrically powered equipment in factories is replacing fossil-fuel-powered machinery. Merging the Information Age with electrical systems for all of these uses allows "smart" energy systems to regulate energy expenditures more efficiently. Fine-tuned, computerized sensors can be designed into most mechanisms that use electric power, thereby conserving energy.

If we are going to create a sustainable, nonpolluting, fully renewable economy, it is critical that we reduce the use of fossil fuels in electricity production. Additional wind, solar, and other renewable sources are needed so that we can phase out coal and oil plants, thereby providing for the growth in electricity that a growing population and a growing economy demand. Currently, only a small percentage comes from these renewable sources.

The US electric grid spans the entire nation; envision high-voltage lines strung from towers throughout the land—a superbly created electronic spider web bringing us power for communication, warmth, entertainment, education, transportation, and manufacturing. The grid can be healthy and beneficial or unhealthy and destructive—all depending on how we produce the electrons that flow through this remarkable life-enhancing web.

Nuclear power plants do not produce climate-change pollutants; however, as we have seen at Chernobyl in Russia, Three Mile Island in New York, and Fukushima in Japan, radioactive spills are disastrous, rendering adjoining population areas and animal habitats devastated for many decades. Their pollution poses risks to the planet's health. Radioactive waste-disposal problems and high capital costs with major financial risks make new nuclear plants infeasible as the basis for electric generation. Likewise, "clean coal" is an oxymoron; it is a pie-in-the-sky industry trick to get new coal-fired plants approved when facing heavy environmental opposition. The term is based on the idea of capturing the smokestack carbon emissions and sequestering them so they do not get into the atmosphere. Although theoretically possible, the engineering challenges and additional costs involved make this process infeasible. If truly clean, it will not be able to produce energy that can compete with other energy sources when the economic playing field is made fair for the clean alternatives.

The Ecological Epoch requires a transformation in electricity production from fossil fuel and nuclear power to alternative fuel; however, this change will not occur in the normal course of business. Although the transition makes economic sense and provides opportunities for businesses and investors to profit, still, it's not that easy. As stated, entrenched interests are invested in the status quo; big oil companies' contributions have elected many legislators, and, therefore, they have major influence over legislation that affects their industry. Millions of stockholders, funds, and pension plans invested in fossil-fuel companies have already valued their shares to reflect the eventual liquidation and sale of *all* the company's known underground reserves. They will resist changes that, although benefiting the many, will cause their shares to fall in value.

This point takes us back to our New Creation Story. The Ecological Epoch has arrived; we can create a healthy economy if we heed our forward-thinking visionaries and implement their recommended systems into our production and consumption strategies, thus creating a sustainable society. It will require immediate action, perseverance, business savvy, engineering genius, and government legislation. Are we up to the task? Maybe. Is it essential that we do our best to make this transition happen? Absolutely!

America has many gifts from nature that provide energy without debilitating life's intricate web of clean water, fresh air, and wildlife habitat. Texas, Kansas, and the Dakotas have sufficient wind to power the entire grid, plus our increased electricity requirements for the next four decades. California, Arizona, and New Mexico have enough sun to feed solar-electric plants and, likewise, provide enough power for the entire country. New developments in geothermal, biomass, and tidal-flow energy may provide additional alternative sources.

Can we capture this energy in a cost-effective manner and disperse it in a satisfactory way? Yes, but only if we dedicate or minds and hearts to a major transformation—remember, the US auto industry converted to tanks, jeeps, and airplanes for World War II in a matter of months. We now have a similar emergency. Will we acknowledge it so we can dive in and get going? We have the technology, the know-how, and the business acumen to make this transition happen; the missing ingredient is will power!

Photovoltaic (PV) panels and entire PV systems have recently declined in price because they are now manufactured on a large scale. Leaders of utility companies, as well as those of local and federal governments, realize it is less expensive to put panels on residential and commercial rooftops than it is to build new power plants. The savings can be passed on from the electric companies to property owners to fund more installations.

My home has a solar system that feeds into the grid and produces all of the electricity we use; I am converting from low-energy florescent lighting to even lower-energy-use LED fixtures and bulbs. I purchased a government-rated "Energy Star" full-size refrigerator that uses the equivalent of one 60-watt conventional light bulb to operate. And, as mentioned, I also purchased a Prius "plug-in" hybrid electric car I recharge using my home solar system. Thus, I have my own personal "integrated design." I know where my energy is coming from and that producing it is not damaging the Earth. This is one small example of an integrated electrical-design system that, when multiplied by millions and combined with a "smart grid," can make a major impact.

Granted, it is still expensive to purchase solar systems and electric cars; however, given government regulations and incentives to make the completion fair, it will soon be cost-effective for many millions of people to follow suit—as long as entrenched interests do not prevent the change. For the past five years, many utilities have allowed grid-tied systems like mine but their regulations have limited the electricity production by giving credit only for the energy used on-site. This year, my local utility regulations have changed so that we can "sell back" excess solar electricity to the company for consumption elsewhere—a logical change that the electric-utility industry opposed and prevented for years. Citizens' pressure and environmental awareness made this change occur.

Another advantage to localized production sources, like my rooftop, as opposed to huge centralized plants, is that they are less like to have large-scale problems all at once; for example, dispersed production is far less subject to terrorist attacks. Wind power, solar arrays, and rooftop PV systems can be locally independent as well as grid-tied so regions can control their own destinies when other parts of the electric grid are in disarray.

Moving transportation, building, industry, and electricity production away from fossil-fuel will require more investment than continuing our present course; however, it also provides economic opportunity. Transitioning to clean, renewable non-fossil-fuel electricity production over the next forty years will be capital-intensive, but it is estimated to cost less than proceeding with the current business-as-usual approach. That is, it would cost no more *in dollars.* In terms of the peoples' and planet's health costs, the difference is astronomically in favor of a new system; by these standards, we certainly can afford to make the necessary changes.

Changing from fossil fuels to alternative energy makes economic sense, even if the environmental consequences of the current approach are ignored. The Rocky Mountain Institute's research indicates that the combined effect from changing to clean energy in transportation, building, industry, and electricity production will cost almost $5 trillion more than proceeding with business-as-usual. The good news is that it will save almost $10 trillion and create a massive new industry, innumerable different products, and millions of new jobs. CO_2 emissions will decline by more than 80 percent from today's levels, maybe in time to divert us from the disastrous path we're following. In short, Ecological Epoch sustainable energy production can serve the people and the planet well.

> *Death is our eternal companion; it is always to our left, at an arm's length. The thing to do when you're impatient is to turn to your left and ask advice from your death. An immense amount of pettiness is dropped if your death makes a gesture to you, or if you catch a glimpse of it.... It is at arm's length. It may tap you any moment.... The only thing that counts is action, acting instead of talking.*
> —Carlos Castaneda

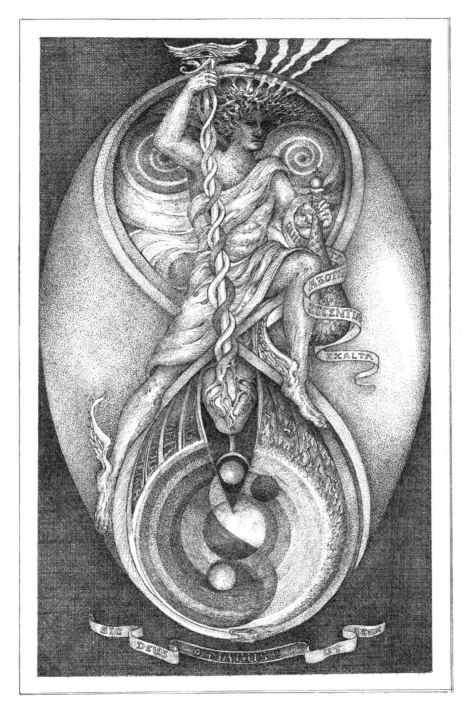

CHAPTER 10

ECOLOGICAL EPOCH MEDICINE

(3:21) By the year 1999, the end of the second millennium, the human species and the Earth's biosphere were left with an immense challenge—a downward spiral that was just beginning to become visible. There are solutions. The Earth will eventually recover. Human beings, however, have just one pathway to minimize their children's suffering—to make a graceful, proactive choice to reimagine and redesign our relationship to nature and, thereby, live in concert with Natural Harmony. The alternative is catastrophic collapse because our abuses make it impossible for the Earth to support us. Temperatures will increase, the oceans will rise up, droughts and floods will run rampant, food production will crash, climate refugees will cause social chaos, world economies will spiral downward, many will starve, diseases will become more pronounced—and human population will suffer a significant decline. If indeed, chaos ensues, after tremendous suffering, we humans will, while mourning our lost relatives, get the message and start behaving as though our best interest is the earth's health, not our individual, personal gain.

Ecological Medicine

Practicing ecological medicine is not the same as fighting illness and disease; rather, it works with nature-based solutions to improve public health and find individual cures. A current US government program called the Human Microbiome Project is attempting to identify all of the micro-organisms in the human body and study their effects on human health—a topic that has had little attention in the past and is not well understood. It includes an analysis of the entire bacteria genome we humans host. We are just recognizing that we are each in relationship with the trillions of bacteria cells residing on and in our body. They are helping protect our health, and we can help them in these efforts. Each bacterial colony's territory is a tiny sector in or on our bodies. To survive, they defend their territory against invading pathogens. They are constantly on duty as our allies in self-defense.

Antibiotics destroy as many "biotics" (that is, living things) as possible, both harmful and beneficial. Isn't it wiser to use probiotics whenever possible to eliminate pathogens? If we recognize the microbiome's beneficial effects in counteracting disease and support it in this endeavor, we will have improved public health while realizing our profound interrelatedness with these bacteria. Trillions of microorganisms are at home on and in the human body. We are just beginning to acknowledge their importance for our own health.

There is an analogy here: just as my body's surface is host to a multitude of living beings, more than seven billion humans reside on the earth's surface. In many respects, we are currently pathogens to the earth; however, this Creation Story describes how we can become healing agents, and, like my own skin's beneficial bacteria, we can each help to protect our planet. At the same time, we are learning about our body's microbiome and also how to make our relationship with the Earth a healthy one. A few personal stories might help illustrate my point.

After sixty-eight years in the Florida and California sun, my fore-arms have precancerous sun damage. For twenty years, I have been going to the doctor for liquid nitrogen treatments to remove twenty or thirty "spots" each time. Last year, I was working in a rural area in Tennessee; a local farmer had the same sun damage on his arms, so I asked him if he was treating it. He walked me about one hundred feet to a pond, reached down, picked a "weed," and broke the stem in half. Milky syrup seeped out, which he dabbed on his skin. "Milkweed," he said. That night, my research revealed that milkweed (*Euphorbia peplus*) contains a poisonous latex sap that doctors in Australia are using to kill squamous and basal cell cancers. This information has saved me some trips to the doctor; the planet's plant pharmacy is now providing care.

My body needs exercise to feel right. I do something vigorous almost every day to "lose" my breath and thereby deepen my breath, which sustains my life. There's a small mountain directly behind my house; I walk part of the way up it several times a week. Along the way, there are a few aloe plants growing beside the road. Knowing aloe has healing properties, about six months ago I started breaking open the succulent, thick leaves and rubbing the raw aloe on my arms and face each time I passed by. My overall skin health has dramatically improved. After being right next door for twenty years, I have discovered a second plant that cures my skin damage; I have become more self-sufficient *and* more intimate with these plants and with my backyard mountain!

My eight-year-old daughter, AnaSophia, had a large and persistent plan-tar wart on her foot. We took her to the doctor, who gave her a treatment that didn't help. I researched alternatives on the Internet. Surprisingly, many people have had success using a sponge soaked in apple cider vin-egar and wrapped with duct tape for forty-eight hours. It worked! Native people who live closer to the Earth know that the more we learn about plants and natural products, the more we will appreciate nature's ability to care for us and the more respectful and self-sufficient we will become.

As mentioned in the prior chapter, about three years ago I was diagnosed with prostate cancer. This news came out of the blue because there was no reason to have suspected that I had cancer. As a young man, I was a three-sport college athlete. I have stayed in shape my whole life, working out three or four times a week. I've never had a serious medical issue. Naturally, I was shocked to hear the news. It caused me to reexamine my entire lifestyle. Why did this happen?

I thought I lived in healthy ways: a little alcohol only, not much meat in my diet, a good amount of exercise compared to my contemporaries, a concern for getting enough sleep, avoiding most environmental toxins, etc. In short, I was paying attention to current medical information while living my life in a business-as-usual way. But now I have cancer. What a wake-up call!

It strikes me that the earth's situation is similar. Her living systems are ill. Allow me once more to use the human body as a metaphor for the earth's body: each planetary life form can be seen as a cell type in Earth's anatomy; it could be said that one cell type—that is, one species—has run amok and is multiplying exponentially. Cancer cells in a human body are not lethal in and of themselves. Although often mutated, they are not poisonous or foreign; rather, they are part of one's constitution that has multiplied out of control until their tumors crowd out other vital cells and organs, which cannot properly function as a result. Ultimately, the body's living systems break down, and death follows.

Cancer cells lack appropriate communication with their neighboring cells; they are selfish. We, you, and I and the other seven billion, are those out-of-control cells on the Earth's body, insinuating ourselves into the Earth's vital systems. Cancer is a lack-of-balance disease. Climate change, including global warming, is the most dramatic breakdown of the earth's life-serving functions; of course, there are many others: acidification of ocean water, polluted fresh-water systems, planet-wide habitat loss, species extinctions, and much more. We are causing these planetary illnesses. The earth's health is in decline.

Tuberculosis used to be called "consumption." It consumes the human body. When we mine the planet's natural resources and use up other life forms at a rate that causes their extinction, we are consuming the earth. Our global society is suffering from the disease of consumption. It is as much a psychological and emotional disease as a physical one. Our wellbeing does not depend on consuming all of the resources that we currently use. As mentioned, the United States makes up 4 percent of the world's population, but we consume 25 percent of its resources. China aspires to our levels of consumption—an impossible objective because too much of the earth's vitality will wither away first.

My cancer was a personal wake-up call; similarly, there will be a wake-up call for the health of the planet. It cannot be otherwise, and the process has begun. Rachel Carson's *Silent Spring* was published in 1962. The first Earth Day occurred on April 22, 1970. Al Gore toured with his documentary, *An Inconvenient Truth*, in 2006. He won the Nobel Prize. These and many, many other efforts are waking us up. But more is needed. The consumption mentality has too strong a hold. Corporations pay for ambiguous climate-science research that produces reports to confuse voters and politicians. There is no clear-cut diagnosis like "You have prostate cancer!"

I was jolted awake. There was a serious possibility that my expected thirty years of remaining life had just been reduced to five years or less. My father and his father before him had no idea that their hard work, along with that of their contemporaries, to build more cars and make more stuff, to provide for their families, was laying the groundwork for planetary and personal disease. Nor did I know that my lifestyle was creating my cancer. What should I do? What could I do?

Upon getting the results of my biopsy, my urologist called me in for a conference. "You have cancer," he said. "Here are your choices." He then laid out the various treatments available to supposedly rid my body of this problem—my own out-of-control cells. He offered a surgical prosectomy to remove the prostate, an operation that would likely include some nasty, life-changing side effects. Another option was radiation treatment, or a freezing treatment called cryoablation, or a more recently developed ultrasound blast that kills off the entire prostate. Being naive, these choices raised my hopes—until I realized that I would be treating the symptom of the disease, not its root cause.

I was shocked into action. Being a progressive guy, with access to lots of alternative sources of information—the web in particular—I got to work to expand my range of alternatives. The situation became, along with my two young children, my life's priority. I suspected Western medicine and my allopathic doctor were not the only choices.

What did ecological medicine have to teach me? My body is a continuum of mind–body–spirit. Trying to heal the body without addressing the entire system would not be the best approach. Looking at the Earth in a similar way, there are a variety of scientific plans that would artificially alter the atmosphere to reduce global warming. All of these ideas come with unknown side effects and are potentially more dangerous than the disease they are addressing. The surgical removal of my prostate would not be taking into account the mind–body–spirit connection; *likewise, these atmosphere-altering ideas look at climate change as a disease when it is actually a symptom. The disease is our cultural outlook—the way we "see" the world and behave as though unsustainable economies can continue without limit.*

I did not know I was sick. I learned that I had cancer and was awakened into action, quickly. I learned that what I consumed was making my body ill. Up to 90 percent of prostate cancer has a dietary connection: animal fats, excessive sugar, alcohol, and acidic-forming foods. These foods and inflammation-causing toxins sometimes contribute to genetic damage and cellular changes that turn healthy cells into cancer cells. It is a disease of consumption and degraded environment. I had a pea-sized lump on my prostate. My PSA score, a test for prostate health, had more than doubled in a short time, from 1.1 to 2.5, indicting a possible problem. And the *coup de grâce*, my biopsy, came back showing malignant cancer. Now I knew. There was no excuse not to take action. Could I restore my health? Could I live long enough to get my two young children through school and started in life?

To address my personal situation, I literally changed my life. Cancer cells do badly in an oxygenated environment. As mentioned earlier, I started exercising, working out, every day to deepen my breath and bring healing oxygen to my out-of-balance system, strengthening my own immune system. I ran the stadium steps, used the machines in the gym, played more tennis and basketball, and walked the mountain behind my house more frequently—not every other day, but *every* day.

I changed my diet. I learned that many cancers, including my type, thrive if one has excessive sugar in the system, partially because they reproduce using an abnormal process involving fermentation. Stop eating sugar! I learned that many cancers, including mine, need an acidic chemistry to survive and that 80 percent of the normal American diet causes acidic conditions at the cellular level. All meats, all refined sugars, most carbohydrates, and many other popular food choices create acidic conditions in the body's cells. Stop eating those foods! I learned that particular foods are especially useful in healing my type of cancer and building my immune system: pomegranate juice, garlic, kale, spinach, broccoli, and others. Eat those foods! Some supplements might be helpful in healing the prostate, including turmeric, cayenne, vitamin D, and berberine. Use them!

I thought, "This may not be the way I prefer to eat, but I can learn to like it, especially if it keeps me alive." It is my own personal chemotherapy, and it builds immunity. The program my doctor recommends makes you feel more ill and causes your hair to fall out. Which would you prefer? After six months on my protocol, I went for another examination, this time to an urologist who was more understanding about alternative therapies. My results: the pea-sized growth was smaller, and my PSA score had fallen from 2.5 to 1.4. I was not cured, but no additional cancer was found in my next biopsy. The existing cancer had remained stable at a low-grade level that could possibly be maintained for many years. Thank goodness! Thank ecological medicine.

I learned about my cancer while it was still in an early stage. Perhaps I can keep it there or perhaps not. I'll readily admit there is a place for allopathic medicine and its brilliant prostate cancer doctors; however, less invasive therapies are being developed every year. For example, in the few years since my diagnosis, doctors have learned how to treat prostate cancer by removing just part of the organ, leaving the prostate largely intact. I may eventually need that therapy and am pleased to know it is available.

In my case, the uncertainty is challenging, but in some respects it is a blessing, deepening my appreciation for life's gifts. Will my future life span be five years or twenty-five years? I don't know, but I can say that the lifestyle changes I've made will mean I am more likely to survive other health challenges as well. Whatever adds flexibility adds strength. My cancer strengthened me. I've decided to change my life priorities: I have more than enough material possessions. Remembering that death can be just around the corner causes one to reexamine priorities. For me, that means no more accumulating; it also means that life's meaning is found by going deeper and appreciating relationships and experiences above possessions.

As we understand our own bodies better, we are able to see the Earth as a contiguous whole. We have recently learned that our planet is ill. Imbalances are creating the Earth's diseases. Her living systems and her plethora of life are quickly deteriorating. We are responsible. This downward spiral is our species' wake-up call! What are we going to do? What is the planetary equivalent of bringing oxygen to the cells and of totally changing our cumulative human diet—not just for food, but also for our addiction to consumable products? This is the challenge we face as citizens of the Earth. Seen as one people on one planet, we are a much more elegant community than we are as a group of competing nation-states driven by corporate interests. Our New Creation Story continues.

(3:22) Numerous preceding creation stories attempt to define humanity's relationship to the physical surroundings. They all use the wisdom available to them in their place and time. Knowledge changes, insights deepen, and new stories emerge from additional depth of understanding. Ecology and Natural Harmony show us our place in the world. It's about relationship. The deeper we explore the natural world, the more we realize that everything is interrelated. It's necessary to untangle innumerable threads to keep each system healthy. The human body is one such system we are just beginning to learn about. Once upon a time, before the knowledge of bacteria and viruses, medicine was based on humans' relationship to plants; for many thousands of years, medicinal plants provided a pharmacopeia for treating people's maladies. A little knowledge is sometimes a dangerous thing. The earliest human-body surgeries were performed without knowledge of bacteria and infection. The results were not good. Upon gaining a rudimentary understanding of microbes and learning to sterilize surgical instruments, we began to more systematically invade the body—to explore its innermost workings. As in other scientific arenas, reductionism was the rule—locate a physical structure and try to determine its function. If the medical wisdom of the moment thought there is no useful function, as was the case with tonsils, then the response was to excise the body part.

I was born in 1945. The function of tonsils was unknown then, but it concerned the medical profession that tonsils sometimes got infected. The solution, with or without a tonsil problem, was surgical removal soon after birth. My tonsils were sacrificed to this perspective. Doctors still argue that tonsils are not necessary for proper body function based on the fact that the body seems to be fine after a tonsillectomy. But what about special conditions? Perhaps the tonsils are designed for less obvious functions that arise only occasionally—as is the case with the appendix.

The appendix is often removed if it has minor inflammation because most doctors consider it to be an unnecessary body part—one that is vestigial, having had a function in the deep past but no longer considered useful. More recently, subtle but important functions have come to light. Under duress, diarrhea flushes the stomach contents. The process eliminates the good with the bad: the beneficial bacteria needed for digestion are also lost. It seems that the appendix can harbor these bacteria, making them available for repopulating the stomach in such conditions. In addition, recent research indicates that the appendix has a role in hormone-related endocrine function in the human fetus. It also plays a role in the adult immune system. The more we learn about relationship, the more we realize that everything is interdependent; nothing is superfluous.

Fighting disease from the outside is not necessarily the best way to heal a disease. For example, chemotherapy is designed to attack a particular problem; the chemical processes involved shock one's bodily functions and often reduce the effectiveness of the body's own immune system. This approach can be at odds with more immunity-supporting methods for stabilizing and curing disease. When one supports his or her immune system in the best possible ways, the individual allows his or her own body to produce a more effective immune response to the pathogen—for example, determining the precise nutrition needed for each particular disease, the type of exercise needed, and the best physical therapies for both body and mind can help the healing process.

There are times when allopathic (including surgical and chemical) intervention is the correct choice to deal with a disease; however, refining these techniques is just one solution to improving our society's health. Ecological medicine refines our *ideas* about how to relate to our own internal bodily functions and about our body's relationship to its surroundings. As a necessary step in the process, we also learn more about the toxins and stresses to which we are exposed.

As discussed with the appendix, the more we know about relationships within the body, the better choices we can make for our own health and for medical intervention. Externally, our population's overall medical health requires us, as a society, to decide such issues as: whether or not smoking is allowed in public places, whether or not obesity is a public health issue, whether or not ozone holes are acceptable, whether or not toxic nuclear waste will continue to be produced, whether or not ground-water contamination is to be allowed from industrial "fracking" for natural gas, and whether or not violent movies are discouraged and taxed to provide funds for the negative social consequences they create. There are, of course, numerous other public-health concerns.

Keeping one's own body as healthy as possible within this chaotic milieu requires attention to basics. We need a healthy amount of sleep, good nutrition, limited stress, and sufficient exercise. Of course, in our advertising-driven culture, these simple requirements are easier said than done. I find it very difficult to keep my nine-year-old daughter from eating too much sugar, which is often available, even at school. Friends are constantly bringing candies, cakes, and pies to my home. Even the YMCA occasionally hands out free candy just for fun. Ronald McDonald is on billboards and TV ads, constantly selling sugar-laden and obesity-generating fast food.

Chemicals are another major concern. As a society, we are confronted with numerous toxins in our immediate environment—in soaps, in home-cleaning products, and even in children's toys. Environmental stress is becoming endemic. There are toxins in our drinking water; more and more seafood is contaminated with heavy metals, including mercury. Damaged nuclear power plants are spewing radioactive particles, some of which migrate around the world. These conditions challenge the body's immune systems and add extensive costs to public-health programs.

Ecological medicine is focused on each person's understanding of her own body so that disease is less likely, as opposed to ignoring one's health, waiting for disease to strike, and then relying on medical experts to solve the problem. All four main factors mentioned above—sleep, nutrition, stress control, and exercise—are directed toward the same thing: They create the optimal conditions for one's own immune system to function at its highest capacity. That is the foundation for a healthy body. Medical intervention is not the only answer and is frequently too little, too late. Even after contracting a serious disease, the immune system, if supported by the appropriate lifestyle, can often—not always—cause the body to respond better than medical intervention can.

Each of us has a somewhat programmed life-span that can be reduced or extended depending on lifestyle. My father's father died in his forties; my father died at age fifty-seven from smoking, bad nutrition, and no exercise, leading to various cancers. I'm sixty-nine and have an early stage of prostate cancer; however, I intend to live another twenty or thirty years. I'm constantly reminded by the medical community that the safe thing to do is to remove my prostate gland before the cancer cells migrate to other body areas, but my intuition and my own review of the most recent medical research is telling me to deal with this potentially life-threatening situation by building up my own immune system. Interestingly, in the three years since my diagnosis, many prostate research doctors are recommending lifestyle changes and longer wait times, which they call "active surveillance," before removing the prostate gland. In most cases, mutilating one's own body should not be the first recourse, provided there are viable alternatives.

Our New Creation Story is about deepening understanding, including attention to one's own immune system. The medical community is continually learning more about the body's operating systems. Recent research shows that one's immune system is more complex than ever imagined. Let's look at some cutting-edge ideas in this arena. When we consider current immunology research, we see that the immune system includes three interlocking defense mechanisms. Until recently, only two of these immune defenses got all our medical attention—the "humeral" and the "cellular". As introduced earlier in this chapter, more recent research about microorganisms living in our bodies indicates that this microbiome also serves as an important immunological defense, perhaps the most important.

The *humeral immune response* (derived from the term "humours," meaning body fluids) involves secreted fluids that are produced by one's body to destroy or neutralize bacteria cells, pollen molecules, or other potentially damaging foreign invaders. Produced by B lymphocyte cells, these fluids contain antibodies that recognize and bind to the foreign substance, virus, bacteria, etc., to eliminate these potential pathogens.

The *cellular immune system* involves white blood cells that engulf and digest pathogens, including harmful bacteria and virus cells. They also are able to recognize and protect against fungi and cancer cells. *Serum antibodies* make up part of the immune system that operates outside the body's cell walls. Until recently, the humeral and cellular immunity mechanisms have been given priority in medical research. Now, a third area is gaining more attention: the *microbiome.*

The story of microorganisms living inside our body becomes part of our New Creation Story because it is about relationship. The more deeply we look into each scientific medical area, the more relationship we find—our new story is based on revealing interactions between all things, including both biological and geological environs. The microbiome inside my body outnumbers my own cells by a ten-to-one margin. Let me repeat that: There are ten times as many foreign cells on my skin, in my mouth, in my intestines, and in my lungs as there are cells that belong to my body proper. My body has about 100 trillion cells in relation to about 1,000 trillion microorganisms living in and on my body. (These bacteria cells are much smaller than the body's cells, so the total mass of microorganisms is much less than the human cells' total mass.) The foreign cells are so important to the body's functioning that some researchers consider these "gut flora" and other microorganisms, such as those living on our skin, to function like an organ.

There are perhaps five hundred different bacteria species that live on the skin's surface, and a similar number reside in the gut. *Sixty percent* of the dry material making up human feces is gut bacteria—that is, more than half of the body's waste material is this bacteria type. Imagine how much bacteria proliferation is constantly occurring in the intestines for this amount to be excreted every day. There is a symbiotic relationship in which the microbiome helps create necessary fermentation for digestion; it trains the immune system to recognize harmful bacteria, produces some needed vitamins such as vitamin K, and creates hormones that regulate fat storage. As always, relationship is about balance. "Right relationship" is a term I use to describe a healthy balance. Excesses can cause a lack of equilibrium and consequent disease. For example, bacteria that are beneficial in the gut can be pathogenic if they penetrate the skin and are allowed to multiply inside a wound.

Staphylococcus epidermidis is a form of bacteria that lives on our skin. If these bacteria are allowed to penetrate your body's inner sanctum—for example, if a medical implant is not sterile, it can cause serious, even fatal, infections. The June 2011, issue of *National Geographic* reported that medical researchers have recently discovered that *Staphylococcus epidermidis* has a beneficial, symbiotic role to play as it resides on the body's skin. It produces a molecule that neutralizes microorganisms that would otherwise cause inflammation in cuts and scrapes on the surface, even small ones.

My body and these particular bacteria are in right relationship. When they are on my skin, they are beneficial; however, if inside my body, they would be pathogenic. *S. epidermidis* is neither good nor bad. When on my skin, it is helpful; when in my body, it is harmful. These relationships are all extremely complex and are interwoven throughout the planet's biological matrix. I call this complexity "Natural Harmony"; it has taken 4.57 billion Earth-years to create. Similarly, hydrocarbons are neither good nor bad. Oil pools in the ground, which the Earth created over many million years, reside in right relationship with all other life. When redistributed from the ground into the atmosphere, they become pathogenic for today's life community—the many species that exist at this particular moment in the Earth's cycle.

Given a few million years, there will be a new cycle; it will include life that has adapted to the higher CO_2 levels and the warmer climate. Adaptions such as these have always taken place when the earth's living systems are stressed, as they are now. Will we humans have a place in this next cycle? How much suffering will be imposed upon our children and their families as this "great correction" unfolds? Wouldn't it be better to let this current cycle, with its elegant diversity, continue its languorous flow onto the future, as opposed to mowing it down with the Grim Reaper's scythe?

In a similar vein, humans are not good or bad; however, there is another question: Are humans good or bad for the planet? Are we good or bad for the biosphere, Earth's life community? It's the same *S. epidermidis* question, and the same answer: beneficial when in right relationship with the earth, unhealthy when inserted into the planet's inner workings in pathogenic ways. In using the terms "good" and "bad," I am not implying moral judgment, as in "good versus bad" or "holy versus evil"; rather, these words help frame existential questions about our children's and our species' survival.

We now know we are creating malignant conditions that affect the Earth. Our planet's biology depends on the earth's immune system. Toxic chemicals weaken the Earth's immune responses—her ability to repair damage. Polluted rivers, lakes, and oceans reduce biological diversity, as do oil and uranium that have been transformed from their proper environment under the ground and deposited onto the land and into the atmosphere.

The evidence is clear—the potential outcomes dire; however, there is a lot the Ecological Epoch can do to mitigate the damage. Our planet's health is important for our species' immunity to disease. To strengthen the Earth's immune systems and improve its healthy functioning, the Ecological Epoch is showing us how to distribute wealth equitably and reduce poverty, create sustainable economies, stabilize the human population, and eliminate toxins from the environment. These actions will enhance nature's living systems and thereby support the planet's seven billion-plus people by creating renewed forests, restored grasslands, healthy waterways, and clean air.

> *Wisdom is that aspect of human reflection that emphasizes the process of personal and communal transformation within a divine presence that encompasses all life and is available to all who seek its transformative power.*
> —Jim Garrison

> *In the last analysis, what is the fate of great nations but a summation of the psychic changes in individuals?*
> —Carl Jung

CHAPTER 11

ART IN THE ECOLOGICAL EPOCH

(3:23) I love running—traversing neighborhood streets, past village stores, around the lake path, and through the woods to get home—iPod playing favorite songs. For today's run, I forgot the iPod; the woods seemed like a new place. "What's so different here?" I asked, compelled to stop and listen. Sophia answered me: "When fully present, you are an empty, spacious vessel. You will often find 'presence' and a calm mind in quiet places that exist between the fullness of opinions and the emptiness of no thoughts. There you can more readily experience singing birds, gentle breezes, and rustling leaves. These are sounds of silence, present but unnoticed a moment before. To always think about what is not present dishonors the moment. To move with rhythm and spontaneity, ah, the joy! The more you think you know, the more contracted you are." I paused a long time and then walked home, listening.

The arts affect culture. Social commentary in the arts can raise awareness and help to bring forth cultural transformation. Artists tend to be more visionary than businesspeople and politicians; thus, the arts are important to society. Conversely, there is often political pressure to reduce support for the arts in difficult economic times. Those in charge do not recognize art's social benefits and dislike artists' attempts to raise awareness because these efforts are a challenge to the status quo.

Rachel Carson's book *Silent Spring* was visionary in 1962. The book raised awareness of the environmental damage that DDT was causing in the United States and introduced ecological concern into the popular culture. Eventually, this awareness led to a ban on DDT. Today, Lester Brown and the World Watch Institute are providing an entire series of visionary books and articles about our relationship to nature and solutions to the ecological problems we have created. Most art communicates viscerally through "showing." The shaman's job is to show; the philosopher's job is to convince by intellectual argument. Ecological Epoch art encompasses a wide gestalt that includes shamanism, art, and philosophy.

Filmmaker Godfrey Reggio and musician Phillip Glass created a series of seven or eight emotionally evocative works, starting with *Koyaanisqatsi* in 1983 and currently continuing with the recent *The Holy See* in 2012—about thirty years of artistic social influence. As is true of many visual arts and most shamanic intervention, the message of these works connects with one's emotional intelligence. Many more people go to films than read books; consequently, the cognitive intellect is somewhat more difficult to reach. Sometimes, artists are our best visionaries and social shamans. The mystical Sufi poet Rumi, who lived in the thirteenth century, is still today's best-selling poet.

Ecological Art

Intuition is often the driving force that inspires art. Most profound art is created for art's sake, not for financial gain. There are reasons we need art in our schools; it teaches us about nature and emotional intelligence. These are the same reasons why art is often cut from school programs when budgets get tight. Priority is given to business-type skills.

Art and culture go hand in hand. Leading-edge art depicts social change. We have entered a new consciousness epoch and need our art to help us integrate our deepening awareness into the culture's behavior. What is ecological art? Nature creates art; for example, a shimmering spider web bejeweled with a thousand dew droplets, or a beaver dam's intricate design. Often, the best human art springs directly from nature. Ecological art complements the natural world. There are many wonderful images, both in photo and film that lead us to a deepened appreciation of our surroundings.

Those of us who are fortunate enough to have access to the Internet have probably seen some amazing images of nature in the past few years. I know I have been astounded many times while viewing images, including remarkably colorful rainbows, animals engaged in their rambunctious daily lives, and humans interacting with curious wild animals. I've been privileged to see incredibly beautiful sea creatures that live beyond the penetrating sunlight, surfers tunneling through giant ocean curls amid the sun's sparkling prism colors, a polar bear playing gently with a tethered sled dog, and a rhinoceros baby being mothered by a huge tortoise. Internet images have become an abundant art form. At their best, these photos convey our New Creation Story to a wide audience. This art, combined with film and music, is helping us to find a new, more supportive mythology.

We are well into our generation's greatest challenge. As mentioned more than a few times, the environmental crisis has been the catalyst for the next step in the evolution of human consciousness. Finding ways to create the necessary cultural changes, thereby standing up to the challenges we face, is the most meaningful way to live one's life. Ecological art will help us negotiate the dangerous waters ahead.

Ecological Epoch Filmmaking

Ever since humans developed sophisticated language, culture has been created, maintained, and passed down to children through storytelling.

For the first 99 percent of this language era, these stories were verbal, often recounted around the evening's campfire. Over the past few thousand years, stories have been written down; however, for a long time, few people could read, and books were not easily reproduced. The spoken word thus remained the primary vehicle for storytelling. For the past few hundred years, books have been a major source of stories in educated cultures; more recently, a new storytelling approach has emerged—motion pictures burst into the scene only a few generations ago.

Much of our cultural lore is now transmitted through movies and the film industry's little sister, television. Almost all of today's decision makers have been influenced by cinema: films with a moral message, films about family relationship, and films depicting war, horror, alien invasions, and lost love relationships. There are musical films, historical films, religious films, and documentary films about real people and real events—like classical Greek theater and its panoply of gods and goddesses that represent human emotions; the themes are all-encompassing.

Screenwriters and producers make decisions and create images they hope will have power to influence audiences. We attempt to reach down into a visceral depth, sometimes to convey a message and sometimes just to persuade an audience to buy tickets so the film is profitable. Of course, the most artistic films are concerned more with creativity than financial gain. A variety of film genres are produced and shown to audiences. After the initial advertising push, potential viewers vote on the film's appeal using their ticket purchases and word-of-mouth recommendations. These referrals affect the movie's success or failure. Total ticket sales show which ideas succeeded in hitting a pop-culture cord.

Some films, books, poetry, and word-of-mouth stories gain wide audiences, become classics, and have cultural longevity; others gain a big audience for a moment and then disappear. Ghost stories are exciting around the Boy Scout campfire; horror movies excite teens; gratuitously violent films come and go, drawing large audiences. But, unlike classic films or Shakespeare plays, their characters and plots have little longevity. Why? Perhaps because they have no roots in life's deeper meaning. By comparison, Walt Whitman's poetry provides insight that deepens many human-to-nature relationships. Rumi's poetry explores the human–divine emotional relationship.

Horror stories and violent films are made to sell tickets, to scintillate. They are designed to distract the viewer from his daily trials and tribulations, providing a temporary thrill. Their characters and stories are not "of" the real world. These are not characters you will meet on the street. The films sell tickets by creating repetitive emotional ups and downs. This temporary thrill often desensitizes the individual from emotionally engaging in his or her normal, everyday life. These films sell tickets, create corporate profits, and can become addicting because the real world seems emotionally flat by comparison. We need more and more artificial stimulation when our natural surroundings seem dull. Fortunately, these stories and films have limited cultural staying power and soon disappear.

Shakespeare, Rumi, and Whitman—this is the substance, the foundation, for a healthy world. If we are fed a constant stream of horror, murder, and war, creating villains that are usually "others"—another religion, another country, aliens from outer space—we are more likely to respond with fear and loathing to all others who are unlike ourselves. Our entire society is affected from this additional tension and existential anxiety. Boys and young men are most often the target audience for violent films and video games. For example, there is a currently popular video game in which a player is able to interact with the game characters—males as young as twelve are allowed to play. The "game" is to beat a young woman to death with a shovel. These products are extremely profitable for their creators and distributers; however, by Ecological Epoch standards, they are unquestionably detrimental to personal and public health.

Culture-wide fears augmented by this and similar entertainment drives us to make unhealthy choices in domestic and international decision-making and foreign policy. When we remove Whitman from our children's education, we lose purpose, depth, and meaning. Fortunately, the new epoch is also providing stories and images that reconnect us to the real world and demonstrate that the Earth's health is a necessary priority for human success.

The Lorax

There is hunger for positive messages. Ecological and social-justice themes have an important role to play in cultural change. For example, the film version of a children's story, *The Lorax*, has been beautifully rendered in 3-D. Its debut was in March 2012, and the movie soon became one of the leading box-office successes in film history. The prescient author, Dr. Seuss, wrote *The Lorax* as a children's story in 1971—one of our culture's first environmentally themed stories. It is a fable that exposes the dangers of corporate greed.

The lorax is a small, orange-mustached, person-like animal creature about two feet tall who walks upright. He speaks for the trees. The Once-ler is an industrious boy who has invented "Thneeds," which are made from truffula trees. Thneeds became so popular, and the demand for them is so great that all the forests were chopped down to make more. The once-blissful lands, filled with cheerful animals, were devastated, and the animals were left homeless.

When the tree cutting began, the lorax confronted the Once-ler and told him in no uncertain terms that it was very wrong to harm the trees. The Once-ler says, "Bring on your lightning bolts and all your other powers to stop me, if you think I'm doing the wrong thing."

The lorax replies, "That's not the way it works." The forest animals shuffle off to try to find another home.

The land was desolated. The trees disappeared and were forgotten; behind the city walls, air pollution mounted. One company made clean air. Because everyone needed healthy air, the company virtually controlled the society. The last thing this industry wanted was a return of trees that cleaned the air "naturally." The fable ends on a hopeful note: The Once-ler saved the last truffula seed. Some concerned young people plant the seed; the people rebel against the industrialists and support the trees' return. Children love this movie, and it gained wide popularity. Thankfully, it has already influenced millions.

Avatar

James Cameron's 2011 film *Avatar* also set box-office records. Like *The Lorax*, its financial success shows that the public wants stories that address their gnawing anxieties about environmental destruction; however, the remarkable thing about this film is not only its theme. It is a story for our time, told through metaphor that resonates with all ages and has a cultural immediacy. Let's examine it further to see how storytelling via film helps communicate our Creation Story.

The main character, Jake Sully, is a former soldier, wounded and crippled on Earth. He is given an opportunity to inhabit an "avatar" body on a distant planet's moon, Pandora. It is light-years away from the earth. In the story an avatar is an artificial body mimicking the physique and behavior of the local indigenous population. Avatars are being used to infiltrate the local population and convince them to leave their homelands. The corporation Jake works for is attempting to mine a precious energy-producing mineral, unobtainium, and will stop at nothing short of annihilating the indigenous people if they will not leave the area that the company wants to mine. This future-day theme recapitulates how Native Americans were treated and includes an up-to-date corporate-greed embellishment.

As a show of propriety (called "greenwashing" today), the corporation also employs some biology and anthropology experts who are attempting to resolve the impasse peacefully; however, the company's military arm is planning an attack. The biology researchers (who are given the avatar bodies) are fascinated with the magical Pandora world full of wondrous life. Meanwhile, the military leader, Colonel Miles Quaritch, preaches to his troops: "Everything out there is dangerous and will try to kill you." These are the diametrically opposed philosophical perspectives that create the film's message and its dramatic tension.

Through three-dimensional filmmaking, James Cameron brings this new-world Garden of Eden alive for his audiences. It is truly mesmerizing as we are transported to Pandora and become part of Cameron's romanticized, harmony-loving Na'vi culture. For a few hours, we participate in an extremely realistic, virtual reality. Reaching into our guts, these magical images are more influential than ideas.

Filmmaking sometimes feels didactic and forced; documentaries can be effective but have a difficult challenge in finding large audiences. Films are normally more impactful when they engage one's artistic imagination rather than the intellect. Evocative images have the potential to influence an audience's emotions and therefore have more cultural-change potential.

Informative filmmaking also has its role. Documentary films can be at once intellectual and gut wrenching. Al Gore's *An Inconvenient Truth* about climate-change perils was an "idea" film that had a small audience but a tremendous influence—a film whose time had come. A worldwide audience was ready for this message in the same way that we were ready for Rachel Carson's popular, first-of-a-kind book, *Silent Spring* in 1962.

The avatar story is an example of pop culture discovering ancient wisdom. Stories are the way humans have communicated and taught since soon after refined language was developed; we learn through stories. This film is a teaching story. It challenges corporate greed and environmental destruction. Today, many more people will see a film than would read a similar book. Images have replaced reading. Only 8 percent of the US population will read a book this year, compared to 57 percent who will see a film.

Whether on theater screens or home screens, filmmaking is our culture's way of telling stories. Modern film technology or virtual-reality computer software sometimes fully immerses the audience, creating an altered state. Whether this is healthy for the individual or the society depends on the material being presented. By identifying with some on-screen characters, through empathy, it is possible to temporarily *become* a harmonious, indigenous person. Conversely, a viewer can temporarily become the callous killer in a virtual-reality video game. Leonard Cohen, the great songwriter and poet, has a lyric: "America, home of the best and the worst." That applies to Hollywood. Economically successful, violent films lead to more violent films. Successful stories about environmental abuse, like *The Lorax* and *Avatar*, will encourage a studio to approve additional, similar stories. Usually it's easy to see which films benefit society and support the Ecological Epoch.

What is the rational mind's role in filmmaking? James Cameron thoughtfully created the *Avatar* story; he devised the plot, created characters, developed those characters, and decided to include various ethical statements—for example, supporting indigenous peoples' rights to their homelands. The rational mind starts the process and determines how to present the story, but the real connection to the audience is through emotions.

All cultures have ingrained myths, including origin stories that explain their beginnings. There are fables that define the socially acceptable treatment of others, plots involving culturally acceptable sexual conduct, and many other social-conduct themes. As demonstrated by their phenomenal popularity, setting records for box-office receipts, *The Lorax* and *Avatar* have added their influence to our modern mythology. This is not random storytelling force-fed to naive theatergoers; rather, the huge numbers of people who set attendance records and were impressed by these films indicate that these particular stories have deeply touched our society. Perhaps our entire culture subconsciously hungers for the Ecological Epoch to take root, for a healthy relationship with nature, for human rights, for more equal wealth distribution, and for politicians who serve the people instead of their corporate sponsors.

While film creates virtual reality, there are many real-world ways to deepen one's life. Nature offers amazing opportunities to find meaning: Go to the snowcapped glaciers. Go under the sea to witness the multicolored luminous tropical fish in their coral reef habitats. Go to the bowels of Mother Earth, down into an ancient Hawaiian lava tube, or into the many European caves where, twenty thousand years ago, Paleolithic shamans created abstract art in communion with sacred Earth.

Unfortunately, these Earth-honoring experiences are not available to many people. We modern humans have busy lives. There are too many people for each one to have a personal experience of lava tubes or sacred cave paintings. But thanks to James Cameron, millions are able to visit the Na'vi; as such, this type of storytelling is important for cultural transformation. *Avatar* was a huge financial gamble that paid off handsomely. Thankfully, there will be more films like *Avatar* and *The Lorax* because the film industry likes to copycat successful productions. Film is playing a role in our cultural transformation.

Ecological Epoch Music

Popular art and entertainment can change awareness. Artistic music is an important medium for cultural change. In many regards, I'm a product of America's '60s culture. We had our social troubadours, including Woody Guthrie, Pete Seeger, Joan Baez, Bob Dylan, and others. Songs, such as "Hard Travelin'," "The Times They Are A-Changing," "Blowin' in the Wind," and hundreds more are all fraught with meaning and concern for others. Some lines from Bob Dylan's "Blowin' in the Wind" address social-justice issues:

How many roads must a man walk down, before you call him a man?
Yes, 'n' how many seas must a white dove sail, before she sleeps in the sand?
Yes, 'n' how many times must the cannonballs fly, before they are forever banned?
The answer, my friend, is blowing in the wind....
Yes, 'n' how many years can some people exist, before they're allowed to be free?
Yes, 'n' how many times can a man turn his head, pretending he just doesn't see?

Union rights, civil rights, human rights, and the Vietnam War: these were the issues of my youth; these American folk-music artists addressed social issues with passion, concern, and love. Their songs affected me deeply. Gender issues and concern about the patriarchal society came later. I don't remember any songs about the destructive, corporate-controlled economy or the unhealthy environment; however, where there's injustice, there's also art to help us see, and there's music to help us feel.

My favorite contemporary musical poet is Eliza Gilkyson; her hard-charging, no-nonsense protest and love-letter lyrics hit today's issues on the head. She's an artistic spokesperson for our time in the ways Guthrie and Dylan were for theirs, and she's helping us find our way. Her audiences are small but growing. Referring to corporate greed and its international ramifications, in "The Great Correction" she sings these words:

people round here don't know what it means
to suffer at the hands of our American dreams
they turn their backs on the grisly scenes
traced to the privileged sons
they got their god, they got their guns
got their armies and the chosen ones
but we'll all be burnin' in the same big sun
when the great correction comes...

213

The biggest issue of our epoch, global warming, is creating climate chaos. Eliza is a visionary troubadour whose music points out this situation; also in "The Great Correction" she sings about human wisdom, the Great Mystery, and the deep past—all telescoping into today's one-point-in-time crisis, "the eye of a needle":

down through the ages lovers of the mystery
been sayin' people let your love light shine
poets and sages all throughout history
say the light burns brightest in the darkest times
it's the bitter end we've come down to
the eye of the needle that we gotta get through
but the end could be the start of something new
when the great correction comes…

Eliza knows that a time of reckoning is upon us—she's not saying "if" the great correction comes. But hers is not only a message of despair. It also encourages us to *see* what's happening and how critical our current decisions are:

down through the ages
down to the wire, runnin' out of time
still got hope in this heart of mine
but the future waits on the horizon line
for our daughters and our sons…

Like awaking from a happy dream and finding one's house on fire, we don't know the ending to our dire circumstance, yet a large community—a "whole lotta people"—are crying out for change.

I don't know where this train's bound
whole lotta people tryin to turn it around
gonna shout til the walls come tumblin down
and the great correction comes

Another Eliza Gilkyson song called "Runaway Train" uses the train as a metaphor for the US economy, referring to the irreparable damage caused from our full-speed-ahead planetary resource use and our insatiable consumption:

everyone said don't pay it any mind
there's a pot of gold waitin at the end of the line
just move with the eye of the hurricane
you'll never get off this runaway train
nobody cared when they piled on board
and the doors snapped shut and the engines roared
they pushed to the front
some fell to the back
buyin and sellin every inch of the track
deep in the engines, fire in the hole
dark-skinned workers shovelin coal
all singin their sad refrain
we'll never get off this runaway train...

so proud of the engine proud of the speed
call for the porter give them everything they need
stare through the glass feel no pain
don't even know they're on a runaway train

long after midnight a pitiful few sound the alarm
don't know what else to do
bangin on the doors of the cabin and crew
hey we gotta slow down or we won't make it through
sleepy riders don't want to wake
or suffer the shock when they put on the brake
don't want to question, don't want to complain
rather keep ridin on this runaway train

Our sons and daughters, our extended families, you, and I are all riding this train with almost no control of the locomotive—interesting word, "loco-motive." You and I are there in the song, the "pitiful few" who see the *motive* as "loco"—that is, crazy as can be. But it is possible for the pitiful few to become the enlightened many. That is what we are doing together; it's the *raison d'etre* for this book. Maybe it's too late; maybe it's not. In any case, for me, a life-denying momentary, wine-consuming distraction on a runaway train is not a meaningful or joyful way to spend my few remaining years on Earth.

Music can be culturally impactful. In 2011, my organization, EarthWays, and UCLA's Center for Intercultural Performance coproduced an awareness-raising project called *The Water Is Rising*, which is a person-to-person message about the climate change crisis we're facing. The program brought a music and dance troupe of forty-five indigenous people from Tuvalu, Tokelau, and Kiribati, islands in the Pacific Ocean. They are three small, culturally distinct islands that are currently being dramatically affected by rising sea levels. Our message was brought to the American people using the exotic song and dance of vulnerable Pacific Island people—performing in person, showing the world firsthand the beauty that the rising ocean is drowning away. *The Water Is Rising* was an artistic attempt to help wake up American audiences.

Peru's Amazon

The year was 2008; I was serving on a board of directors, helping a friend who had initiated a project in the Peruvian Amazon. She was supporting a local village to develop their own artisan handicraft products, providing employment for some women in the village. She also was helping the men expand production of a local food crop. Her work was pro bono—that is, without pay. She was well loved in the village and invited me to accompany her to assess the project's progress. We flew to Iquitos, a city on the Amazon's upper regions with no road connections to the outer world. Then we traveled on the river by dugout canoe with a large outboard motor; the journey soon wove away from the half-mile-wide upper Amazon into jungle-surrounded, winding tributary eddies. I was totally out of my element—lost in many ways.

We finally arrived in a strange dreamscape: about thirty thatched-roof homes in a jungle clearing beside a twenty-foot-wide, flowing stream. The village elder, its patriarch, was named Ramon; he was the shaman, the "medicine man," and was knowledgeable about the properties of more than two hundred plants—both their potential healing and also their toxic effects. During the following days, he and his assistant held ceremonies for us. Each night, they used a different plant; in effect, we created a relationship with that particular plant—to learn from the plant itself about its core essence. The ceremony extended through the night, involving chanting and local music, emphasizing rattles. Each event included ingestion of the night's special plant.

Some plants that are normally poisonous can be medicinal when consumed in tiny amounts. It was necessary to trust our host. I often experienced a variety of emotional and psychological impacts from ingesting a particular plant. Sometimes it was necessary for me to excuse myself from the tiny, candle-lit room to go outside and throw up.

Each of these long nights provided time to contemplate life. In one session, I just couldn't shake a recurring concern and an amorphous fear: "What about all the world's chaotic craziness? What about the huge oil spills, nuclear power plant meltdowns, global warming, and increasingly extreme weather?" The shadows were flickering; Ramon's feather headdress, bone necklace, rattles, and the earthen floor made a surreal scene. I was immersed in jungle sounds from beyond the thin walls.

217

The light wind breathed an answer: "To be present in the moment, to be fully human, and to accept life's gifts requires that we experience our deepest emotions—from despair and anxiety to joy and exaltation. All is a gift from life's mystery. Tangled in the modern-world web of emotional denial and repression, you are unable to appreciate your own magnificence. Let go of the fear. There may be grief beneath it; feel deeply, uncover the joy, and see where this takes you. Take time away from troubling problems when feeling overwhelmed—restore your inner strength and wholeness. Remember your relationship to the community of all life. The first step toward bringing renewed health to the human community is a personal one. An increase in consciousness within any individual elevates planetary consciousness. This is why Ramon is here for you, this moment. Pay attention!"

CHAPTER 12

SOCIAL SOLUTIONS: TRANSFORMING INSIDE

*Yes, ours is a world…in which too many are dancing to the individual-ism of "My Way." In such a world, how does the beautiful, spirited human being blossom out of the militaristic politics, oversize scale, sterile alienation, and brash egoism that have, in one way or another, infected every one of us and every institution in our midst?…I am aware of the multitude of intelligent projects afoot…. In a world laden with fires, tor-nadoes, hurricanes, tsunamis, volcanoes, earthquakes, and technological disasters; unending wars over land, oil, and water…increasing corporate power; decreasing social liberties; out-of-hand control by drug cartels; cancer epidemics; mass addictions; and growing social chaos—**in this world, hope is a precious thing** (author's emphasis).*
—Chellis Glendinning, *When Technology Wounds*

Our Creation Story has described some of the solutions that can be employed to create sustainable economies: clean energy, nontoxic manufacturing, and recycled appliance cores; all are important if we are to avoid ecological calamity. In the same breath, our story has consistently maintained that the damage we are attempting to heal with these strategies is a symptom, not a disease. The disease is our myopic, contracted perspective; we do not *see* the world clearly enough.

The Creative Source is a great mystery; however, the human species has a collective soul, and each person carries within her body a core essence from the universe's original creation. This Creation Story attempts to focus more clearly the human-to-nature relationship and thereby reveal that essential soul. We examine the areas that are functioning well and those that have become dysfunctional. The story is a collaboration involving thousands of insightful people; they have carefully observed how the world is structured and have explained the appropriate relationship for our species within nature's complex matrix to whoever will listen. This information has been gleaned from science and, just as importantly, the human body's remarkable capacity for subjectivity—our own self-examination. As Earth shamans, these visionaries are observers first, witnessing the surroundings, *seeing* what works and what does not.

Data are not enough; soul searching is needed to get to the depth of a problem, whether it is personal, social, scientific, or economic. For complicated problems, including our current ecological crisis, we are more likely to understand the issues and find solutions if we are fully versed in our culture and, at the same time, able to temporarily step outside its cultural influences. This "stepping out" includes inward soul searching, our own and that of our society and our entire species—science, mysticism, spirituality, and love are all critical to *seeing* with the necessary depth to understand Natural Harmony.

Society in general is looking through outdated lenses. We are seeing the same world that Wilbur Wright saw when he achieved the first successful airplane flight. That was a time when automobiles were a curiosity, and the world's cumulative industrial output was not large enough to negatively impact the earth's regenerative capacity. It was a time when there were one and a half billion people alive, not seven and a half billion. Times have changed, and new confrontations have arisen. The good news is that we know what to do to reverse today's ecological deterioration. Unfortunately, many institutionalized barriers inhibit the required transformation. To successfully remove these obstacles, we need to treat the underlying disease—that is, the truncated vision and limited depth of field our old lenses provide. A New Creation Story will help lead us to new social priorities.

Expanded Self

In this story, one's personal body is the small self. Interrelatedness among all living things is the big self. Realizing these connections exist provides a bridge that allows an individual to expand the small self into the big self. This process is called self-realization. When one comes to know, appreciate, and love his or her fellow life travelers, that person also realizes that to unnecessarily harm another being is to diminish one's self. This worldview, based on appreciation and gratefulness, brings meaning to one's life.

John Trudell is a Native American leader, social philosopher, and inspiring orator. He describes how we have become trapped in a destructive social system. When we can see what binds us, we are better able to extricate ourselves. Our Creation Story describes the necessity to awaken to Natural Harmony. As mentioned earlier, it is the mutually beneficial reciprocity woven into the web of life that allows life on Earth to endure and evolve over billions of years. John calls this awakening "clarity and coherence of mind." I have taken license to summarize John's outlook below as part of our New Creation Story:

(3:24) A human being is composed of human (the flesh and bones) and being (the spirit). When we lose ourselves, we've lost the being, the spirit. Then we are no longer human beings; we are only human. Political, corporate, industrial, military, educational, religious, media, and entertainment institutions are able to capture your being, your spirit, and take it away from you, causing you to lose your empowerment. Some of these systems purposely do this for their own benefit. Others unintentionally do it. Clarity and coherence are what give a human his or her "being" and therefore his or her power. Through our own awakening to clarity and coherence, we realize these political, corporate, industrial, military, educational, religious, and media entities are not powerful, especially because **they** are out of clarity and coherence; as such, they have no authentic power. If we give them power over us, or even think that they are powerful, this means we have no clarity and coherence ourselves. This way of seeing the world drains away our own power. When this is the case, these social institutions have captured our spirit and caused us to become downtrodden.

To awaken is to see beyond these destructive social institutions— to have a grander perception and see the system itself is powerless and confused. It lacks clarity and coherence. Its confusion is destroying the world. When we awaken to these realizations, we regain our own spirit and thereby become powerful.

Our story has also shown how various social leaders are using their own clarity to provide new perspectives for the entire society: ecologists like Joanna Macy and Lester Brown, cosmologists like Brian Swimme, theologians including Thomas Berry; artists like filmmaker James Cameron, and songwriters such as Eliza Gilkyson. Many other examples have been mentioned. These leaders need support from a larger cadre, including you. There are many million individuals from all walks of life who viscerally know we humans have painted ourselves into a corner; they are telling us how to extricate our species and ourselves. Naturally, this includes people in every professional field imaginable—influence that can effectuate change by helping to bring transformation to bear within their own areas of expertise.

"Social science" is an umbrella term that covers many subjective disciplines; among them are sociology, psychology, economics, and politics. Because it involves so much interpretation and judgment, this science has limited objectivity. In our current era, social character is malleable; it changes over short time frames. The Ecological Epoch is crying out for cultural transformation. Eventually, all professions will be reoriented to accommodate this deeper understanding of the nature of reality.

> *We are crying for a vision that all living things can share.*
> —Kate Wolfe, Singer, Songwriter

Ecological Epoch Psychology

Whether one realizes it or not, one's personal psychological health is ultimately tied to the earth's healthy functioning. There is a relatively new branch in the psychology profession called "ecopsychology." This psychological perspective provides an analogy between the human body and our planet's physical operating systems, including the atmosphere, the oceans, and all living beings. The earth's ecology is inconceivably complex, as is a human body. Each person has her own inner ecology composed of body, mind, and spirit. The health of her psychological terrain determines her emotional flexibility; it provides skills to meet her daily challenges, and this skill-set determines how well she will function under stress.

When the Earth is environmentally stressed, it loses species and, therefore, diversity. Likewise, in emotionally traumatic times, an individual usually becomes emotionally contracted, retreating to a safer, more walled-in defensive position, resulting in less inner diversity and more physical stress. When the planet loses species, all of its biological systems are weakened. The Earth requires connectivity among its ecosystems to maintain them in a healthy state. Likewise, our own body needs connectivity among body, mind, and spirit to stay healthy.

Today's economic and environmental challenges continue to mount, producing psychic trauma in individuals and, cumulatively, in society as a whole. Species losses, natural disasters, pollution, chemical toxicity, and warnings about climate chaos weigh heavily on many people, resulting in psychological malaise. Energy use and resource wars are intertwined with ecological health. Extracting fuels often causes environmental damage.

Personal psychology defines social behavior and influences cultural values. Culture informs and, thereby, forms an individual's psyche. A culture's psychological attitude toward nature affects how its citizens treat animals, plants and oceans. A society that prioritizes relationship and kindness will "grow" more kind people than one that values power and aggression. A brutal culture will more likely produce people who are more psychologically capable of committing violent acts. Nations who pursue military excursions, engage in capital punishment, and encourage violent entertainment establish a social context for school shootings, higher murder rates, and indifferent attitudes toward nature's health.

A healthy environment is important to a person's psychological well-being. In today's cultures, most individuals are disconnected from nature. When a person breaks out of this disconnect, he diminishes distracting cultural influences. Ecopsychology emphasizes self-examination techniques that show the importance of the human/nature relationship, thereby transforming the ingrained, unconsciousness narratives that affect an individual's behavior. This outlook relieves elevated anxiety levels and emotional discomfort.

Human organizations and institutions can also be analyzed as ecosystems, including agricultural operations, schools, corporations, and governments. These human-made systems can be compared to our planet's ecosystems. Are they healthy and sustainable, or not? Are they functional or dysfunctional? In nature, diverse systems have more flexibility—that is, they have resistance to disease and decline. Less diversity equates to less resistance; for example, when large tracts of land are used to grow just one crop, a system called "monoculture," diversity is lost, and the crop is more vulnerable to disease. Similarly, in any society, fundamentalism in politics or religion lacks diversity and leads society toward ill health.

Despoiling the planet and despoiling one's own body are similar. Respecting one's physical and psychological integrity is analogous to caring for the planet. The less respect we have for our own health and for our society's healthy functioning, the harder it is to value other life, both human and animal. The more willing we are to allow abuse and destruction, the more we destroy the planet's living systems, the more diversity we lose, and the more diminished we become as individuals and as a species.

How does our society cope with the destruction surrounding us— the despoliation and ecological damage we are accumulating—and still stay sane? We create defenses. We shut down. In clinical psychological terms, we practice denial, compensation, transcendence, or misplaced forgiveness. Whether consciously or unconsciously, when we turn a blind eye toward the declining environment, our collective self-esteem suffers, often resulting in more destruction. It becomes a debilitating downward spiral. We are in its midst as I write. Our emotional and spiritual connections to nature and the Creative Mystery are fraying. Prior generations enjoyed a vibrant, living, ecologically healthy landscape; conversely, our consumption-first corporate outlook often sees the planet as dead matter to be exploited and used up.

With challenge comes opportunity. As species go extinct, people who are awakening to what is happening also realize we humans are in danger, and change is essential. This realization provides an incentive to expand into new territory—that is, new consciousness. In biological evolution, because extinctions provide vacancies, new species emerge within the ecological niches that have opened up. This principle applies to our personal psyche also; new niches have opened to reveal a worldview that shows our interrelational nature.

When we cultivate the soil using permaculture principles, we build up its creative potential and make it more productive. The same applies to one's body, mind, and spirit: As we cultivate ourselves using Ecological Epoch principles, we add diversity and deepened understanding. This approach provides more meaning to one's life and helps us build healthy bodies. As we change ourselves, we are then in position to change the way we treat the planet. As Shakespeare wrote in "Hamlet" five hundred years ago, "To thine own self be true and thou canst not then be false to any man." It is important to become familiar with the shadow elements in one's own psyche to recognize our society's shadow side and thereby change society. Cultivating personal insight can be likened to cultivating soil to build its strength—hence the term "ecopsychology."

To know myself, to be intimate with myself as Shakespeare suggests, is to delve as deeply as possible into life's mysteries. Self-inquiry invariably leads to knowing oneself better—to deepening understanding and more emotional flexibility. What Jungian cultural archetypes are driving my behavior? What family history is influencing my emotions, both positive and destructive? In my personal case, I ask, what influences from my father's sadness, alcoholism, rampant cancer, and early death are affecting my own decisions and actions?

On a grander scale, what larger-vision influences are motivating me to serve society and the planet because my grandfather founded a still-thriving hospital in Winnipeg that has helped so many people? What am I hopeful about? Where does my hopelessness come into play? This self-renewal, introspective process provides comfort and healing.

When my children were younger, as with all children, they were sometimes physically or emotionally in pain for no apparent reason. Of course, there were reasons. I could not discern what they were but could feel their pain. I found with AnaSophia that just holding her helped a lot. It usually did not cure what was ailing her in the moment, but it gave her the security she needed so that she did not feel compelled to lash out at others.

We've had many recent examples in which our society has lashed out at others from impetuous misunderstanding—much like a child in pain.

When Richard Nixon met with China's leader Mao Tse-tung for the first time, Mao, who had gained wisdom in hindsight, told Nixon that they had each caused great suffering because of their own emotional damage in childhood—Mao, by promoting his country's "cultural revolution" that killed thousands and also destroyed Tibet's cultural heritage; and Nixon, by pursuing the Vietnam War, which killed hundreds of thousands.

Accessing my personal shadow and holding it in awareness, like holding my child, allows me to work through difficult emotional moments. Loving myself, including my deficiencies, helps me heal my emotional wounds—this provides new energy to embrace the world, not destroy it. Ecological health applies to me as well as the Earth. Healing one's self helps heal the collective.

Ecological Epoch Parenting

A society's education system plays a prominent role in establishing its culture's worldview and consequent ethical makeup. Each new generation of children provides an opportunity to renew our society. Parenting and teaching play the leading roles. As demonstrated in example after example from this Creation Story, our world is primarily relational, wherein each being plays a part in a remarkably intricate composite whole. This is what the thirteenth-century Zen teacher, Dogen, meant when he said, "Enlightenment is intimacy with all things." When we ignore the relational implications of our actions, we usually create difficulties. When a person is in a position of power, he or she has choices: to act with force or to proceed in relationship—that is, in consideration of all the variables that affect all the parties. Take child rearing, for example, in my own ongoing story:

(3:25) My eleven-year-old boy, Leo, is a "sweet" person; he's kind, he's helpful, he's focused, he tries hard and has self-discipline. These are qualities I do my best to protect, so I almost never have to be forceful in parenting Leo. His sister, AnaSophia, on the other hand, until the age of seven was sometimes moody and difficult, causing considerable disruption. Parents are the authority in relationship with young children. I have a choice to be forceful or to be patient and loving. The latter is often the harder course when a child is frequently annoying and when this behavior interrupts the family's daily plans and activities.

AnaSophia's aunt thought she should be punished—sent to her room, for example—when she misbehaved—the forceful approach. This treatment might "work" for Leo, whose personality is well formed and whose psychological adjustment in the world is strong. He's older and may respond to a forceful lesson, such as a "time-out." But this is not the case with all children. AnaSophia was "acting out," because she was suffering in ways that were not easy to discern. They may have been physiological, psychological, hormonal, or caused from some other difficulty. Punishing her may have changed her behavior but would not address the underlying disharmony. It may also break her spirit.

What is this "spirit" that is susceptible to being broken? It is life's joy, curiosity, and adventuresome nature that accompany an open heart and mind. To take away a child's spirit because she is annoying is a crime against nature; it is to sever the relational fibers that give life meaning; fibers that create connection, compassion, and understanding—this spirit is essential for healthy relating to family, friends, and all other living beings, both as a child and as an adult. If lost in childhood through impatient parenting, it is difficult to reestablish. For the sake of the child, the society, and a healthy planet, I have learned to use my utmost ability to protect my children's open hearts and minds.

With AnaSophia, the forceful, authoritarian parenting style would be the easiest course to follow; it takes less time and less patience. It eventually creates a compliant child, thereby eliminating the irritating behavior and allowing the parent to pursue his or her interests undisturbed. But the last thing I want for AnaSophia is a broken spirit. The alternative is to give her more love, more kindness, and more patience with the hope that she will grow through her suffering without losing her spirit—the deeply connected Natural Harmony roots that accompany all newly born, little people into the world.

Love heals many wounds. When AnaSophia was difficult, she was crying for love, without knowing it. I have watched her; when there is enough love to steady her, she focuses her will on constructive activities in healthy ways. The story has a good ending. Soon after turning seven, her petulant fits and difficult behavior almost completely disappeared. Now, two years later, she needs little special attention and has more friends; her spirit is more secure and readily accessible to her.

Of course, each child is different, and parenting is about guiding a child through good times as well as difficult episodes. My relationship with AnaSophia, or with my son, Leonardo, will not provide a foolproof formula to use for another child's parenting; a relationship is a flowing, living process. Discipline can be part of the guidance, but loving, empathetic discipline is the best way to provide guidance while keeping a child's spirit intact. Respect for the child and his or her world is the guiding principle, not attempts to control a particular behavior. Love and patience compose the relational approach, not force, not convenience, and not a parent's own frustrated emotional reaction to his or her child's behavior.

There are parallels in our adult life. Most workplaces have the bosses and the workers—those in positions of authority and those working for them. Each institution has its own culture. Emotional abuse, usually based on authoritarian management, is sometimes part of that institutional culture; for example, sexual misconduct might be overlooked when bosses force themselves on subordinates who fear losing their job if they rebuff these advances.

Are bottom-line profits higher in authoritarian organizations? Normally they are not. Do society and the world benefit from patriarchal authoritarianism? Almost never! The world needs more personal interaction, empathy, and kindness—from parenting to corporate management to government. "Tough love" is part of that formula when required, but always with the "other" in mind and in heart. Hal David was right in 1965 when he wrote the lyrics to the often-recorded popular song, "What the world needs now is love, sweet love." Millions who bought the recordings likely agree.

Ecological Epoch Education

Various higher-education institutions have moved ahead of their peers in providing environmental research and ecological philosophy. Duke University's Nicholas School of the Environment was created in 1991 by combining the school's Environmental Studies Program with its Marine Lab. In 1997, Duke's Geology Department joined the fold as the Division of Earth and Ocean Sciences. The merging of these departments created one of the most formidable environmental programs in the world and represents the Ecological Epoch's continuing cultural influence. Ecology can be examined in part, but it cannot be separated; it is the whole cloth. And it encompasses more than the Nicholas Schools' combined Earth Science departments can possibly teach; in actuality, it is the context for all scholarly disciplines.

Ecological Epoch education is more effective when it begins at the youngest ages. The hope is to present all subjects within the context of their ecological reality. Human population is growing dramatically. Resources available to feed, house, transport, and entertain all of these people are dwindling. The younger we are when we begin to see this reality, the better chance we will have to find sustainable alternatives—and a lifestyle that adapts to the coming challenges.

California has created a leading-edge educational program that is promoting environmental education; it's called the California Education and the Environment Initiative (EEI) and was developed by the California Environmental Protection Agency. Kindergarten students through twelfth graders are taught English arts, science, and history/social studies within an environmental context. The lessons have been developed as an up-to-date replacement for older course material and have been fully approved for use in the California public school system. Correlation guides in the form of teaching materials have been made available so that teachers can

232

integrate this new approach into their core courses. Teacher trainings and continuing education credits are provided.

Because the EEI is new territory, only a small percentage of teachers have adopted it. At least one California not-for-profit organization, Ten Strands, has as its mission to facilitate this program's adoption into the school system. This private group is, in effect, partnering with California's school system. Ten Strands locates funding to promote these objectives so that the EEI teaching materials are incorporated sooner than later into California's system of 150,000 teachers and six million students.

Ecological Epoch Media

As described in previous chapters, art and music are media platforms. Television, newspapers, books, magazines, and weblogs also have powerful social influences. The media disseminate cultural information; therefore, social transformation involves all media. Traditional newspapers have begun to pay attention to climate change issues. In March 2014 The *American Association for the Advancement of Science* published a report citing possibilities of "abrupt, unpredictable and potentially irreversible changes" from global warming. The association is the world's largest general scientific society. A panel of thirteen climate scientists prepared the report, which was front-page news in the Los Angeles Times.

In addition, Congress mandates "the National Climate Assessment" report to provide policymakers with information. It gained media attention in May 2014. This government report predicts increased flooding, extreme heat, more wildfires, droughts, and insect outbreaks causing tree diseases and habitat loss. Per the report, if current policies and business practices continue, temperatures will rise between 5 and 10 degrees Fahrenheit by this century's end, with disastrous consequences.

Another report, written by the *Chicago Council on Global Affairs*, also in May 2014, notes that extreme heat, drought, and flooding threaten to dramatically reduce food production. This scenario will become a worldwide phenomenon. The most fragile regions, those most susceptible to crop failures and starvation, are poor countries with high population densities; however, the world economy is intertwined. Disruption in one region can destabilize even the most developed economies.

Thankfully, the US for the most part still allows open, unrestricted media, especially the World Wide Web, where less conventional stories can be disseminated. On October 29, 2012, a colossal storm hit the North American East Coast, combining Hurricane Sandy, coming from the east, with another heavy-weather system that had rolled in from the west. This was not just another storm; its ferocious intensity was a product of climate change, and we can expect more and larger such disruptions to continue impacting our society. New York subways were flooded, 286 people died, and millions of people had no electricity many days after the storm. Economic losses in the United States were estimated to be $68 billion.

Events like Superstorm Sandy will happen more frequently in the future. How these occurrences are presented in the media will affect our attitude toward climate change and our resolve to do something about it. Ecological Epoch reporting deepens consciousness. Canada has a progressive, web-based publication called *The Vancouver Observer*, which published an article written by Barry Saxifrage that used research from meteorologists and climate scientists to show how climate change influenced Sandy. Because the climate is warmer now, there is more energy in the atmosphere, which "fuels" a storm's power. Warmer air causes more water evaporation and also holds more water in the atmosphere; this means that the deluge will be larger when storms hit. Condensation that converts water vapor to rain also releases energy into the atmosphere, adding to the storm's fuel. Warmer ocean temperatures add heat to the storm system; heat provides additional energy. More powerful tropical storms and hurricanes also cause more ocean wave surge along the coastlines; therefore, more flooding occurs.

Most of the early news articles about this devastating weather event just related the facts and the damage. Saxifrage's article gets behind the scene to describe why the damage was so severe and to warn about climate change's continuing impact. Cause and effect is occurring. For example, the arctic ice is melting and is much reduced in volume; less ice and warmer air create pressure systems that block the winds so hurricanes moving in from east to west are able to penetrate farther over westerly land masses, causing more havoc.

As we continue to warm the environment, we invite more dramatic weather into our proverbial front yard. Even conventional media are beginning to connect the dots. Although not as analytical as the *Vancouver Observer* article, several days after the storm, the October 31, 2012, issue of *The New York Times* said, "The resulting storm surge along the Atlantic coast was almost certainly intensified by decades of sea-level rise linked to human emissions of greenhouse gases." The article emphasized that Hurricane Sandy, whatever its causes, should be seen as a foretaste of trouble to come as the seas rise faster, the risks of climate change accumulate, and the political system fails to respond.

People want to know whether or not storm damage is tied to climate change. The corporate-owned media are often slow to address climate change, for fear of ruffling establishment feathers, but this elephant in the room can no longer be ignored. Mass-media images are also important tools for change. In 1969, Ohio's chemically toxic Cuyahoga River "caught fire." Photographs of the fire were seen throughout the country; this event became iconic and led to the passing of major environmental legislation over the next ten years. The fire was a turning point in efforts to address industrial pollution.

In 2012, intense drought occurred in the Midwestern United States, extensive wildfires burned in the Western states, and Sandy hit the East

Coast. These weather patterns will be amplified during this decade and those to follow. Most of today's cell phones have built-in cameras. Person-to-person images transferred over the Internet provide unedited media communication that is not corporately controlled. Perhaps the images of Sandy's destruction in New York City, parched farms, and destructive tornadoes in the Midwest will draw more attention to climate change than the more abstract newspaper article descriptions of melting artic ice and dying coral reefs.

Ecological Epoch Politics

Many landmark environmental laws were passed during the Nixon and Reagan presidencies. The Clean Air Act was passed by the US legislature in 1963; The Clean Water Act was passed in 1972. I live in California. Under Governor Jerry Brown's auspices, this state is leading the way with innovative social and environmental initiatives. In October 2013, legislation was signed into law that breaks new ground in addressing the causes of global warming; in addition, several laws were passed that reduce income disparity between the poor and the wealthy. For example, the minimum wage was raised substantially, and the state provided many additional civil rights for undocumented immigrants.

In addition, a law was passed reducing taxes on urban land that has been converted to farming, provided that it is restricted to growing crops for at least five years. In addition to feeding inner-city residents, this law encourages the conversion of trash-catching, vacant lots into green spaces, thereby adding beauty to the urban environment. The importance of these laws is not restricted to California. Governor Brown acknowledges that his polices are meant to affect the national political scene. Per Brown: "Things happen in California that are not happening in Washington. We can do a lot of things in California that shift the [political] climate throughout the whole country."

In another example, Governor Brown serves as one regent (a trustee-like position) for the massive University of California's multi-campus system. At the May 2014 regent's meeting, he encouraged the group to sell the shares of all the companies in its endowment fund that were associated with coal mining. Student activists prodded this initiative. Stanford University has already implemented this coal-divestiture policy.

In 2006, the California State Legislature passed a law that is meant to reduce CO_2 pollutants significantly. Its "cap and trade" provisions took effect in November 2012. The intention is to reduce California's emissions by 17 percent from current levels down to those that prevailed in 1990. Businesses earn credits by reducing their pollution below 90 percent of the prior level. To begin, current pollution from industrial businesses is measured; within a specified number of months, each company is allowed to produce only 90 percent of its current pollution without penalty. If a company does not reduce pollution to the 90 percent level, it must buy "pollution credits" from the state or from other companies that have reduced pollution by more than 90 percent. Increased pollution and failure to reduce pollution both result in significant lost profits. Proceeds that California collects from the polluters are used for environmental cleanup. Some experts consider the law to be a pollution tax. No matter how it is defined, it is a valid attempt to require businesses to bear some costs of the pollution they cause.

Cap-and-trade legislation is also in place in several New England states and in Europe. Although they agree it is much better than nothing, most environmental experts believe that these programs are too little too late and that a much more concerted effort is necessary. Notwithstanding the immense size of California's economy (it would be seventh largest were it a separate country), it produces just 2 percent of the world's CO_2, so the state's goal of a 17 percent reduction will not be impactful on its own; however, California is in a position to demonstrate how this program could produce positive results nationwide, were it to be implemented nationally. In addition, Governor Brown is initiating international agreements in countries where the US federal government is unwilling to tread. In the spring and summer of 2014, Brown traveled to China and Mexico. He had success in both countries establishing preliminary agreements to implement CO_2 emission standards.

We are playing with a short-fused time bomb. Dramatic action is needed, not baby steps. Cap and trade is not enough. It is absolutely necessary to find the resolve to implement high-impact programs. It's time for large-scale integration of ecological consciousness into our energy-use policies. Other approaches are available that are both politically expedient and functional; for example, as a cost of doing business, energy companies could be required to pay a fee based on the amounts of pollution they are creating. This could be a nationwide program, not just one required by a few states. The money collected would be allotted to every US resident because the pollution is damaging each individual.

Economic studies have shown that this dividend-like transfer of resources from the capital-intensive fossil fuel companies to individual consumers would produce growth for the economy because the money would be spent on job-producing retail purchases, healthcare, and similar labor-intensive industries. The government's tax income would not change; the same amounts collected would be distributed, making the plan "revenue neutral." Increased economic activity generated when the dividends were spent would eventually augment government revenue.

The additional costs would mean either lower profits or raised prices for fossil-fuel products. Either effect would help level the playing field so that alternative fuels would become more competitive, their production would expand, and their cost to consumers would decline. This is a model that, if successful, would be adopted by other large economies. Politics have a big role to play in ushering in the Ecological Epoch. Some politicians, like Jerry Brown, are willing and able to take the lead; however, more often it is the people who must lead the politicians by insisting on progressive change and voting for a healthier world.

Innovation

Innovators find it difficult to be taken seriously. Barry Commoner died in October 2012; he was perhaps, along with Rachel Carson, the preeminent US environmental hero. He earned a PhD from Harvard in biology, was a scientist, was a professor at Washington University in St. Louis—and also was a bestselling author. Barry started the Center for the Biology of Natural Systems in 1966, which was the first environmental organization of its kind. In the 1960s and 1970s, his research and his dramatic concern for ecology were considered radical; he railed against pollution, nuclear tests and their toxicity, corporate greed, and environmental damage, all at a time when no one paid any attention.

It took forty years and a new generation—one with thousands of environmental activists whom he influenced—for his warnings to eventually sink in with a larger audience. His ideas were so different, so visionary, that he was pigeonholed as a mad scientist by the corporate world, thus allowing their PR media to marginalize his legitimate concerns and thereby reduce his public influence.

Those times are, thankfully, past. We are beyond the early warning stage that decries imminent ecological destruction—we now know that it's not *if* it will happen, it's how bad will it get—and we can now buckle down to the serious tasks of making changes that will fix the problems. We have a great deal of information, and we know the necessary steps to take on the path to solutions. The issue now is how to integrate this knowledge into our world-community awareness. Some needed changes include: new energy sources, nonpolluting industry, local economies, revamped transportation systems, and, most importantly, new cultural attitudes—a deeper connection to spirit and nature. These solutions would result in more meaningful lives, a sustainable world economy, and a healthy planet. The more open-hearted a relationship we create, the more intimacy we will have with other people, with Earth's animals, with the mountains, the oceans, and the air. Natural Harmony is all about relationship; you can't have one without the other.

> *The vast majority of human beings dislike and even dread all notions with which they are not familiar. Hence, it comes about that at their first appearance, innovators have always been divined as fools and madmen.*
> —Aldous Huxley

CHAPTER 13

TAKING ACTION

(3:26) Our story proposes that only a major intervention to bring about personal and cultural transformation will prevent social chaos and economic collapse in coming decades.

I have a friend and work colleague who spent her early years in El Salvador. She was struggling with the cultural values here in Los Angles and had developed an addiction to distract her from her anxieties—an eating disorder had rendered her a hundred pounds overweight. She belonged to a Native American church group in Northern California. They agreed to do a special ceremony to encourage her healing. She invited me to attend and support her efforts. We chanted, prayed, and told metaphorical stories that related to her condition. There was no debate or instruction. What resulted was community building among different people who were there for a common purpose.

At the beginning I knew only my colleague and the friend I brought with me; the remaining twenty people were strangers. Sitting up throughout the night in that setting offered time to contemplate deeply. Inevitably, today's environmental disasters surfaced: A Japanese Nuclear power plant in Fukushima had recently melted down, causing a large, heavily populated land area to be rendered toxic with radiation. Many people had become environmental refugees. My mind churned through other current events; there was yet another oil spill in the Gulf of Mexico. I felt saddened. Then, as I envisioned more and more damage to the sea life in the Gulf, near my childhood home, sadness became a sickening feeling in my stomach.

I decided to try connecting with Sophia, who often answered my existential concerns—that is, if I approached her with reverence. My question was, "Are scientific discoveries and technology causing more problems than they are helping to solve?" I sat quietly.

Emanating from my own meditative silence, I heard: "Today's challenge is to discover how to appropriately use our technological genius—including splitting the atoms' nuclei and deciphering the human genome—in healthy ways. This is an enormous trial and a maturity test for the human species. Amazing ingenuity has allowed humans to thrive on Earth and has also created an enormous paradox. One billion people have multiplied into more than seven billion in just two hundred years. This population explosion and the social values that have accompanied its rapacious appetite have caused us to lose touch with the living Earth.

"Overconsumption has damaged the earth, but as a result, humans have come to recognize that the Earth is a live body, with living systems. People are interdependent with all life. These realizations are propelling human consciousness into the next level of awareness. People are learning how to live together and to create a healthy relationship with the natural world."

The tent was lit with flickering candlelight. Various natural items bedecked a carefully constructed altar. My mind came to focus on the addictions we suffer in our culture, including the many distractions we provide the masses to numb our anxieties. Another question came to me in the nighttime darkness: "What can be done to change our course?"

Was it Sophia who answered or my own inner voice? "To prevent an ecological collapse, build relationships with nature; to protect our delicate natural habitats, confront the bulldozers where they work in the field. At the same time, look for solutions: create organizations, ideas, plans, and inventions to support and empower those people who are working toward a better world; show others their immutable connection to Earth and life itself. By doing these things, each of you can become a vessel for the evolution of human consciousness." The ceremony continued hour upon hour. By dawn, I had become an integrated part of this caring community.

Some scientists are now referring to our current geological era as the "Anthropocene," because mankind has begun to have a tremendous impact on the planet's geology. For the first time in Earth's existence, we humans are creating indelible geologic changes. Evidence is everywhere. In reviewing publications from the past four years it is evident to me that the popular press has began to pay closer attention to previously less known ecological issues, including the following topics:

Rising sea levels: Environmental deterioration continues to occur more rapidly than scientists had anticipated. Arctic temperatures in the last six years are the highest since measurements began. A report by the Arctic Monitoring and Assessment Program, an eight-nation scientific effort, estimates that sea levels could rise more than five feet by the year 2100, an estimate that is three feet higher than expected in the prior 2007 report. This could inundate low-lying islands, major oceanfront food-production areas in Bangladesh, and other low-elevation population centers. Much of Florida would be flooded. Global warming causes sea water to expand in volume, glacier melt from Greenland and Antarctica adds height to ocean levels, and the loss of ice on the oceans' surfaces reduces sunlight reflection, heating the exposed water, and further increases ambient temperatures causing higher sea levels.

Fossil-fuel pollution: Hydraulic fracturing of subterranean rock formations, called "fracking," is a relatively new process that uses highly pressurized water combined with chemicals, sand, and pebbles to fracture shale-rock deposits, releasing natural gas. There are massive deposits of shale gas in Pennsylvania, New York, and many other states. Fossil-fuel companies have geared up to take advantage of this bonanza, but at what social and environmental cost? The fracking process relies on chemicals that are forced underground using pressure. Energy companies are not required to identify the chemicals that they use, some of which are harmful if they leach into local water supplies.

Thousands of backyard fracking wells have been drilled on land that has been leased from farmers. The chemicals that the companies inject to facilitate the extraction process are proprietary, meaning they are secret information. There is little governmental control, and not even the government oversight agencies know what potentially harmful chemicals are being used. Much of the high-pressure water used in the process flows back to the surface. It's briny, containing the fracking chemicals, and is therefore capable of polluting the adjacent land and the local water table. Contamination and methane leaks often accompany the fracking process.

Endangered species: Petitions listing various animal and plant species as endangered are overwhelming the US Fish and Wildlife Service. A "listing" helps protect a species by providing special regulations for it. Until the past four years, there were about twenty listing requests per year. Things changed: There have been more than 1,200 in the most recent four years, reflecting more species in trouble and more focus on saving them. But the increased numbers have paralyzed the agency's listing process; therefore, it is asking the US Congress to limit the number of annual applications. Currently, even large, elegant species, including the North American wolverine, cannot be added to the list and therefore cannot be protected, all because we lack administrative resources.

Foods: Food activists contend that up to 75 percent of processed food in the supermarket contains genetically modified ingredients. Is this food entirely safe to eat? Is it environmentally responsible to create so much genetic alteration? Many scientists, including Don Huber, an emeritus professor at Purdue University, feel that genetic engineering is producing life forms that are pathogenic. Research convinced him that the combination of the Monsanto Company's genetically engineered soybeans and their pesticide, Roundup, has enabled a new life form to appear that could be highly dangerous. This situation fuels an ongoing debate: What is a responsible balance between increased crop yields from engineered food compared to their potentially high environmental risks and questionable nutritional value?

Addressing the Issues

Has this media scrutiny led to solutions for any of the issues, or are the problems worse? The answers: Ocean levels are rising at increasing rates. Fracking has become even more widespread—rather than mitigating the pollution, new legislation has been proposed to loosen federal regulations and make it harder for individual states to control this extraction technique through their own laws. The endangered species' laws are still in a bureaucratic bottleneck. And citizen rights' groups have been unable to get their legislators to require food companies to label genetically engineered foods so that shoppers can make intelligent choices about their purchases. Although ecological consciousness is seeping into our cultural awareness, on the material plane things are continuing to worsen.

A worldview that sees production and consumption as the first priority creates disease. We function within a structure that allows corporations to operate without moral values. There is little place for corporate social ethics or ecological concern. Executive-compensation incentives are paid based on bottom-line profits, and stockholders clamor for more return on investment. This circumstance was created through legislation and can be changed in the same way.

Because corporations are legally provided many rights and privileges of "personhood," they also should be held to the same ethical standards required of a person. An individual's profit motive is tempered with family and social concerns; society holds each person fully accountable for his actions. Although we have not done so in the past, corporations could be held to the same standards as individuals; profit motives can be recalibrated, and new operating criteria can be developed that include socially responsible behavior.

Corporations control mass media. It could be called the "corporate media." Vast transnational corporate entities pay other companies to create advertisements and promote their "stuff." The system is based on selling products and maintaining a very profitable social status quo. The Internet and other social-media platforms are making inroads but have some distance to travel before changing the overall media equation. Because we are, in many respects, an existentially disconnected culture that lacks deep meaning in our lives, we are vulnerable to corporations' ubiquitous artificial stimulation.

Violence sells; however, violence in media and entertainment is desensitizing. As in war, the more exposed we are, the more we shut down our emotional connection and our compassion for others. This includes our concern for the world at large. In many respects, our culture is so bombarded by violent media images that we suffer from collective posttraumatic stress disorder, and the trauma persists. This insidious cycle makes us more violent within and outside our own society.

Violent media help create a fearful, more violent society. The resulting dysfunctional angst is projected onto the outside world, objectifying and dehumanizing those cultures that are different from ours. Reasons for conflicts can always be found or manufactured. Fossil-fuel shortages are an important impetus for today's wars in the Middle East. Resource wars are not new, and it's likely that the scarcity of clean water will catalyze conflicts in many developing countries in the near future.

As energy companies continue to convert fossil fuels into the atmosphere from natural in-ground reservoirs, numerous additional ecological problems are created. Some of the most polluting are Alberta's tar sands, oil pipeline breaks and leaks, and the numerous new coal-fired plants, especially in China. Alternative energy know-how and resources are available in the United States that, if implemented, would begin to heal the atmosphere, reduce climate-change impacts, and eliminate oil-based conflicts.

The solution to climate chaos is enfolded in the Ecological Epoch worldview. Most auto manufacturers are now offering electric cars. These can be charged from the grid, or better still, with electricity generated from home solar systems, like the one on my house. We know the solutions and have the technical wherewithal to incorporate them into our social fabric, but do we have the will, the resolve, or the courage to do so? We do not—that is, not until we integrate Ecological Epoch consciousness into our economy and allow this approach to drive our personal and collective decisions. Sustainable economics is especially critical.

The first step in solving the problems we are creating is to acknowledge our responsibility for what is occurring. The solutions to our human-versus-planet dilemma are known and widely available. Various obvious changes are needed: slowing climate change requires that we elect more sympathetic legislators. There is no democracy when, as is the current situation, money interests choose all of the candidates. Corporations control the money and, therefore, the government officials. The campaign money required to compete for the US presidency or a congressional seat is ludicrous. Our society needs campaign finance reform and publically financed elections.

Education could be environmentally focused. Ecological approaches that demonstrate healthy interactions and relationships in economics, psychology, sociology, media, medicine, and all other educational disciplines could be given priority in our schools, from the earliest grades to post-doctoral work. Perhaps social media can offset corporate influence on our culture, resulting in less media violence and a kinder society.

Four Conscious Activism Strategies

Joanna Macy is an author and environmental philosopher. I've talked with her numerous times about ways to intervene in an effort to change our society's destructive course. A number of years ago, I wrote a book

249

called *Consciousness in Action* and included a section based on Joanna's activist philosophy. She describes three strategies for environmental activism: The statement "Just say no!" captures the first. For her second strategy, Joanna does everything possible to encourage and support the visionaries who are dedicating their lives and creativity to developing practical solutions to the industrial and economic challenges we face. The third strategy is to change people's attitudes by transforming awareness, deepening consciousness, and promoting intimacy with the natural world.

I've added a fourth strategy: Ecological Epoch product development and business activity that is part of our everyday, normal business—that is, simply selling and using products and services that result in economic sustainability. The products in this category do not have to solve our current problems; rather, they are made so that they do not create additional burdens on the systems. Those are the items to purchase. Each dollar spent on products that sustain the planet's health is a form of activism; it is a vote for solutions.

These four conscious activism strategies offer solutions to every challenge we face in our efforts to restore the earth's healthy functioning. Everyone can participate. This is a way to practice "right livelihood," as Buddhist teachings would say. There are examples by the thousands: food that is healthy to consume and harmless to grow; the all-electric Tesla automobiles; socially responsible investment funds; carpets made from 100 percent reused materials; and rooftop solar energy, wind power, and other nonpolluting alternative energy sources.

Activism

Joanna Macy's "Just say no!" strategy takes the position that it's not all right for corporations or other institutions to create toxicity in the planet's commons—particularly in the oceans and the atmosphere. The Rainforest Action Network (RAN) is an activist organization with a mission to protect and restore the world's rainforests. Early in 2013, RAN's chairman, Jim Gollin, wrote an e-mail to supporters with the following success story:

RAN discovered that a huge amount of pulp and paper ripped from Indonesia's rainforests was going into children's books. [When confronted by RAN] eight of the major children's publishers fairly immediately shifted their paper supply to more environmentally friendly sources, once they learned that they were killing forests to entertain kiddies. But the largest, Disney, was intransigent. RAN activists, dressed as Minnie and Mickey, chained themselves to Disney's HQ. Typical RAN-style corporate office pressure followed. Disney, to their credit, did more than cave in. After a year and a half of intense negotiation, today they are rolling out their new policy, which aims to eliminate all paper products that endanger forests and forest peoples from their supply chain. And not just Disney the publisher, but also the theme parks around the world; subsidiaries from ABC, ESPN, Pixar, and Touchstone; their cruise line, etc. And…they will require that their 3,700 licensees follow the new protocols. This is big. Disney products are made in 25,000 factories worldwide, including 10,000 in China alone. This agreement will help lift pressure from forests around the world. And it will put pressure on rainforest destroyers such as Asia Pulp and Paper and Asia Pacific Resources International Holdings to improve their policies or lose further business. RAN aims to use this as a model for other major publishers and users of paper.

The activist group I founded in 1985 is called EarthWays. We have three themes in our work: (1) to support social justice throughout the world, (2) to promote an economy that is environmentally sustainable, and (3) to bring more spiritual meaning into our culture. EarthWays, in cooperation with other groups, has been trying for many years to protect Los Angeles's last remaining large wetlands, called "Ballona." We started with representatives from four groups, meeting in my kitchen; this eventually expanded to include one hundred more organizations. We coordinated protest marches, sat in front of bulldozers, conducted media campaigns, and embarrassed celebrity movie producers who were involved in the development. We were told that one developer pulled out when his son, having heard about Ballona at school, confronted his father about the pending wetlands development.

The project is named Playa Vista and, as originally proposed, was to be one of the largest residential land developments of its kind in the United States, with thirty thousand people living and working within its boundaries. To get local government approval, the builders claimed that it was an environmentally friendly development. It included the most up-to-date recycling systems, the buildings were highly insulated, they used low-wattage light bulbs, etc. However, no amount of environmentally friendly design features can offset habitat loss. Wetlands are a nursery for many thousands of marine animals. California has filled in more than 90 percent of its original wetlands; the few remaining are precious indeed.

About seventeen years have passed since the project started. The efforts of the Ballona coalition eventually reduced the project to one half its original size and preserved half the wetlands. Today, there are "Just say no!" environmental protectors everywhere on the planet. Almost every ecologically sensitive area, no matter what country, has at least one watchdog group concerned about its preservation. This is helping; at the same time, more effort is needed to stem the political and economic tide. Even with the most sophisticated environmental organizing and access to significant resources, our coalition was only able to preserve half of the Ballona wetlands when, in actuality, we cannot afford to lose *anymore* impossible-to-replace habitat.

I am involved as a board member with five other public charities; each one has its own activist style—that is, each has its own strategy to influence society and to promote positive change. Atossa Soltani started Amazon Watch more than fifteen years ago. I have served on the group's board of directors since its inception. Our mission is to protect the Amazon Basin from overly large industrial projects: large dams, mines, forest clearing, new highways, and similar nature-destroying activities.

Amazon Watch peels back corporate anonymity. When indigenous people are becoming ill from toxicity due to oil extraction and fouled water, we often bring their leaders all the way from the Amazon to attend the company's shareholders meetings. When this occurs, the victims are no longer faceless to company officials and stockholders. We mount information campaigns so that irresponsible practices become fully visible. For example, when oil-production methods are tainted, often resulting in depression, illness, and death for those people living in the production areas, we inform the oil company's customers.

Transparency helps. We hang massive banners from the polluting company's corporate headquarters, identifying the harmful practices, attracting media attention, and embarrassing the company's officers and directors. In the Amazon River basin countries, including Ecuador, Peru, and Brazil, Amazon Watch trains indigenous people to nonviolently protect their territories, using video cameras with satellite uploads to document human-rights and environmental abuses.

The potential impacts of global warming, although widely recognized, are rarely fully understood at a human level. Often it is the indigenous peoples of the planet, still living a lifestyle that contributes little to global warming, who are the first to suffer. For example, in addition to the Amazon's polluted rivers, many native peoples' low-lying ancestral lands will be lost to the rising oceans as the world's ice melts. Some evacuations are occurring right now, as I write, creating more climate refugees.

Visionaries

Joanna's second activist strategy, as introduced earlier, is to promote visionary solutions to our current challenges. For example, Amory Lovins and Hunter Lovins cofounded a think tank called the Rocky Mountain Institute to research alternative, sustainable fuels that can replace fossil fuels. The institute demonstrates how business can take the lead in developing renewable energy, and do so in profitable ways. Their innovative synthesis that I have referred to previously is called *Reinventing Fire: Bold Business Solutions for the New Energy Era*. Another visionary, Lester Brown, has written many books, including *World on the Edge* and *Plan B 4.0: Mobilizing to Save Civilization*, that are visionary in scope; they examine the connection between business and ecological destruction and propose solutions to some of our most vexing challenges.

Paul Hawken is a leader in the activist movement for social-justice and environmental restoration. He spent ten years researching organizations that are dedicated to progressive change—most of them functioning within the Ecological Epoch's ethical envelope. This work is a compendium dedicated to activists and visionaries. Called *Blessed Unrest, How the Largest Movement in the World Came into Being and Why No One Saw it Coming*, it describes how thousands of people are doing their part to recreate our world.

Hawken worked with researchers to create a database that includes more than 110,000 organizations doing environmental and social-justice work—groups that are attempting to implement changes so that our society is able to thrive. If we are able to make the adjustments these cutting-edge activists propose, we will have a chance to live peaceably and to develop economies that protect the natural world.

Lovins, Brown, and Hawken are all visionaries. They see the future and know that a change in direction is critical. They are also able to see solutions that will, given a chance, create a healthier environment, potentially avoiding the chaos that is otherwise looming in our children's future. These are different pathways with one ultimate objective—building sustainable relationships between people and the planet, thereby stopping the destruction and healing the damage we have inflicted.

Changing Consciousness

Joanna Macy's third activism category, *changing consciousness,* is necessary so the Ecological Epoch can be integrated into modern culture—the economy, the arts, the media, education, science, and all other areas. When we see the world with fresh perspective, one that is in alignment with the earth's inner workings, we are able to relate to the living Earth in healthy ways. This deepened intimacy is our guide to an economically sustainable, mutually beneficial future.

We are face to face with a critical moment in time. We are saying no, but the bulldozers keep rolling; our visionaries are designing and creating excellent alternatives—"a vision that all living things can share"—but the entrenched economic powers-that-be ignore these solutions. Unless we make new social–ecological agreements and immediately begin to implement solutions, then Earth's core systems will continue to decline.

Changing the way we see the world has a critical role to play. As mentioned earlier, *human consciousness has always been engaged in change and is evolving at this moment. Today's worldview is creating tomorrow's world. Changing our way of seeing will change the future.*

There's an adage I like to paraphrase: "You can't go back and make a new start, but you can start again and make a new end." In my book *Consciousness in Action,* I use the term "liberation pathways" to describe various methods to facilitate personal transformation: meditation, yoga, ceremonial dance, poetry, shamanistic practice, intellectual pursuits, and many more. Through these practices, we realize we are all intimately imbedded with one another. Personal transformation leads to experiencing reality in more profound ways. In the initial phases, while building a critical mass, cultural transformation happens person-by-person, transforming and enlisting visionary politicians, business innovators, artists, filmmakers, and authors—all have important roles to play in changing consciousness.

Private and Public Sector Intervention

There are many ways to participate in the economy and also create constructive changes. Some people work within charitable organizations, others as government employees, and still others in the private sector, providing much-needed services while gaining substantial returns for their efforts and products. Ron Jones is the chief financial officer for a private, environmentally focused engineering company called Ecolotree. This company has patented various processes that use trees to decontaminate toxic areas, such as military bases, old factories, and dump sites—locations that have built up toxicity over long periods of industrial use, leaving solvents, paint thinners, aircraft fuel, engine lubricants, dry-cleaning fluids, and similar contaminants in the soil.

Over dinner, Ron described one of his projects to me. The objective is to use fast-growing, deep-rooted trees to encourage microbial degradation of contaminants. A hundred years ago, the railroads were expanding in the southeastern United States. For durability, the wood ties used to connect the parallel tracks were impregnated with creosote, which is an oil-based product. There was little concern for spillage, so the locations where the ties were treated became contaminated during many years of use.

Ecolotree was given the cleanup job at one of these sites. Willow and poplar trees are well suited for this challenge; finger-width cuttings about six feet long can be planted three to four feet deep and will grow roots all along the planted cutting—that is, for the entire underground depth. The three-foot-deep cutting, with roots sprouting all along the whole depth, creates an interconnected root mat that intersects with roots from the adjoining cuttings. The fast-growing roots infuse their immediate soil area with carbon from the root growth and from excretions. This process stimulates the soil's microbes, whose population greatly expands. The additional, more active microbes break down large, hard to degrade creosote molecules into new, harmless substances.

Because poplars sprout from cuttings, thousands of trees were planted in short order and at low cost. The site was decontaminated because Ecolotree's engineers discovered the connection among the poplars' mat-forming root characteristics, the microbes, and the fossil-oil contaminants. Entrepreneurial, affordable solutions exist for many such environmental problems. This project solved the problem while enhancing the surroundings with many thousand new trees. The cost was much less than that for different cleanup proposals made by other companies, and Ecolotree made a profit from the work.

The public sector has its own innovators. The Smithsonian Conservation Biology Institute is part of the National Zoo in Washington. Its director, Dr. Steven Monfort, is attempting to transform the zoo's mission: instead of just displaying animals for entertainment, he wants the institute to participate in conserving endangered animal species by both emphasizing this aspect of the zoo's operations and by funding programs to protect animals in their wild habitat. As many species continue to go extinct and others enter the danger zone, zoos are logical institutions to intervene; however, this has never been their mission. Dr. Monfort is an innovator, and he will have a major influence in conservation biology if he is able to get other zoos to participate in this approach.

We live amid incredible beauty; yet the natural world is withering around us. If we can't see the beauty, we won't see this deterioration. When we are able to see nature's magnificence, we will also realize the damage we are inflicting. As a whole, the human species has been *careless* in its attitude about the survival of other species—that is, we couldn't *care less*. Ancient, giant mammals, including the woolly mammoth and the saber-toothed tiger that are familiar to us from museum displays, were condemned to extinction by highly skilled Paleolithic hunters. The British Isles lost their last wild wolf centuries ago. More recently, human activity has caused thousands of extinctions, including the demise of the magnificent passenger pigeon, the Chinese river dolphin, the dodo, the great auk, the thylacine (a marsupial called the Tasmanian tiger), and the Pyrenean ibex, which disappeared as recently as 1999.

Deextinction

The April 2013 issue of *National Geographic* ran a long article about "deextinction," the process of bringing a species back from extinction by reconstructing its DNA. Spanish scientists in Madrid carried out one such experiment to bring back the Pyrenean ibex. By using newly developed germ-cell and stem-cell technology to create a viable zygote, then implanting these dividing cells into a surrogate mother from another ibex species, a living offspring was born. It died shortly thereafter.

A similar project is being pursued to bring back the woolly mammoth. Well-preserved blood and tissue samples have been recovered as glaciers retreat in Siberia. According to an article in the *Los Angeles Times* in June 2013, a woolly mammoth was found perfectly preserved on an Artic island off the Siberian coast; melting ice is exposing numerous mammoth bones, but this is an entire intact specimen. Blood had drained into ice cavities below the animal's belly and was discovered in liquid form. Cloning this animal would probably be successful. Scientists are confident that they can succeed because the technology has greatly advanced in the past fifteen years.[27]

---

27. Most experts say woolly mammoths went extinct about ten thousand years ago. Some scientists believe that small groups survived to a later date. Others theorize that a temporary climate change occurred about thirteen thousand years ago, caused by a large meteorite that disintegrated in the earth's atmosphere and resulted in an "all-year" winter. This occurrence, it's

It is highly unlikely that we will ever be able to reproduce a living dinosaur, à la Jurassic Park, because DNA deteriorates over so many million years, even when frozen. Humans had no hand in dinosaurs' demise; however, we most likely did cause the extinction of all of the elegant species listed above—perhaps we can reverse some of the damage we have caused by bringing them back to life.

This possibility epitomizes human creativity—quite literally! But is it the correct path for the Ecological Epoch? There are good reasons to pursue deextinction and just as many reasons not to. Stewart Brand is the well-known founder of the *Whole Life Catalogue*, which was especially popular with 1970s-era environmentalists. As quoted in the *Earth Island Journal*, Brand makes the case in favor of bringing back extinct species: "To preserve biodiversity, to restore diminished ecosystems, to advance the science of preventing extinctions, and to undo harm the humans have caused in the past."[28]

The same article provides five compelling arguments against deextinction, which is also called "revival biology":

First, these programs will use limited funds that could be better-spent protecting habitat and pursuing other much- needed conservation strategies.

Second, bringing back one species at tremendous expense distracts attention from today's continuing losses and deteriorating conditions; consequently, people lose focus on the bigger picture.

Third, revival biology provides the business-as-usual community with a fallacious but confusing argument: "Don't worry about what's happening because we can fix it."

---

thought, eliminated the plant-food sources for the mammoth and other megafauna. If correct, it would counter the argument that *H. sapiens* was entirely responsible for the woolly mammoth's disappearance.

28. Jason Mark, "Back from the Dead," *Earth Island Journal*, Autumn 2013.

Forth, the revival techniques do not profess to produce the actual species that went extinct, just an approximation, because nonextinct, related species are employed as part of the process. The revived animal is really a hybrid.

Fifth, there really is no place to relocate an extinct species in the wild. Most went extinct because their habitat was diminished. With no place to return a species to the wild, even a successful project would leave its offspring confined to zoos. They would remain scientific curiosities, not the magnificent life forms their foreparents once were.

Notwithstanding the debate, revival biology's molecular research will benefit the Ecological Epoch because the same research is also being employed to protect endangered species. Given proper attention, genetic recombination and breeding programs might save some still-living, elegant species, including the magnificent white rhino. It likely makes more sense to use our limited environmental restoration resources to protect habitats that harbor endangered species; however, deextinction work and its exorbitant cost might provide a valuable lesson. As a species, we humans are becoming more careful—that is, we are concerned enough about restoration that we are willing to allocate significant resources in attempts to restore nature. When we see the price tag for one revived ibex, perhaps this will help us realize the immense valuable of each living creature. As a result, we will try harder to prevent their eternal loss.

We are an amazing species engaged in a noble experiment, attempting to find our way through a complex world. The more complicated our circumstances, the greater are the moral dilemmas we face. The more we destroy, the more we are compelled to awaken. Those individuals who are participating in the Ecological Epoch can feel the angst. This pain of loss also brings about more awakening—including new creation stories.

(3:27) Alone in the kitchen, after getting the kids off to school, I sat reading an article in The New York Times about genetic engineering. It's possible, in years to come, that we will be creating as many new life forms as we are causing to become extinct. I paused, paper in lap, staring out the window. A thought arose: "We humans are as natural as starfish, moss and wild deer—why not consider these newly created life forms to be an extension of nature's fecundity, as expressed through nature's own human co-creators?" The question hung silently for in the kitchen air, as though it were a meditation focus.

Time passed. Mysteriously, an answer rose up: "Unlike nature-based communities, our current social values encourage a gold-rush mentality that turns a blind eye toward other species' welfare—and are ignorant of most intricacies contained in the delicate interactive weaving that protects life's overarching presence.

"Humans rush in where angels fear to tread; we are too impatient to allocate hundreds of years and multiple generations of interaction, as is nature's normal process, so we can be confident that a new life form will fit within the existing matrix. Nature's innovations are implemented gradually—any initial harm is slowly absorbed and rectified so that a viable equilibrium is attained. Human experiments come on suddenly and can be toxic to life; and yet, we are also nature's creation and have been gifted with the tools to carry on this enterprise. This conundrum can be resolved only by using our deepest emotional, psychological, intellectual, and spiritual insight when making nature-changing decisions. If we can do this, we may be able to hold this profound, life-creating responsibility as a sacred trust."

Social Entrepreneurs

Last week, I had a gathering for various social entrepreneurs at my home so that they could meet one another and describe their work. One man was selling a technologically innovative product that monitors, using a home-based computer, every aspect of a home's energy use: the lights, the refrigerator, the air heating system, the hot water heater, and all other electrical devices. Learning which electrical uses are excessive helps the homeowner make adjustments. The monitors even send out alerts when lights are left on. This system typically helps a homeowner reduce electric use by 30 percent or more. Investors are jumping into this for-profit venture and hope to make a good living from the environmentally responsible work. The monitoring system was just one example. The circle of twenty-two people in my living room all had their own approach to doing beneficial work while also finding ways that these efforts would provide income for themselves and their families.

I recently participated in a wind-farm tour near Mojave, California. The windmill industry is booming; newer, more efficient technology is continually emerging. Land owners, equipment installers, operators, and investors are excited about this rapidly expanding clean-energy field. Regulated capitalism can be an effective system in replacing destructive business practices with healthy economic solutions. These clean, renewable technologies need government protection in their early stages so that they can attain economies of scale; afterward, they can become fully competitive with fossil-fuel industries.

The preceding examples are profit-making ventures. The not-for-profit community provides additional opportunities to build a healthier society. My group, EarthWays Foundation, operates an environmental education center in Sonoma County, California. The land has giant redwood trees, rolling grassland meadows, and distant ocean views. Called Ocean Song, this beautiful location "speaks" to people who visit. The land inspires its guests. With its 250 acres of ecologically protected area, Ocean Song also encourages meditative interaction with the land. My young children, nine-year-old AnaSophia and eleven-year-old Leonardo, attend an environmental summer camp at Ocean Song. They recently discovered a four-foot-long gopher snake scurrying into its in-ground lair. Upon passing by hours later, we were all delighted to discover a baby snake poking its head out from the hole.

The problems we face as a species are diverse. One EarthWays project purchases medical supplies and helps deliver them to the oppressed Karen people in Burma—an area where the Burmese government has, until recently, not allowed foreign aid. To provide even the most basic medicine, porters using backpacks have to carry supplies over the mountains. These efforts were not without danger. When I made this trip eight years ago, as mentioned earlier, our guides had to monitor where we walked in several areas that had landmines planted beside the jungle trails.

Several other EarthWays projects fit into this *social entrepreneur* category. For fifteen years, we have been working to help women in Guatemala's high mountains in a village called Casaca. Working with a local partner called AFOPADI, we provide funding and jointly design the projects to be pursued. These include providing health-care education, manufacturing grain-storage bins, installing more efficient stoves, and teaching organic gardening. AFDOPADI implements the projects in the villages.

In Ecuador, EarthWays has been working for ten years with several other groups in an attempt to protect parts of the upper Amazon River from pollution-causing oil exploration. For various reasons, this effort has met with almost no success. The pollution is growing, and the local people continue to suffer its consequences—unhealthy fish to eat and unsanitary waterways in which mothers bathe and children swim.

Our sister group, Amazon Watch, was instrumental in winning a multibillion-dollar judgment against the Chevron Oil Company, which was held responsible for pollution in the Peruvian Amazon. The money is meant to compensate the local people, whose health has been impaired from decades of oil-industry toxicity. The dollar amounts received will never make up for the losses these families have suffered, and the polluted waterways will take nature generations to restore. In defiance, even after losing their legal appeals in Peru's highest courts, Chevron has publicly vowed to never pay the judgment.

I started another organization about seventeen years ago called SEE, an acronym standing for Social and Environmental Entrepreneurs. SEE is a catalyst to encourage progressive activism. We facilitate the start-up of not-for-profit projects by providing administrative controls, tax-exempt status with the US government, funding consultation, and operating advice. Our SEE staff currently shepherd $7 million of activist projects per year, more than ninety programs, each operating in various capacities to solve social and ecological problems. The social entrepreneurs in each project conceive and initiate their own program. We help them succeed. These activists usually have other jobs to pay their own living expenses; however, some of the programs do generate enough operating income from grants and donations to pay a living wage.

EarthWays continues to be focused on "conscious activism," which I define as: "engagement in the world that reveals and expresses our most profound understanding of the nature of reality." This awareness-raising is one form of social entrepreneurship. Our work encourages each individual to dig down as deeply as possible into his or her psyche and intuition—as dark and unknown as this universe might seem to be—to more fully understand what is most important in life. Each person who succeeds at this endeavor will then know how to live in tune with his or her surroundings and help others to do the same.

My own activist work and writing projects promote social change. For example, EarthWays has coproduced the World Festival of Sacred Music every three years in Los Angeles, comprising thirty-five performances in different venues over sixteen days. The last festival featured a performance called "Water Is Rising" that was mentioned previously. This program brought to the United States music and dance troupes comprised of indigenous peoples from three culturally unique Pacific islands.

The musical entourage visited fourteen prestigious venues in the United States, presenting global warming's human face to the American people. Climate change became more real as audiences experienced these artists whose homelands are being dramatically affected—the beautiful cultures will be swallowed in tomorrow's expanding oceans. The exotic songs and dances, performed by the very vulnerable and sweet Pacific Island peoples, show us the beauty we are drowning.[29]

These island cultures have not contributed to global warming, yet much of their ancestral land will be lost to the sea. They are among the first of many climate-change refugees. In coming years, more intense floods, droughts, hurricanes, and other climate-related emergencies will create numerous additional weather-related refugees, especially in the developing world, where there is little margin for the infrastructure to absorb extreme conditions.

Although it is a musical performance, the "Water Is Rising" tour allowed these culturally diverse indigenous voices to be heard and also provided the core content for our environmental message. Led by Judy Mitoma of UCLA, we developed educational material in partnership with environmental science departments in the schools where the troupe performed. We helped educate grade-school children, university students, and the public, especially through newspaper and TV news articles in the venue cities. These music and dance performances gave us opportunities to introduce distant cultures and also bring awareness to the catastrophic threat posed by climate change.

The world-famous activist, Nobel Peace laureate Wangari Maathai, used tree planting in Africa to help the local people by providing shade protection, firewood, and animal fodder. We humans have deforested the planet and continue to do so in many places; however, we are just as capable of reforestation. Considering the planet's entire remaining forest cover, many people are still engaged in tearing it down; however, just as many are beginning the necessary regeneration.

These are two competing cultural phenomena. One represents rapacious economic growth, and the other stands for sustainable living on the planet. I anticipate a time when, from that moment on, more trees

---

29. "Water Is Rising" is a collaborative project among EarthWays Foundation, the UCLA Center for Intercultural Performance, and the Foundation for World Arts.

are planted than are destroyed. Perhaps that moment is near; however, destructive corporate influence is growing, not declining. It often feels as though our EarthWays' projects are just dust in the wind, but the renewal has to start somewhere. Although logic and facts can help, action is essential; talking is not enough to get us through this dangerous birth canal.

EarthWays' previously mentioned tree-planting project called the Green World Campaign is attempting to plant millions of trees in fertile tropical regions to sequester carbon from the atmosphere and offset CO_2 buildup. Per Mark Barasch, the project founder, "Our staff in Mombasa, Kenya, has established a Green Schools program in which each of the twenty participating schools plants one thousand trees and students learn about ecology and global citizenship. We've been asked to help plant two million indigenous trees, build an elephant fence to reduce human conflict with these magnificent creatures, and develop nontimber forest products to help people make a tree-friendly living." GWC hopes to create a holistic model of regeneration that could spread throughout the country.

At times it is necessary for activism to combine nonviolent civil disobedience with visionary solutions to bring awareness to the issues. Dr. Mark Jaccard is a Simon Fraser University economist whose career is focused on sustainability. He is a Nobel Prize Laureate, recognized for his work as a leader with the International Panel on Climate Change, and he has advised numerous governments, including the United States and Canada, as well as California, British Columbia, Ontario, and Québec. On May 5, 2012, Dr. Jaccard was arrested because he was taking part in a peaceful protest to bring attention to the Canadian government's support for "dirty" coal that is being imported to Canada from the United States to be used as power-plant fuel. Dr. Jaccard sat on the railroad tracks to block a train that was delivering the coal.

He told reporters, "I now ask myself how our children, when they look back decades from now, will have expected us to have acted today.... When I think about that, I conclude that every sensible and sincere person, who cares about this planet and can see through lies and delusion motivated by money, should be doing what I and others are now prepared to do."

He was also quoted in the *Vancouver Observer* news magazine:

I've never broken a law in my life.... If governments were acting to reduce greenhouse gas emissions, or slow the rate of increase, I wouldn't be here today; I'd be helping those governments to do that. But in the last few years, especially in Canada under Harper, the emphasis has been on accelerating the rate at which we are destroying the planet. So I have to ask myself and I have to ask everyone else, ethically, what is the right thing to do? It's made me read more about civil disobedience, people like Mahatma Gandhi, Martin Luther King, and Henry David Thoreau...I really think that we should all be doing this...I'm here drawing attention to myself for ethical reasons, but I don't want to be a martyr. I'd much rather that there were ten thousand of us out here. Everyone has the ability to know how dangerous the current situation is.... Over one hundred coal plants in the United States were cancelled or put on hold because of people like us. It created a big increase in renewable energy, and it is happening rapidly.

The *Vancouver Observer* noted that US climate scientist Dr. James Hansen, who is also a Nobel Laureate, has been arrested while participating in similar civil disobedience. Taking to the streets in nonviolent protest actions gets the attention of governmental decision makers. US leaders take heed more than leaders in most other countries: segregation was ended partially from public outcries; protests led to the end of the Vietnam War. In a later decade, citizen activists, a half million strong, gathered in New York's Central Park in the 1980s to initiate a nuclear weapons freeze. Similar protests are beginning to occur, drawing more attention to climate chaos. On September 21, 2014, climate activists gathered in New York City with the largest numbers ever assembled.

I live in California. This summer, 2014, is the hottest ever recorded. The National Weather Service also reported that, in California, 2014's first six months have been the hottest on record—about five degrees warmer than the average during the hundred years from 1900 to 2000. The state is also suffering its worst drought on record. These circumstances do not provide scientific proofs of global warming, but a sensitive person's intuition will tell him or her a great deal just from experiencing this "new normal" and its voracious appetite for destruction.

Taking action is critical if the Ecological Epoch is to have a chance to succeed. The British Royal Family is doing its part. Although Queen Elizabeth has not been an environmental advocate, her son, Prince Charles, is passionate about promoting conservation and protecting endangered species. Even more promising, England's next-closest heir to the throne, Charles's and Diana's son, William, has inherited his father's concerns. In the fall of 2013, William left his seven-year military tour of duty to focus on public service. According to a statement issued by the Royal Palace, William would expand his activities related to environmental conservation, particularly concerning endangered species. It is likely that William will eventually be England's king. This highly visible semi-political position will help his ecological wisdom filter into the culture.

Most of us need encouragement to jump into the lake for the first time. Dr. Jaccard pointed to Gandhi and King for inspiration. Nonviolent activists set the example and provide impetus. Others witness this resolve and get involved themselves. When the time is right, when our damaged surroundings become so visible that we are called to act, then more of us will *see* Dr. Mark Jaccard's actions and be willing to dive in.

Personal Actions

There are things one can do individually to mitigate the problems and promote solutions. These constructive actions sometimes require significant resources, which are beyond those available to the average family. The all-electric cars, for example, are currently more costly than comparable gasoline ones; however, for those able to afford a plug-in car that is energized from a solar-energy system installed on one's own house, doing so will help make affordable electric cars available to others. The increased production volume from early sales will encourage auto manufacturers to build more of these models, thereby providing economies of scale that bring prices down for later buyers.

If you have funds to invest in securities, there are socially responsible firms whose stock and bond securities sell on public stock exchanges; there are also funds that specialize in alternative energy: solar, wind, geothermal, biogas, and other eco-friendly energy sources. If carefully chosen, these investments sometimes even outpace the market indexes and provide a better investment return than other security investments. If you are a businessperson, do your best to transform your business using environmental-impact criteria, including the sustainability index mentioned above, as a guideline.

For those without funds to invest, there are other actions to take. As a consumer, you are able to support local, socially responsible businesses so that products are not transported all over the world, wasting energy in the process. This strengthens your local community and provides nearby jobs. Buy produce at your farmers' market—if your area does not have one, lobby for one.

LED light bulbs use a fraction of the electricity that incandescent bulbs do, and they last many times longer. More droughts are on the way; consider replacing your lawn with drought-resistant plants and installing a gray water system (using water recycled from sinks and showers) to water your home's landscaping. Ride your bike to work; if this is hard to do, or too far to go, then just do it once a week or once a month to model what can be done. Your co-workers will notice. Take your own grocery bags to the market and avoid purchasing products with extensive packaging.

Each US consumer can offset his carbon footprint by planting and maintaining eight hundred trees; keeping these trees alive and replacing those that die provides a lifelong carbon offset. This may seem onerous, but starting with seedlings and doing the work oneself is not as hard as it sounds, and it is personally rewarding. Find someone with land that will benefit from reforestation and partner with that person. Another personally rewarding and planet-enhancing strategy is to join a local activist group that is protecting an ecologically sensitive place in your region—while doing so, you will find new friends with similar values and thereby strengthen your region's ecological community.

Pay attention to your carbon footprint. Attempt to reduce your driving and the airplane flights you take each year. Insulate your home better so that you use less energy to heat and cool it; perhaps eliminate air conditioning altogether—just wear light clothing on hot days. I know from my experience that this lifestyle is more liberating. Without air conditioning in my home, I am not breathing stale, "conditioned" air. These actions also save money; a win–win for you and the planet.

Eat as though the Earth matters. Greatly reduce your meat consumption. Get more minerals and vitamins from eating vegetables and fruits. Eat closer to the earth—that is, eat food that is lower on the food chain, and you will get more bang for your buck; the grains that currently feed the cattle we eat can directly feed us. This is a lot more efficient than first converting them into bovine muscle and then using that animal muscle for our food.

A friend of mine is vegan—that is to say, he's vegetarian, and he eats no eggs or dairy products, including cheese and milk. He reads labels assiduously. Once I was given several vegetarian cookies. I offered one to my friend. He took a bite and immediately spit it out, somehow detecting that a little milk lurked in the offering. Another time, he refused a veggie submarine sandwich because originally it had had cheese on it. (I removed the cheese prior to giving him the sandwich.) Was this extreme? Perhaps it was, or maybe not.

His point is that he does not want to participate in the system that produces eggs and cheese in ways that are abusive to animals. My removing the cheese from the sandwich was not sufficient for my friend. His broader philosophy comes into play: the cheese is an animal product. As such, it represents to him our systemic food-production problems, including an overabundance of methane-producing cows, in addition to animal cruelty issues, which include the inhumane treatment of farm animals.

When you create your own ecology-benefiting strategies and start adhering to them, let your friends and family see what you are doing, how you are doing it, and what it means to you. It is not necessary for them to agree with you. Just modeling this behavior will have its own effect. Others will consider following suit.

It's not too important what you decide to do; any activity, any contribution at all will help solve our many environmental challenges. Often, actions speak louder than words, although at times you will want to speak out so that your children and neighbors know what you have discovered for yourself. The speaking combined with the actions create a healthier community. One's own world becomes bigger just from the participation, and life gains meaning.

> *It is my deep conviction that the only option is a change in the sphere of the spirit, in the sphere of human conscience. It's not enough to invent a new machine, new regulations, new institutions. We must develop a new understanding of the true purpose of our existence on Earth. Only by making such a fundamental shift will we be able to create new models of behavior and a new set of values for the planet.*
> —Vaclav Havel, former Czech Republic president, professional teacher, and poet

CHAPTER 14

CONCLUDING THOUGHTS

(3:28) The Earth has a propensity to evolve biological consciousness. Consciousness is continually advancing. Large-brained mammals, for example, whales, elephants, and some primates, are all examples of this evolution.

All progressive human endeavors, including science, religion, philosophy, social organization, and, therefore, history are products of evolving human-consciousness stages. The change and development of consciousness is the scaffolding for advances in each human discipline.

Human consciousness has recently entered a new level of awareness that we are calling the Ecological Epoch. This consciousness stage is more aligned with Natural Harmony than were the most recent prior epochs, which were the Philosophical Epoch and the Scientific Epoch.

How we humans see the world determines how we behave and dictates our interactions with nature. Given our current capacity to impact the environment, our worldview will change the physical world. A healthier perspective can heal the Earth.

The Fukushima Story

In the coming decades, humanity will face grave perils. In times past, facing pandemic disease, war, or natural disaster, the human spirit has risen to meet the most difficult challenges. Calamities that result from the now-ongoing climate chaos will help us find our appropriate place in the earth's community of life. In a recent microcosm of things to come, on March 11, 2011, a giant tsunami wave, following a major earthquake, hit Japan's coast, causing three nuclear reactors at Fukushima to fail and leak radioactive material into the surrounding environment. More than three years later, radioactivity is still leaking into the nearby ocean.

There are many stories describing how the affected people came together to help one another. One coastal area was devastated with more than nineteen thousand deaths, and the area's main economic engines were lost: agriculture, fishing ports, and a small boat-building industry. In the days following the disaster, cut off from outside support, the people helped one another, quickly creating a local barter economy for goods and services. Fisherman helped other fisherman; farmers helped farmers. The people had to trust one another. In 2012, an unsigned letter from someone at the Soto Zen School that is in Sendai, near Fukushima, was published on the Internet:

Things here in Sendai have been rather surreal.... I am now staying at a friend's home. We share supplies like water, food, and a kerosene heater. We sleep lined up in one room, eat by candlelight, share stories.... If someone has water running in their home, they put out a sign so people can come to fill up their jugs and buckets. Utterly amazingly, where I am there has been no looting, no pushing in lines. People leave their front door open, as it is safer when an earthquake strikes.

Quakes keep coming. Last night, they struck about every fifteen minutes. Sirens are constant, and helicopters pass overhead often....We got water for a few hours in our homes last night, and now it is for half a day.... No one has washed for several days. We feel grubby, but there are so much more important concerns than that for us now. I love this peeling away of nonessentials… living fully on the level of instinct, of intuition, of caring, of what is needed for survival, not just of me, but the entire group.….There are strange parallel universes happening…people lining up for water and food, and yet a few people were out walking their dogs. All happening at the same time. There are other unexpected touches of beauty. The silence at night. No cars. No one out on the streets. And the heavens at night are scattered with stars. I usually can see about two, but now the whole sky is filled…. People talk to complete strangers asking if they need help. I see no signs of fear. Resignation, yes, but fear or panic, no.

They tell us we can expect aftershocks, and even other major quakes, for another month or more. And we are getting constant tremors, rolls, shaking, rumbling…. Somehow at this time, I realize from direct experience that there is indeed an enormous cosmic evolutionary step that is occurring all over the world right at this moment. And somehow, as I experience the events happening now in Japan, I can feel my heart opening very wide…. I feel as part of something happening that is much larger than me. This wave of birthing (worldwide) is hard, and yet magnificent.

According to the March 11, 2012, *Christian Science Monitor,* "The shutdown of fifty-two of Japan's fifty-four nuclear power plants over safety concerns has also led to proposals to build solar and wind projects in the tsunami-hit zone. This idea of energy self-reliance reflects a desire to build up a local economy that is not dependent on the rest of Japan."

On the positive side, Japan's tsunami and its aftereffects, although probably not directly caused by climate change, demonstrate how ecological consciousness will be forced upon us when climate chaos results in numerous destructive events. Alternatively, perhaps we can institute the policies needed to minimize these calamities by immediately beginning to create nonpolluting, sustainable economies on a worldwide basis. Our New Creation Story is begging the question: "Can we change course before we further endanger our own children?"

Our society has critical choices to make at this moment in time. Will nature be revered as our provider and protector so that the whole world might prosper? Or will our myopia and disrespect continue to lead us into chaos and eventual despair? Two national news articles in on consecutive days in July 2014 symbolize the paradox: In Hawaii a dead whale washed ashore in the midst of the US Navy's powerful underwater sonar exercises that flood the marine world with deafening sound waves. For every whale that is found dead, many more are mortally wounded without anyone knowing. Activists have been protesting these navy practices for more than a decade, to little avail—the sonar use has been scaled back, but the undersea blasts continue and are known to destabilize vast marine mammal habitats.

In contrast, the following day, July 27, 2014, the *LA Times* ran a story by Geoffrey Mohan, "Ships on Collision Course", about a marine mammal ecologist that led a fifteen-year study to track the magnificent blue whales' feeding habits, in order to reduce the number of times that cargo boats hit these whales while they are feeding in shipping lanes. We have a choice to make: The Ecological Epoch will do its best to protect the remaining whales, tigers, elephants, and hummingbirds. The old order, business-as-usual corporations, military, and shortsighted politicians for the most part continue to ignore the risks. But in the end, people control institutions, and people can change. The social choices are ours to make, here and now.

(3:29) There are currently two fields of consciousness competing for the soul of each human: the destructive, industry-based, unsustainable worldwide economic juggernaut versus the new epoch's interdependent, Earth-life-as-priority worldview. The competition is fierce; the potential outcomes differ drastically. Business-as-usual will prevail unless there is a major intervention, starting now, to avoid collapse and chaos during the next thirty to sixty years. It is of critical importance that each able person participates in finding and implementing solutions.

Change Is upon Us

The ways in which we perceive the world are changing. Many positive developments are occurring that provide hope for a healthier future. One hundred fifty years ago, US society agreed that slavery was unacceptable and forcibly ended the practice. Fifty years ago, US society realized that segregation was dysfunctional and cut it away. More recently, we accepted the premise that smoking is a public-health problem that needed to be regulated, taxed, and discouraged. Likewise, unhealthy food that promotes obesity is now seen as a public-health issue. Social values can, and do, change. Our collective worldview is currently changing our values about how we see ecological destruction.

Promoting fear and thinking of different races and religions as "other" has allowed governments to pursue "resource wars." Our rapacious desire for cheap energy is a major variable behind the "war on terrorism" that has occurred in Iraq, Afghanistan, Libya, Syria, and other volatile regions. The public is beginning to see through government pretense that blames terrorism and promotes distrust of other societies. Our Creation Story applauds cultural diversity. Blossoming out from African roots, we settled and populated the Earth's most remote regions; local adaptations that modified skin color made people appear to be different. The idea that different colors indicate varying "races" was adopted. That misperception is changing in the Ecological Epoch.

(3:30) The human collective unconscious suffers from the delusion that "races" are scientific categories. The Ecological Epoch professes something different: We all started in Africa, offspring of "Mitochondrial Eve," our common Mother ancestor; we were all black-skinned (more precisely, dark chocolate); we spread throughout the world; during forty thousand years of migrations, groups became relatively isolated, each settling in their own region. We developed various facial features, body types, and skin color (called the four races) based on our geographic and climatic situation. During the past century, mobility, more open borders, acceptance of mixed marriages, and modern transportation have begun to intermingle all these physical features.

In a few hundred years, there will be predominately one "world race." The majority of our planet's human population will have various gradations of "tan" skin. Only remnant pockets of lighter-skinned and darker-skinned people will remain. We will have come full circle from dark chocolate brown to light chocolate tan, a cycle that started in Africa about sixty-five thousand years ago and resulted in worldwide population diffusion. Everyone was dark-skinned; migrating groups reached every habitable niche; territories were established; geologic features often set the boundaries; agriculture began; cultures were born; political boarders resulted in isolation and segregation; cities flourished.

Then something different occurred: Science shrank the distances between "foreign" places; human population exploded; people intermingled—reintegration had begun. In reality, "race" is not a valid scientific category. We are all one people, although in our desire to gain an upper hand, we confused ourselves for a long time by what appeared to be different skin colors—each claiming to be a superior race when, in fact, what we call "race" indicates nothing more than uniquely distinguished body features shared by a large group.

Unsustainable economics have, to a large extent, created climate instability and environmental crisis. Ecological Epoch economics gives first priority to policies that help the Earth restore itself. Many churches, synagogues, and mosques are teaching their members that ecological preservation is a spiritual concern. In this global society, we are all neighbors, even with those who live on the planet's farthest reaches. Loving thy neighbor includes not drowning low-lying Pacific atolls in rising seas.

We are beginning to change to more local economic systems. For example, farmers' markets are appearing in most cities as well as in small towns. Their village-like gatherings promote community, emphasize "localism," and support independent farmers. Young people are becoming more concerned with environmental issues and are paying more attention than their elders; many are skilled in using social media to communicate solutions.

Technology is our ally in many respects: we are exploring the solar system and beyond; quantum physics has recently made important, mind-expanding discoveries, including verification of the Higgs field; we are making ingenious advances in understanding and curing human illness; DNA research is revealing our relatedness to one another and to extinct hominids; and the entire world has become more networked by using social media, thus providing communication and information systems that allow more equitable dissemination of up-to-the-minute information, while reducing information-control tyranny. These technologies help to integrate the Ecological Epoch.

Scientific discoveries tumble forth at a remarkable pace. Given our higher population density, more researchers, much better interactive communication through the Internet, and an ever-expanding knowledge base, our factual grasp of our universe and our DNA continues to grow. In 2014 radio telescopes at the South Pole discovered the first direct evidence of the Big Bang's unexplainable "cosmic inflation," a theory that describes the universe's violent, faster-than-light expansion from the most miniscule physical size imaginable. The BICEPT2 project also theorizes that our known cosmos, as determined from faint light generated 13.8 billion years ago, is just a tiny puzzle-piece of some larger reality that extends beyond these light-defined boundaries. This scientifically based conjecture helps to blow apart the conventional worldview and, as in biological evolution, opens niches for new perspectives to take hold and grow.

Nature's double helix DNA structure is built from nucleotides called adenine, thymine, guanine, and cytosine, arranged in base pairs and forming the rungs of the double helix. In 2014 bioengineers at the Scripps Research Institute in California successfully inserted a man-made base pair of nucleotides into E. coli's genetic code; the bacteria was able to reproduce with these artificial DNA molecules intact. This procedure may provide a delivery system for future cancer treatment and other biomedical disease challenges. Is this progress, or does it present more potential for nature's abuse? All discoveries are expressions of human creativity. How they are used is based on society's consciousness level. Will DNA manipulation, artificial intelligence, and robotic exploration of Mars be blindly used to create further planetary dysfunction, or will these and other amazing new discoveries be integrated responsibly to help us integrate the Ecological Epoch?

> (3:31) The Scientific Epoch began about five hundred years ago. Its remarkable inventiveness took control of human consciousness and culture; however, this ingeniously productive worldview brought with it industrial expansion that overwhelmed the earth's ability to heal the wounds that industry's onslaught caused. During the past seventy years, our production and consumption priorities have modified the planet in detrimental ways. We have impacted Earth's physical integrity—our children will inherit a withered environment.
>
> We are an amazingly adaptive species. The destruction we are causing is forcing the next step in the evolution of human consciousness—the Ecological Epoch. The damage has become so significant in the past seven decades that many more people all over the world are waking up and addressing the challenging issues we now face.

World population has tripled in the past seventy years; framed in this context, our Creation Story is about a new epoch in human evolution— how to awaken to an intimate rapport with the natural world and the importance of bringing world economies into healthy relationship with all the Earth's living beings. Ecological awareness is a guide for our behavior. Activism and protests are most effective when they are nonviolent and include solutions. Corporate decision makers and others who degrade our surroundings are usually ill informed. Labeling them wrong, or bad guys, or evildoers will not help them change. Providing a different context with which to examine a situation, more profound insight, and alternative solutions **can** catalyze change.

There are encouraging social signs that things are changing. For example, in September 2013, although retail stores complained vehemently, West Hollywood, California, became the first municipality to ban sales of clothes that are made from animal fur. The governing council declared their city a "cruelty-free zone for animals."

Michael Vick, a star quarterback for the Philadelphia Eagles football team, is another example. Surprisingly, his excellent career was sidetracked several years ago because he was sent to prison after a conviction for animal cruelty. At the time the animal incident occurred, Vick was a revered celebrity. There are few societies that would have the courage to put a popular athlete behind bars for treating animals badly.

These events show that we are paying attention. We care about animals enough to enforce social rules that protect them. Vick later resurrected his football career and appears to be a changed man. These examples would not have happened prior to the recent advent of ecological consciousness. They foretell further municipal, state, national, and international regulatory changes to protect the planet's dwindling biosphere.

Whale protection exemplifies changing worldviews and transforming economies. In the late eighteenth century and early nineteenth century, whales were hunted and killed for their fatty tissue; it was rendered into lamp oil. Whales became endangered. In 1859, a new fuel was found in large enough quantities that whales were no longer needed to light lamps. Fossil-fuel oil reservoirs were discovered in quantity and refined for lamp oil. Whales survived, barely. No longer an economically viable activity, the whaling industry disappeared in the following twenty-five years. Considering today's fuel situation, alternative energy could, likewise, replace the entire fossil-fuel industry. Not just one species, but entire ecosystems could be saved.

New spirituality is also emerging from ecological consciousness. On September 8, 2013, in Huntington Beach, California, twenty-five surfers paddled into the ocean and formed a circle using their surfboards. Holding hands, they all participated in a "Blessing of the Waves" ceremony, in appreciation for the ocean.

Social transformation begins with the individual; culture is changed one person at a time. Letting go of self-importance, goals, and egotistical strife helps one change. There are processes, technologies, disciplines, and practices that can liberate your ego, enhance your spirit, and open your heart. I call these "liberation pathways." They encourage each individual to perceive the world with broader, more expanded insights—new perspectives about fairness in society, about the health of the planet, and about spiritual meaning in one's own life; these ways of *seeing* results in deepened understanding about how to live together on the planet. Integral to our story is the necessary coming together of the man with the woman, creating a more balanced masculine and feminine culture:

(3:32) Carl Jung used the term "syzygy" to connote the integration of disparate parts into a complete whole. When applied to a man or a woman, it indicates merging with one's soul and, as a couple, finding one's soul mate, which creates the divine couple. Both the words "health" and "holy" have a common root in their original Anglo-Saxon language derivation. The root is "hale," whose definition is "whole" or "wholeness." So, to be healthy is to be whole, and to be holy is to be whole. Holy and healthy are branches of wholeness. For the human species to be healthy, it must be whole. As mentioned, the Ecological Epoch is joining together, for the first time, the divine feminine and the mature, rational masculine. This dance has begun; however, for it to gain momentum, doors must be opened for women to find greater influence in social and cultural institutions and affairs. The Ecological Epoch provides new opportunities for women. Research and experience tell us that by empowering women in developing countries we can end poverty, starvation, and war. Giving women, and especially girls, the help they need—leadership development, education, violence-prevention training, and economic empowerment—will bring about more gender balance.

My friend, Jack Zimmerman, is an educator and a wise elder. His fifty years of professional work with men and women has convinced him that love and intimacy between couples is where the tire meets the road in solving our current planetary challenges. When men and women learn to live lovingly and peaceably together, it will teach us how to resolve racial and international conflicts. Female and male reconciliation is important work that will also help to save the planet. Male mistreatment of the Earth is a reflection of distain for the feminine. If we solve this imbalance through more conscious man-to-woman relating, we will create the sygyzy needed to heal the human-Earth relationship.

Integrating the Ecological Epoch

We can all participate in Joanna Macy's strategies for creating social change. She and David Horton call it the "Great Turning." As discussed earlier, activism is needed on several fronts, including nonviolent action to protest or prevent activities that are destroying the "commons." These include civil disobedience where needed; creating visionary, cutting-edge technologies and organizations dedicated to finding alternative approaches to destructive business as usual; the expansion of awakened awareness— changing consciousness—resulting in "a vision that all living things can share"; and a sustainable, mutually beneficial economic future.

A concise strategy for integrating ecological values into our social fabric begins with seeing our circumstance in a new light, that is, creating new stories that more accurately reflect the realities of human life in relationship to our planet's health. This occurs person by person through participation in activities (liberation pathways) that expand one's awareness, thereby, endowing one with more insight, kindness and peacefulness. Personal strength grows when one is extricated from the draining propaganda of corporate media and the consumer society.

This liberation increases one's capacity to create and implement programs that help to solve the many impediments to planetary health and reduce current and future human suffering. To a large extent, social justice is a function of sustainable economics, population control, and wealth distribution. These are primary objectives for the new epoch. Sustainable economics requires climate protection so that weather abnormalities and natural calamities do not prematurely derail human life—and to preserve the awe-inspiring arrays of plants and animals that comprise Mother Nature's biological guts. Along with policies to cleanse the atmosphere of toxins, concurrent environmental activism is essential to end ongoing deforestation, to protect habitat, to bring back endangered species, to eliminate chemical toxins, and to minimize plastic waste.

There are numerous strategies to address these objectives: developing and delivering alternative education for children and adults; personally participating in some form of sustainable development while earning a living provides a model for others to follow suit; legal challenges and new legislation influence changes; restoration on all environmental fronts advances the cause; each individual's consumer advocacy educates other shoppers about harmful products; while social media and filmmaking also help to spread the word.

There is no scarcity of specific project areas that need attention. They include climate change work, fossil fuel and alternative energy issues, animal and habitat protection, pollution and toxicity reduction, new means for producing healthy food and eliminating damaging agricultural policies, protecting and restoring the oceans' health, and developing education platforms to efficiently deliver ecological values throughout our school and university systems. With deepened insight you will find inner strength—passion and appreciation for life will grow, opening pathways for your own participation in this most important endeavor of our human epoch.

(3:33) Natural Harmony is mutually beneficial reciprocity; its nature-based principles can be used as an ethical guide for finding solutions to our most vexing problems. There are many techniques available for a person to connect to Natural Harmony and thereby participate in this evolutionary human transformation. When practiced, these techniques reveal their sacred nature and help liberate the human spirit: for example, meditation, yoga, nature contemplation, immersion in wild nature, music, art, heartfelt science, Earth-based philosophy, Native American sun-dance ceremony, and even long-distance running. With practice, one's worldview eventually aligns with a healthy planet and brings personal fulfillment. To embrace the Ecological Epoch is the most meaningful life one could have, so why not participate? It is a sacred adventure that brings intimacy to one's life. As Dogen said in the thirteenth century, "Enlightenment is intimacy with all things."

My yoga-teaching friend recently brought to my attention the term "waking down." Not only do we have to "wake up," but it is also necessary to wake down. This New Creation Story has been about waking up through the process of waking down. Expanding and integrating human comprehension of Earth wisdom, which manifests as Natural Harmony, results in waking down.

How can we accomplish this? The Earth has given us the intuition and sensibility to recognize Natural Harmony and to use it to guide our actions. Conscious activism is a start. Activist Julia Butterfly lived hundreds of feet up in a redwood tree named Luna for two years, preventing it from being cut down. Luna taught Julia ecological wisdom. Others have learned from the dolphins and the whales or from the million examples of "mutually beneficial reciprocity" that make up our Earth home. All of this teaching can be boiled down to two words: "Be kinder."

Kindness

Empathy, compassion, concern for others: in a nutshell, a solution to our human-created disharmony is "kindness." Its value is extolled in ancient Greek and Chinese philosophies; it is prominent in Jesus's teachings; and it is a personal virtue that builds relationship. Kindness is both emotion and action that stems from letting one's ego dissolve and feeling the interconnections among all things.

Finding kindness is a step toward finding Sacred Presence, God, the Great Spirit, and the unnamable Creative Source. Kindness is a love poem, existing in our world side by side with the many other motivations that invigorate our individual behaviors: meanness, greed, self-importance, and power. Kindness promotes attraction and intimacy; it builds trust and dissolves barriers. Building kindness into human behavior is as important as any solution we can pursue.

Aldous Huxley was born in 1894 and died in 1963; he was a British writer, humanist, and pacifist with an avid desire to understand mysticism and parapsychology. Known for the novel *Brave New World* and numerous other works, he wrote books, poetry, and philosophical essays. He lived in America for his last twenty-five years and was a world-leading intellectual during his lifetime. Asked for words of wisdom near his life's end, he stated that he had no more to offer than: "Try to be a little kinder."

Aung San Suu Kyi is a world-renowned courageous woman—a Myanmar (Burma) national who was elected to be head of state, then promptly incarcerated for decades by the ruling military junta. She was awarded the Nobel Peace Prize in 1991. While under arrest, she commented about the importance of peace in the world: "Absolute peace is an unattainable goal, but it is one toward which we must continue to journey, our eyes fixed on it as a traveler in a desert fixes his eyes on the one guiding star that will lead him to salvation." Commenting on the importance of kindness, she is quoted as saying: "Of the sweets of adversity, and let me say that those are not numerous, I have found the sweetest, the most precious of all, is the lesson I learned on the value of kindness.... Every kindness I received, small or big, convinced me that there could never be enough of it in the world.... Kindness can change the lives of people."

Kindness

Before you know what kindness really is
you must lose things,
feel the future dissolve in a moment
like salt in a weakened broth.
What you held in your hand,

what you counted and carefully saved,
all this must go so you know
how desolate the landscape can be
between the regions of kindness.
How you ride and ride
thinking the bus will never stop,
the passengers eating maize and chicken
will stare out the window forever.

Before you learn the tender gravity of kindness,
you must travel where the Indian in a white poncho
lies dead by the side of the road.
You must see how this could be you,
how he too was someone
who journeyed through the night with plans
and the simple breath that kept him alive.

Before you know kindness as the deepest thing inside,
you must know sorrow as the other deepest thing.
You must wake up with sorrow.
You must speak to it till your voice
catches the thread of all sorrows
and you see the size of the cloth.

Then it is only kindness that makes sense anymore,
only kindness that ties your shoes
and sends you out into the day to mail letters and purchase bread,
only kindness that raises its head
from the crowd of the world to say

it is I you have been looking for,
and then goes with you every where
like a shadow or a friend.
—Naomi Shihab Nye[30]

We Have a Choice

We are truly amazing animals: our ability to adapt, create remarkable inventions, and manipulate our surroundings is unparalleled in this planet's existence. So, too, is our incredibly ingenious destructiveness. We are running ourselves into the ground; however, because we are so intellectually and intuitively resourceful, our scientific minds are now expanding even further. This expansion is the foundation for our New Creation Story. Its culmination is the Ecological Epoch, in which we deepen our awareness and discover a newly perceived divine presence in the universe—one that is born from both science and mysticism, from intuition and intellect. In this deepening, this practical as well as mystical relationship, there are solutions to resolve the challenges that our desire for overabundance has created.

There is little time to avoid chaos and catastrophe. This is the confrontation of our era. It can be solved, but if it is not, there is nature to pay. Our Creation Story is coming to a rest, providing a broader perspective from which to view human's relationship with the Earth and with life's greatest mystery, the Creative Source:

(3:34) During Homo sapiens' 200,000-year-long existence, there has never been an era in which transformation proceeded so rapidly as is occurring today. In the past eleven thousand years, we settled into agricultural communities, Old Europe developed ancient goddess cultures that lasted several thousand years, and patriarchal societies took over the world using violent masculine domination principles to create empires. In more recent historical times, 2,600 years ago,

30. Naomi Shihab Nye, *The Words under the Words: Selected Poems* (Eighth Mountain Press, 1995).

feminine values created numerous new philosophies within patriarchal societies. In Europe, religious institutions co-opted these
compassionate teachings, using them for political dominance; science liberated society from this fundamentalist trap—Copernicus,
Bruno, Galileo, Kepler, Descartes, and Newton reformulated how we
perceive the world; innumerable inventions followed; human population expanded many fold; industry churned out more and more
stuff. Science's shadow side came into play, creating pollution, toxic
chemicals, nuclear weapons, and war machines.

Now, another epoch has arrived, one that is necessary for human
survival: our scientific-minded population is beginning to awaken to
a new relationship with the living Earth.

The Ecological Epoch is a new way to perceive reality—a deepening of the human mind and psyche, resulting in a more expansive awareness. Many threads are being used to weave this fabric, which is creating renewed respect for life's sacred nature and the earth's living systems.
Our ongoing Creation Story has no end because human consciousness is
continually changing; however, this trilogy has brought us to a present-
moment pause:

(3:35) Stars are children of the cosmos. Our sun was born more than four
and a half billion years ago; Earth coalesced soon thereafter. The sun,
the earth, and all of Earth's living things exist in erotic embrace originating before life began; the sun's photons are in constant intercourse with
green leaves—providing energy for obtaining carbon to grow plants and
nourish animals. Eros is the universal attractor that binds and weaves
together everything from galaxies to subatomic particles.

Earth-life has developed as a unified whole that reveals itself
as an interdependent matrix. Life conjoins with and survives from
erotic intimacy with Earth's atmosphere, geology, and water. Our
story sees these interactions as Natural Harmony, which is the mutually beneficial reciprocity woven into Earth's physical and biological
matrix that has allowed life on Earth to endure and evolve over billions of years.

On a small scale, with manageable population densities, increasing production benefited the human community. On a large scale, it

resulted in overproduction and has become destructive. The production-consumption social priority, a rational economic philosophy for centuries, has now exceeded its healthy limits. It has lost touch with reality—the definition of psychosis. *Homo sapiens* as a species have been aggressively disruptive. We humans are releasing CO_2 into the atmosphere so quickly that we are upsetting the earth's biological and geological cycles.

Cutting away a species by destroying its habitat is an action that diminishes the world and demeans us all—a crime against nature. We have initiated an extinction spasm, potential massive human starvation, and a multitude of environmental refugees looming on the horizon. We know how to correct these imbalances, but will we?

Other animals have not yet developed self-reflective consciousness. They are not predisposed with our appetite for invention. Their past is built into their genetic makeup; they carry all they need to "know" within their cells. No ecological urgency compels them to know more, to be more in order to serve the Earth community. They already serve to their full capacity and will continue to do so. We humans are unique, not better or worse than the other animals but certainly more influential. We have been given an unusual gift, self-reflective consciousness—a special privilege and responsibility. Whether or not this gift is a positive innovation for the planet is as yet unknown.

No matter what humanity's fate, Earth will survive and produce more incredible life forms. Left to its own devices, the Earth will heal; however, we do not have the vast time spans required for the planet to restore CO_2 to healthy-for-human levels. Over multimillion-year periods the Earth possesses a self-correcting dynamic system—the geologic CO_2 weathering cycle will eventually adjust today's atmospheric imbalances. In the process, the Earth will blossom forth with new life forms. Perhaps another species will come forward in six or seven million years to advance biological consciousness further than we have been able to accomplish.

The natural world, with its many species, stands as a whole. When we humans stop betraying this community's trust, we can once again become constructive partners with the other life forms. We have brilliant possibilities, but we are as yet an experiment in evolutionary complexity—thankfully, one that still has a precious window of opportunity to become more intimate with Divine Nature. If the lesson is learned, and we begin to behave based on Ecological Epoch values, Earth's entire life-community will buoy up *Homo sapiens*, in which case we can become healthy, functional partners and stand in our appropriate place—one founded on humility and respect for sacred Nature.

In this scenario, we can succeed. In any event, success or failure, the current environmental crisis has provided the catalyst for the next step in the evolution of human consciousness. Participating at the forefront of this new movement—awakening to Natural Harmony—is the most meaningful and passionate way for any individual to live his or her life, no matter what the eventual outcome.

(3:36) Built upon erotic interconnections, life on Earth is an ephemeral, flowing process that is constantly in flux. Our solar system and planet will burn up with the sun's demise about five billion years hence. All Earth's species come into existence and eventually melt back into the Creative Source. We humans are no different; as such, our Creation Story is currently unfolding in spectacular fashion.

THE END
AND NEW BEGINNING

BIBLIOGRAPHY

Abram, David. *The Spell of the Sensuous: Perception and Language in a More-than-human World*. New York: Pantheon Books, 1996.

Andres Edwards, David Orr. *Sustainability Revolution*. New Society Publishers; First Edition edition, 2005.

Armstrong, Karen. *A Short History of Myth*. Edinburgh; New York: Canongate, 2005.

Begley, Sharon. *The Plastic Mind*. London: Constable, 2009.

Berger, Lee R. *In the Footsteps of Eve: The Mystery of Human Origins*. Washington, D.C.: National Geographic Society, 2000.

Berman, Morris. *Coming to Our Senses: Body and Spirit in the Hidden History of the West*. New York: Simon and Schuster, 1989.

Berry, Thomas. *The Dream of the Earth*. San Francisco: Sierra Club Books, 1988.

———. *The Great Work: Our Way into the Future*. New York: Bell Tower, 1999.

Brower, David Ross. *Let the Mountains Talk, Let the Rivers Run: a Call to Those Who Would Save the Earth*. [San Francisco, Calif.]: HarperCollins West, 1995.

Brown, Lester R. *Eco-economy: Building an Economy for the Earth*. New York: W.W. Norton, 2001.

———. *Plan B 3.0: Mobilizing to Save Civilization*. New York: W.W. Norton, 2008.

———. *Plan B 4.0: Mobilizing to Save Civilization*. New York: W.W. Norton, 2009.

———. *World on the Edge: How to Prevent Environmental and Economic Collapse*. New York: W.W. Norton, 2011.

Calvin, William H. *A Brief History of the Mind: From Apes to Intellect and Beyond*. New York: Oxford University Press, 2004.

Capra, Fritjof. *The Tao of Physics: An Exploration of the Parallels Between Modern Physics and Eastern Mysticism*. Berkeley; [New York]: Shambhala ; distributed in the U.S. by Random House, 1975.

Childs, Christopher. *The Spirit's Terrain: Creativity, Activism, and Transformation*. Boston: Beacon Press, 1998.

Combs, Allan. *Consciousness Explained Better: Towards an Integral Understanding of the Multifaceted Nature of Consciousness*. St. Paul, Minn.: Paragon House, 2009.

Davies, P. C. W. *The Cosmic Blueprint*. London: Heinemann, 1987.

Davis, Mike. *Ecology of Fear: Los Angeles and the Imagination of Disaster*. New York: Metropolitan Books, 1998.

Diamond, Jared M. *Collapse: How Societies Choose to Fail or Succeed*. New York: Viking, 2005.

———. *Guns, Germs, and Steel: The Fates of Human Societies*. New York: W.W. Norton & Co., 1998.

Doidge, Norman. *The Brain That Changes Itself: Stories of Personal Triumph from the Frontiers of Brain Science*. New York: Viking, 2007.

Douglas-Klotz, Neil. *The Hidden Gospel: Decoding the Spiritual Message of the Aramaic Jesus*. Wheaton, Ill.: Quest Books, Theosophical Pub. House, 1999.

Duhm, Dieter. *The Sacred Matrix: From the Matrix of Violence to the Matrix of Life ; the Foundation for a New Civilization*. [Wiesenburg]: Meiga, 2006.

Edelman, Gerald M. *Second Nature: Brain Science and Human Knowledge*. New Haven: Yale University Press, 2006.

Edwards, Andres R. *The Sustainability Revolution: Portrait of a Paradigm Shift.* Gabriola, BC: New Society Publishers, 2005.

Ehrman, Bart D. *Misquoting Jesus: The Story Behind Who Changed the Bible and Why.* New York: HarperSanFrancisco, 2005.

Elgin, Duane. *Living Universe.* San Francisco: Berrett-Koehler Publishers, Incorporated, 2009. https://ezproxy.siast.sk.ca:443/login?url=http://proquest.safaribooksonline.com/9781576759882.

Ferris, Timothy. *Coming of Age in the Milky Way.* New York: Morrow, 1988.

Flannery, Tim F. *The Weather Makers: How Man Is Changing the Climate and What It Means for Life on Earth.* New York: Atlantic Monthly Press, 2005.

Forest, Ohky Simine. *Dreaming the Council Ways: True Native Teachings from the Red Lodge.* Red Wheel / Weiser, 2009.

George, Demetra. *Mysteries of the Dark Moon: The Healing Power of the Dark Goddess.* [San Francisco, Calif.]: HarperSanFrancisco, 1992.

Hansen, James E. *Storms of My Grandchildren: The Truth About the Coming Climate Catastrophe and Our Last Chance to Save Humanity.* New York: Bloomsbury USA, 2009.

Hartmann, Thom. *Screwed: The Undeclared War Against the Middle Class--and What We Can Do About It.* San Francisco: Berrett-Koehler Publishers, 2006.

———. *The Last Hours of Ancient Sunlight: Waking up to Personal and Global Transformation.* New York: Harmony Books, 1999.

Hawken, Paul. *Blessed Unrest: How the Largest Movement in the World Came into Being, and Why No One Saw It Coming.* New York: Viking, 2007.

Hedges, Chris. *Empire of Illusion: The End of Literacy and the Triumph of Spectacle.* New York: Nation Books, 2009.

Humphrey, Nicholas. *A History of the Mind.* New York: Simon & Schuster, 1992.

International Forum on Globalization., Cavanagh. *Alternatives to Economic Globalization.* San Francisco: Berrett-Koehler, 2002.

J.G.Speth. *J.G.Speth'sThe Bridge at the Edge of the World(The Bridge at the Edge of the World: Capitalism, the Environment, and Crossing from Crisis to Sustainability (Hardcover.* Yale University Press, 2008.

Jackson, Tim. *Prosperity Without Growth: Economics for a Finite Planet.* London; Sterling, VA: Earthscan, 2009.

Kasser, Rodolphe. *The Gospel of Judas: From Codex Tchacos.* Washington, D.C.: National Geographic, 2006.

Ken Carey. *The Third Millennium,* n.d.

Khanna, Parag. *How to Run the World: Charting a Course to the Next Renaissance.* New York: Random House, 2011.

Kolbert, Elizabeth. *Field Notes from a Catastrophe: Man, Nature, and Climate Change.* New York: Bloomsbury Pub. : Distributed to the trade by Holtzbrinck Publishers, 2006.

Korten, David C. *The Great Turning: From Empire to Earth Community.* San Francisco, CA; Bloomfield, CT: Berrett-Koehler ; Kumarian Press, 2006.

Krosney, Herbert. *The Lost Gospel: The Quest for the Gospel of Judas Iscariot.* Washington, D.C.: National Geographic, 2006.

Lipton, Bruce H. *The Biology of Belief: Unleashing the Power of Consciousness, Matter and Miracles.* Santa Rosa, CA: Mountain of Love/Elite Books, 2005.

Lovelock, James. *The Vanishing Face of Gaia: a Final Warning.* New York: Basic Books, 2009.

Lovins, Amory B. *Reinventing Fire: Bold Business Solutions for the New Energy Era.* White River Junction, Vt.: Chelsea Green Pub., 2011.

Macy, Joanna. *Coming Back to Life: Practices to Reconnect Our Lives, Our World.* Gabriola Island, BC, Canada; Stony Creek, CT: New Society Publishers, 1998.

———. *The Work That Reconnects.* [Gabriola Island, British Columbia]: New Society Publishers, 2006.

Marcus, Gary F. *The Birth of the Mind: How a Tiny Number of Genes Creates the Complexities of Human Thought*. New York: Basic Books, 2004.

McIntosh, Steve. *Integral Consciousness and the Future of Evolution*. 1st ed. Paragon House, 2007.

McKibben, Bill. *Deep Economy: The Wealth of Communities and the Durable Future*. New York: Times Books, 2007.

———. *Eaarth*. New York: Time Books/Henry Holt, 2010.

———. *The End of Nature*. New York: Random House, 1989.

McTaggart, Lynne. *The Field: The Quest for the Secret Force of the Universe*. Updated. Harper Perennial, 2008.

Mehl-Madrona, Lewis. *Narrative Medicine: The Use of History and Story in the Healing Process*. Original. Bear & Company, 2007.

Metzner, Ralph. *The Expansion of Consciousness*. Berkeley, CA: Green EarthFoundation & Regent Press, 2008.

Miller, Tyson. *Dream of a Nation: Inspiring Ideas for a Better America*. [Asheville, NC]: See Innovation, 2011.

Morton, Oliver. *Eating the Sun: How Plants Power the Planet*. Reprint. Harper Perennial, 2009.

Narby, Jeremy. *The Cosmic Serpent: DNA and the Origins of Knowledge*. New York: Jeremy P. Tarcher/Putnam, 1998.

Nelson, Melissa K. *Original Instructions: Indigenous Teachings for a Sustainable Future*. Rochester, Vt.: Bear & Company, 2008.

Orr, David W. *Down to the Wire: Confronting Climate Collapse*. Oxford; New York: Oxford University Press, 2009.

———. *Hope Is an Imperative the Essential David Orr*. Washington, DC: Island Press, 2010. http://site.ebrary.com/id/10430950.

Pogacnik, Marko. *Christ Power and the Earth Goddess*. Chicago: Findhorn Press, 1999. http://www.msvu.ca:2048/login?url=http://www.msvu.eblib.com/patron/FullRecord.aspx?p=839132.

Powell, Diane Hennacy. *The ESP Enigma: The Scientific Case for Psychic Phenomena*. New York: Walker, 2009.

Radin, Dean I. *The Conscious Universe: The Scientific Truth of Psychic Phenomena.* New York, N.Y.: HarperEdge, 1997.

Rifkin, Jeremy. *The Empathic Civilization: The Race to Global Consciousness in a World in Crisis.* New York: J.P. Tarcher/Penguin, 2009.

Roberts, Paul. *The End of Oil: On the Edge of a Perilous New World.* Boston: Houghton Mifflin, 2004.

Rosenblum, Bruce, and Fred Kuttner. *Quantum Enigma: Physics Encounters Consciousness.* 2nd ed. Oxford University Press, USA, 2011.

Sagan, Carl. *Pale Blue Dot: a Vision of the Human Future in Space.* New York: Random House, 1994.

Sahtouris, Elisabet. *Gaia: The Human Journey from Chaos to Cosmos.* New York: Pocket Books, 1989.

Shlain, Leonard. *Sex, Time, and Power: How Women's Sexuality Shaped Human Evolution.* New York: Viking, 2003.

———. *The Alphabet Versus the Goddess: The Conflict Between Word and Image.* New York: Viking, 1998.

Swimme, Brian. *The Powers of the Universe.* [San Francisco, CA?]: Center for the Story of the Universe, 2004.

Voth, Grant L. *Myth in Human History.* Chantilly, VA: Teaching Co., 2010.

Walker, Evan Harris. *The Physics of Consciousness: The Quantum Minds and the Meaning of Life.* Cambridge, Mass.: Perseus Books, 2000.

Wikman, Monika. *Pregnant Darkness: Alchemy and the Rebirth of Consciousness.* Berwick, Me.; York Beach, ME: Nicolas-Hays ; Distributed to the trade by Red Wheel/Weiser, 2004.

Wilber, Ken. *A Brief History of Everything.* Boston: Shambhala, 1996.

Wright, Robert. *The Moral Animal: Evolutionary Psychology and Everyday Life.* New York: Vintage Books, 1995.

Zajonc, Arthur. *Catching the Light: The Entwined History of Light and Mind.* New York: Bantam Books, 1993.

Zimmer, Carl. *Soul Made Flesh: The Discovery of the Brain-- and How It Changed the World.* New York: Free Press, 2004.

Made in the USA
San Bernardino, CA
18 November 2014